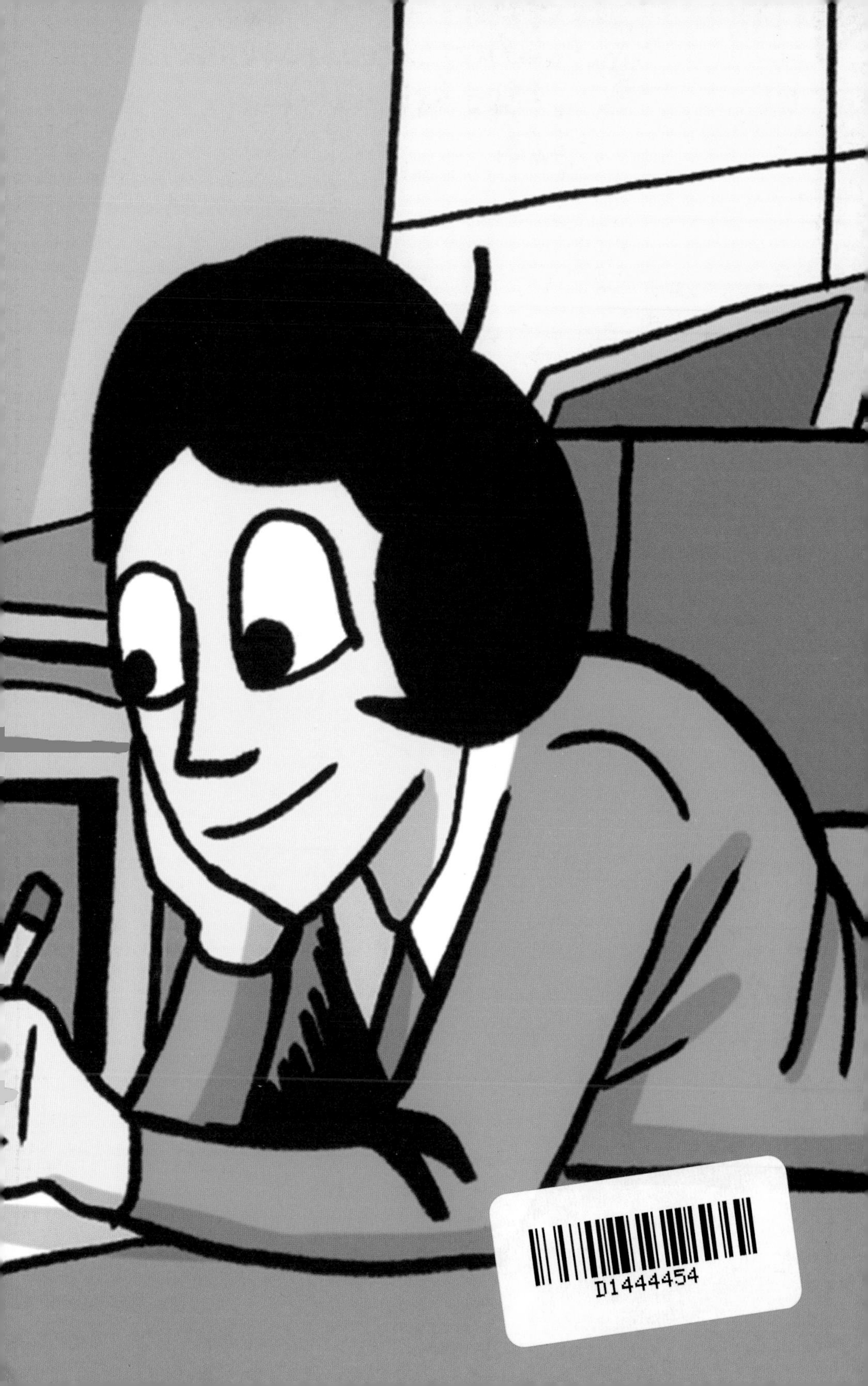

SHOW ME HISTORY!™

ANNE Frank
WITNESS to HISTORY!

BY
MARK SHULMAN

ILLUSTRATED BY
JEFF MARTIN

LETTERING & DESIGN BY
SWELL TYPE

COVER ART BY
IAN CHURCHILL

PORTABLE
PRESS

SAN DIEGO, CALIFORNIA

Portable Press
An imprint of Printers Row Publishing Group
9717 Pacific Heights Blvd, San Diego, CA 92121
www.portablepress.com • mail@portablepress.com

Printers Row Publishing Group is a division of Readerlink Distribution Services, LLC. Portable Press is a registered trademark of Readerlink Distribution Services, LLC.

Correspondence regarding the content of this book should be sent to Portable Press, Editorial Department, at the above address. Author and illustrator inquiries should be sent to Oomf, Inc., www.oomf.com.

Portable Press
Publisher: Peter Norton • Associate Publisher: Ana Parker
Art Director: Charles McStravick
Senior Developmental Editor: April Graham Farr
Editor: Stephanie Romero Gamboa
Production Team: Julie Greene, Rusty von Dyl

Produced by Oomf, Inc., www.Oomf.com
Director: Mark Shulman
Producer: James Buckley Jr.

Author: Mark Shulman
Illustrator: Jeff Martin
Assistant Editor: Michael Centore
Researchers: Christine Fulton, Diane Bailey, Esther Shulman
Lettering & design by Swell Type: John Roshell, Forest Dempsey,
    Sarah Jacobs, Drewes McFarling, Miles Gaushell
Cover illustrator: Ian Churchill

Library of Congress Control Number: 2021930584

ISBN: 978-1-64517-432-5

Printed in China

25 24 23 22 21   1 2 3 4 5

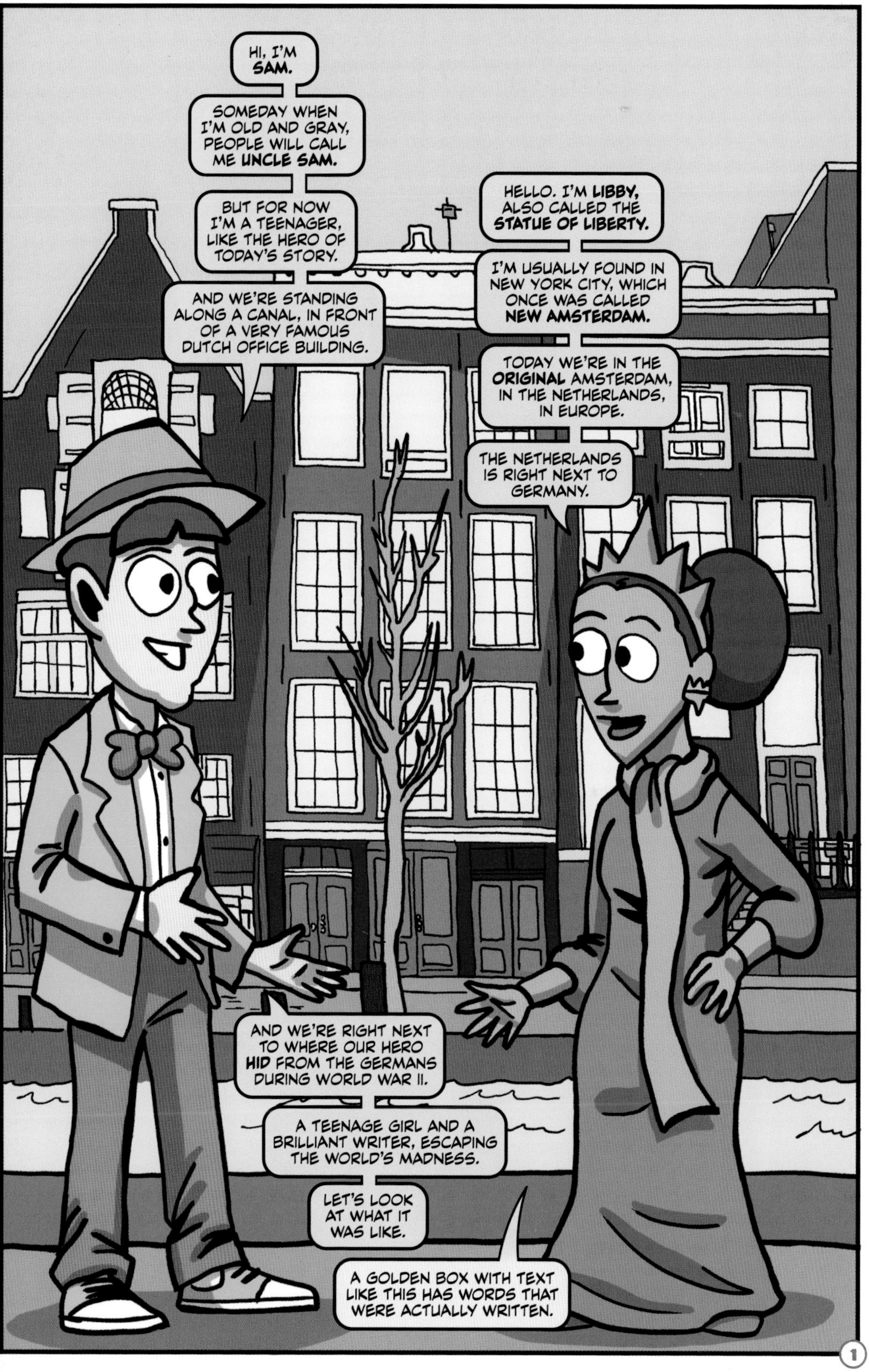

HI, I'M **SAM.**
SOMEDAY WHEN I'M OLD AND GRAY, PEOPLE WILL CALL ME **UNCLE SAM.**
BUT FOR NOW I'M A TEENAGER, LIKE THE HERO OF TODAY'S STORY.
AND WE'RE STANDING ALONG A CANAL, IN FRONT OF A VERY FAMOUS DUTCH OFFICE BUILDING.
HELLO. I'M **LIBBY,** ALSO CALLED THE **STATUE OF LIBERTY.**
I'M USUALLY FOUND IN NEW YORK CITY, WHICH ONCE WAS CALLED **NEW AMSTERDAM.**
TODAY WE'RE IN THE **ORIGINAL** AMSTERDAM, IN THE NETHERLANDS, IN EUROPE.
THE NETHERLANDS IS RIGHT NEXT TO GERMANY.
AND WE'RE RIGHT NEXT TO WHERE OUR HERO **HID** FROM THE GERMANS DURING WORLD WAR II.
A TEENAGE GIRL AND A BRILLIANT WRITER, ESCAPING THE WORLD'S MADNESS.
LET'S LOOK AT WHAT IT WAS LIKE.
A GOLDEN BOX WITH TEXT LIKE THIS HAS WORDS THAT WERE ACTUALLY WRITTEN.

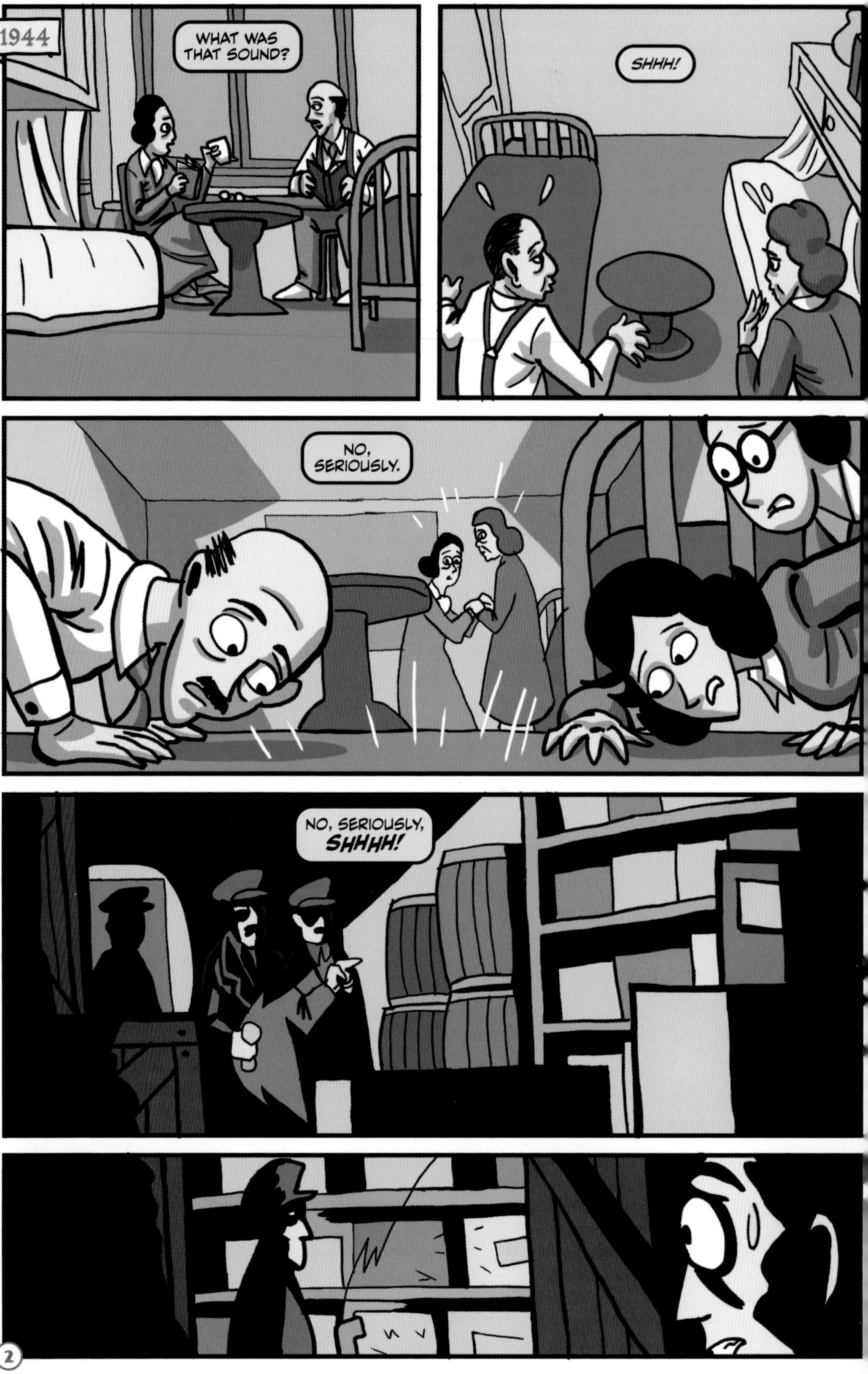
1944
WHAT WAS THAT SOUND?
SHHH!
NO, SERIOUSLY.
NO, SERIOUSLY, SHHHH!

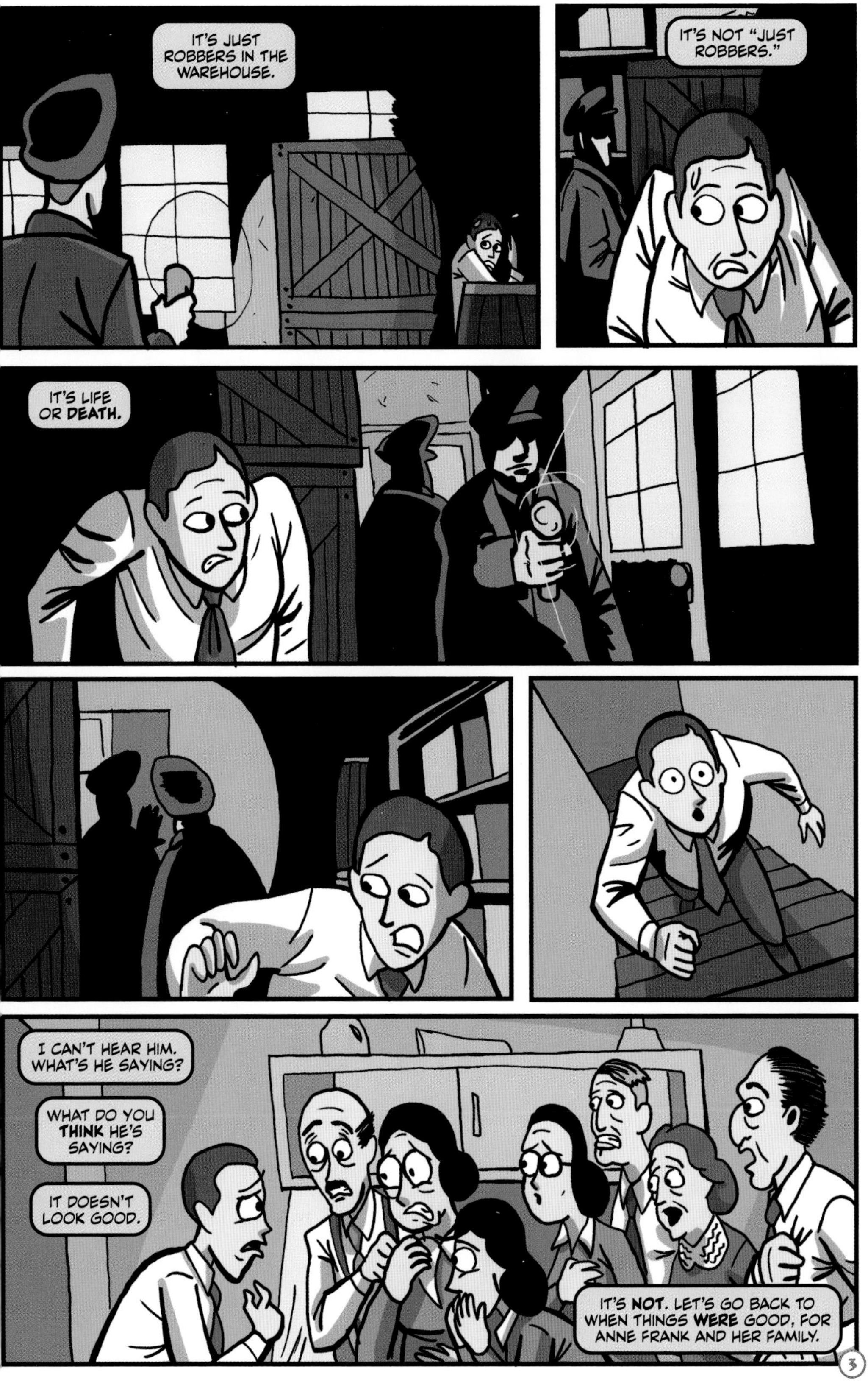
IT'S JUST ROBBERS IN THE WAREHOUSE.
IT'S NOT "JUST ROBBERS."
IT'S LIFE OR **DEATH.**
I CAN'T HEAR HIM. WHAT'S HE SAYING?
WHAT DO YOU **THINK** HE'S SAYING?
IT DOESN'T LOOK GOOD.
IT'S **NOT.** LET'S GO BACK TO WHEN THINGS **WERE** GOOD, FOR ANNE FRANK AND HER FAMILY.

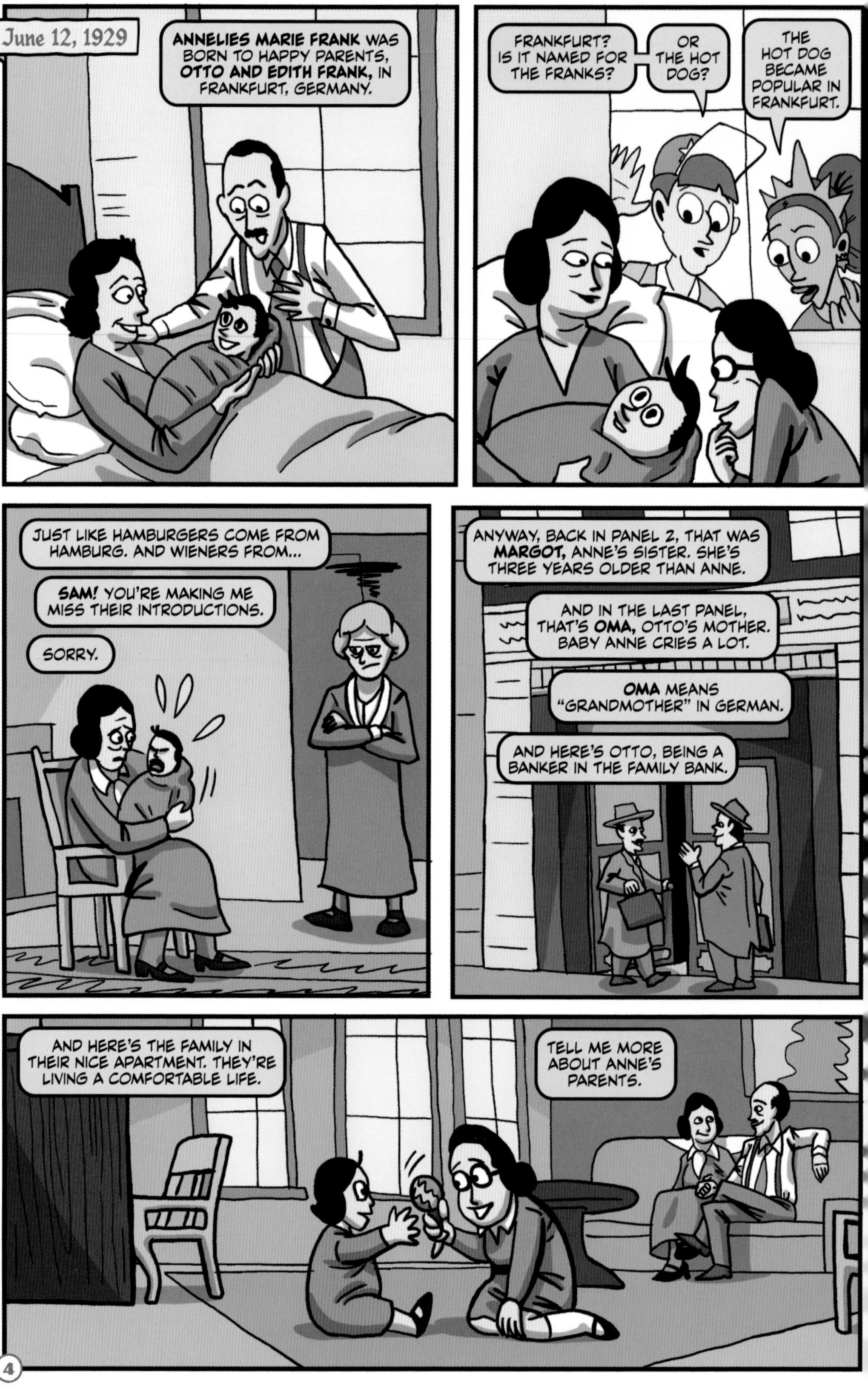
June 12, 1929
ANNELIES MARIE FRANK WAS BORN TO HAPPY PARENTS, OTTO AND EDITH FRANK, IN FRANKFURT, GERMANY.
FRANKFURT? IS IT NAMED FOR THE FRANKS?
OR THE HOT DOG?
THE HOT DOG BECAME POPULAR IN FRANKFURT.
JUST LIKE HAMBURGERS COME FROM HAMBURG. AND WIENERS FROM...
SAM! YOU'RE MAKING ME MISS THEIR INTRODUCTIONS.
SORRY.
ANYWAY, BACK IN PANEL 2, THAT WAS MARGOT, ANNE'S SISTER. SHE'S THREE YEARS OLDER THAN ANNE.
AND IN THE LAST PANEL, THAT'S OMA, OTTO'S MOTHER. BABY ANNE CRIES A LOT.
OMA MEANS "GRANDMOTHER" IN GERMAN.
AND HERE'S OTTO, BEING A BANKER IN THE FAMILY BANK.
AND HERE'S THE FAMILY IN THEIR NICE APARTMENT. THEY'RE LIVING A COMFORTABLE LIFE.
TELL ME MORE ABOUT ANNE'S PARENTS.

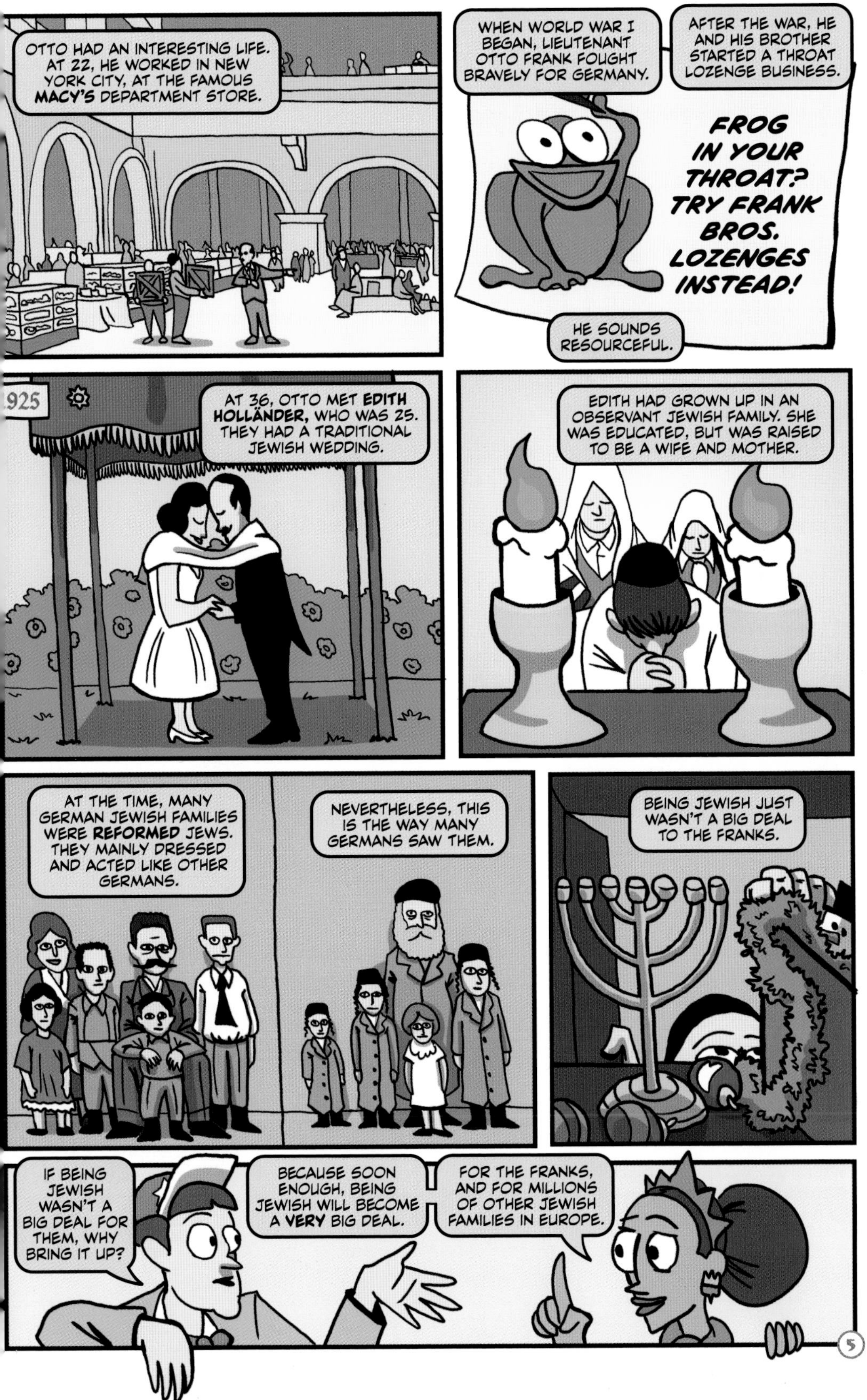
OTTO HAD AN INTERESTING LIFE. AT 22, HE WORKED IN NEW YORK CITY, AT THE FAMOUS **MACY'S** DEPARTMENT STORE.
WHEN WORLD WAR I BEGAN, LIEUTENANT OTTO FRANK FOUGHT BRAVELY FOR GERMANY.
AFTER THE WAR, HE AND HIS BROTHER STARTED A THROAT LOZENGE BUSINESS.
FROG IN YOUR THROAT? TRY FRANK BROS. LOZENGES INSTEAD!
HE SOUNDS RESOURCEFUL.
1925
AT 36, OTTO MET **EDITH HOLLÄNDER,** WHO WAS 25. THEY HAD A TRADITIONAL JEWISH WEDDING.
EDITH HAD GROWN UP IN AN OBSERVANT JEWISH FAMILY. SHE WAS EDUCATED, BUT WAS RAISED TO BE A WIFE AND MOTHER.
AT THE TIME, MANY GERMAN JEWISH FAMILIES WERE **REFORMED** JEWS. THEY MAINLY DRESSED AND ACTED LIKE OTHER GERMANS.
NEVERTHELESS, THIS IS THE WAY MANY GERMANS SAW THEM.
BEING JEWISH JUST WASN'T A BIG DEAL TO THE FRANKS.
IF BEING JEWISH WASN'T A BIG DEAL FOR THEM, WHY BRING IT UP?
BECAUSE SOON ENOUGH, BEING JEWISH WILL BECOME A **VERY** BIG DEAL.
FOR THE FRANKS, AND FOR MILLIONS OF OTHER JEWISH FAMILIES IN EUROPE.

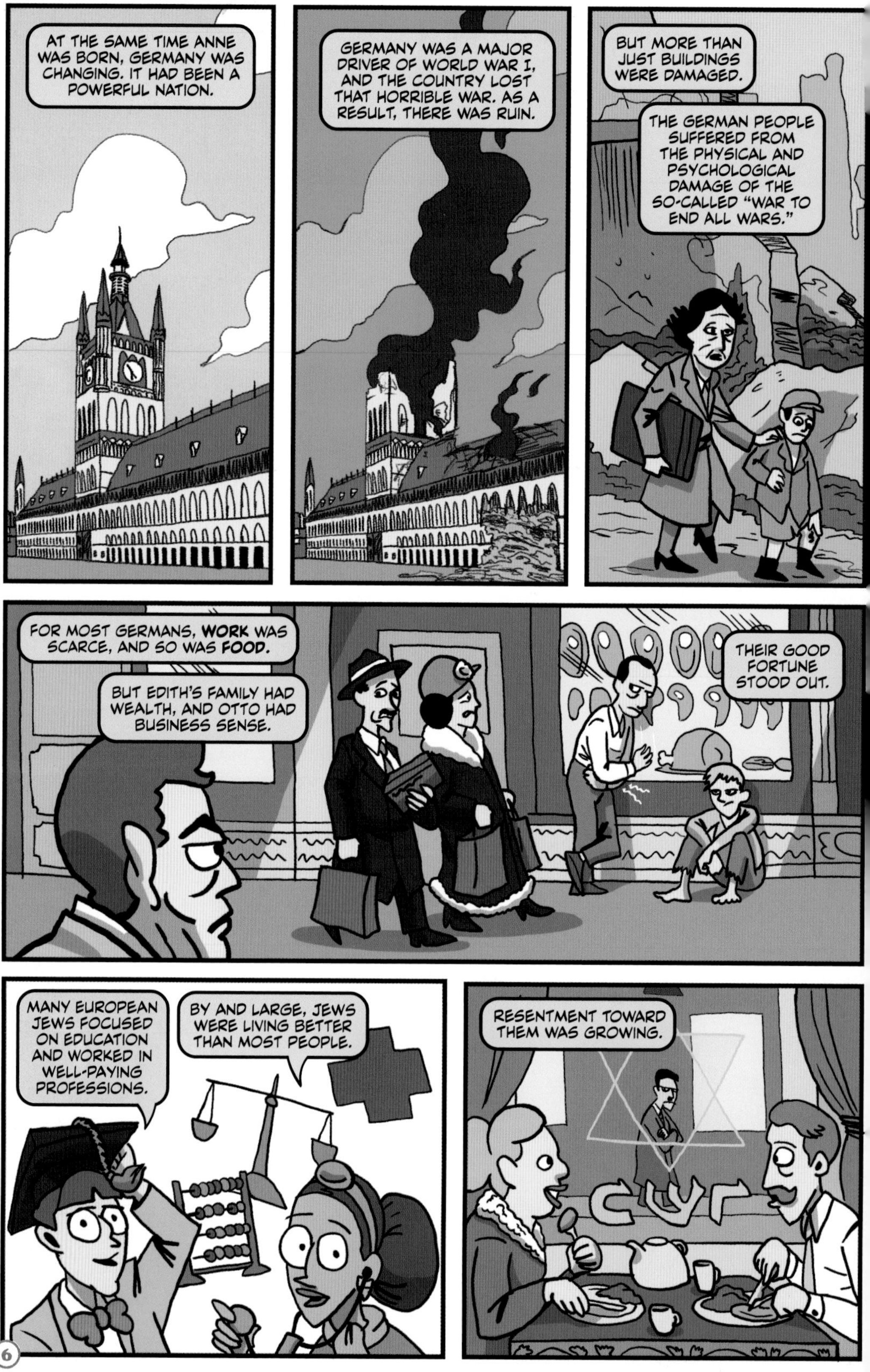
AT THE SAME TIME ANNE WAS BORN, GERMANY WAS CHANGING. IT HAD BEEN A POWERFUL NATION.
GERMANY WAS A MAJOR DRIVER OF WORLD WAR I, AND THE COUNTRY LOST THAT HORRIBLE WAR. AS A RESULT, THERE WAS RUIN.
BUT MORE THAN JUST BUILDINGS WERE DAMAGED.
THE GERMAN PEOPLE SUFFERED FROM THE PHYSICAL AND PSYCHOLOGICAL DAMAGE OF THE SO-CALLED "WAR TO END ALL WARS."
FOR MOST GERMANS, WORK WAS SCARCE, AND SO WAS FOOD.
BUT EDITH'S FAMILY HAD WEALTH, AND OTTO HAD BUSINESS SENSE.
THEIR GOOD FORTUNE STOOD OUT.
MANY EUROPEAN JEWS FOCUSED ON EDUCATION AND WORKED IN WELL-PAYING PROFESSIONS.
BY AND LARGE, JEWS WERE LIVING BETTER THAN MOST PEOPLE.
RESENTMENT TOWARD THEM WAS GROWING.

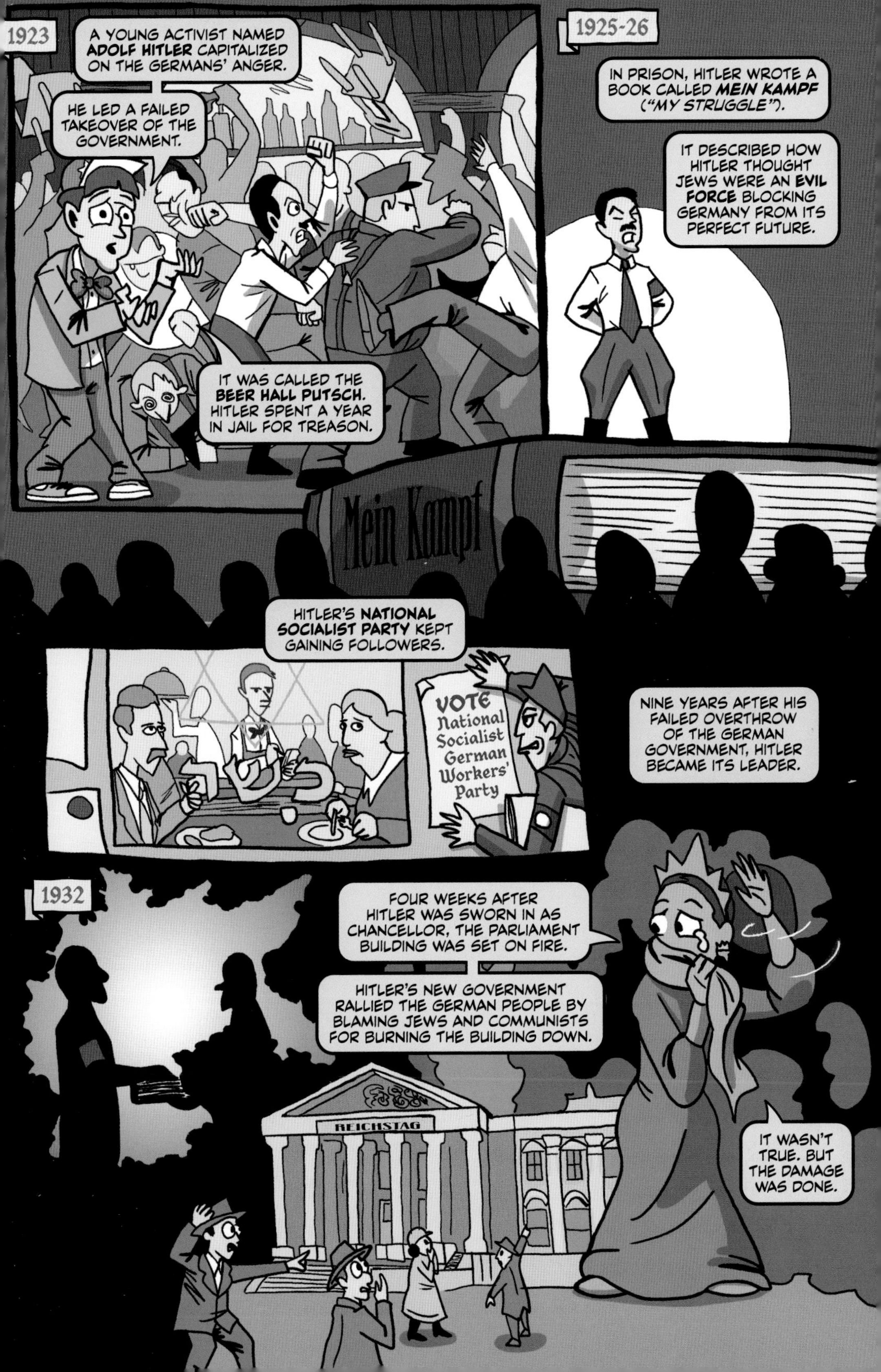
1923
A YOUNG ACTIVIST NAMED **ADOLF HITLER** CAPITALIZED ON THE GERMANS' ANGER.
HE LED A FAILED TAKEOVER OF THE GOVERNMENT.
IT WAS CALLED THE **BEER HALL PUTSCH.** HITLER SPENT A YEAR IN JAIL FOR TREASON.
1925-26
IN PRISON, HITLER WROTE A BOOK CALLED ***MEIN KAMPF*** (*"MY STRUGGLE"*).
IT DESCRIBED HOW HITLER THOUGHT JEWS WERE AN **EVIL FORCE** BLOCKING GERMANY FROM ITS PERFECT FUTURE.
Mein Kampf
HITLER'S **NATIONAL SOCIALIST PARTY** KEPT GAINING FOLLOWERS.
VOTE National Socialist German Workers' Party
NINE YEARS AFTER HIS FAILED OVERTHROW OF THE GERMAN GOVERNMENT, HITLER BECAME ITS LEADER.
1932
FOUR WEEKS AFTER HITLER WAS SWORN IN AS CHANCELLOR, THE PARLIAMENT BUILDING WAS SET ON FIRE.
HITLER'S NEW GOVERNMENT RALLIED THE GERMAN PEOPLE BY BLAMING JEWS AND COMMUNISTS FOR BURNING THE BUILDING DOWN.
REICHSTAG
IT WASN'T TRUE. BUT THE DAMAGE WAS DONE.

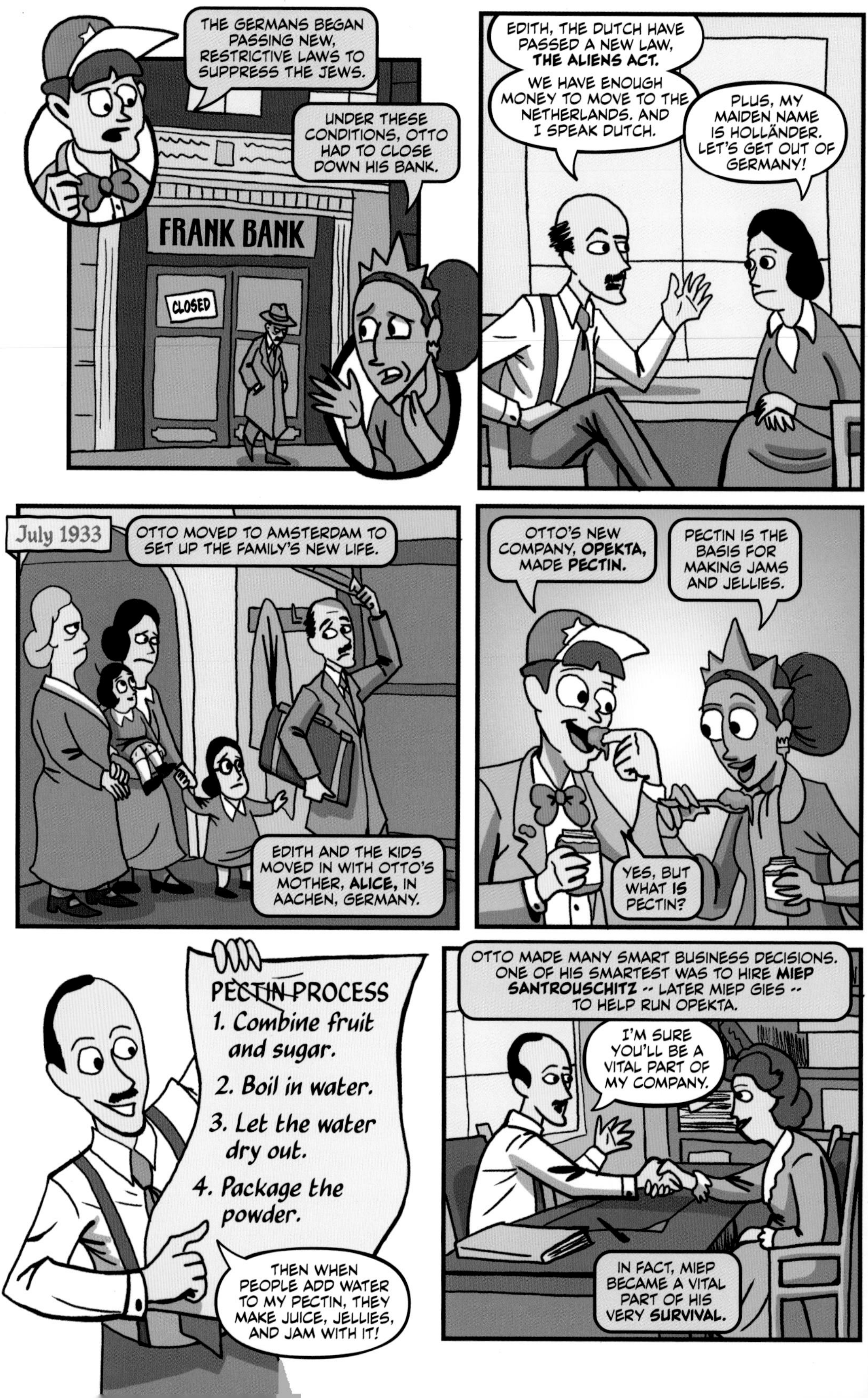

THE GERMANS BEGAN PASSING NEW, RESTRICTIVE LAWS TO SUPPRESS THE JEWS.
UNDER THESE CONDITIONS, OTTO HAD TO CLOSE DOWN HIS BANK.
FRANK BANK
CLOSED
EDITH, THE DUTCH HAVE PASSED A NEW LAW, **THE ALIENS ACT.**
WE HAVE ENOUGH MONEY TO MOVE TO THE NETHERLANDS. AND I SPEAK DUTCH.
PLUS, MY MAIDEN NAME IS HOLLÄNDER. LET'S GET OUT OF GERMANY!
July 1933
OTTO MOVED TO AMSTERDAM TO SET UP THE FAMILY'S NEW LIFE.
EDITH AND THE KIDS MOVED IN WITH OTTO'S MOTHER, **ALICE,** IN AACHEN, GERMANY.
OTTO'S NEW COMPANY, **OPEKTA,** MADE **PECTIN.**
PECTIN IS THE BASIS FOR MAKING JAMS AND JELLIES.
YES, BUT WHAT **IS** PECTIN?
PECTIN PROCESS
1. Combine fruit and sugar.
2. Boil in water.
3. Let the water dry out.
4. Package the powder.
THEN WHEN PEOPLE ADD WATER TO MY PECTIN, THEY MAKE JUICE, JELLIES, AND JAM WITH IT!
OTTO MADE MANY SMART BUSINESS DECISIONS. ONE OF HIS SMARTEST WAS TO HIRE **MIEP SANTROUSCHITZ** -- LATER MIEP GIES -- TO HELP RUN OPEKTA.
I'M SURE YOU'LL BE A VITAL PART OF MY COMPANY.
IN FACT, MIEP BECAME A VITAL PART OF HIS VERY **SURVIVAL.**

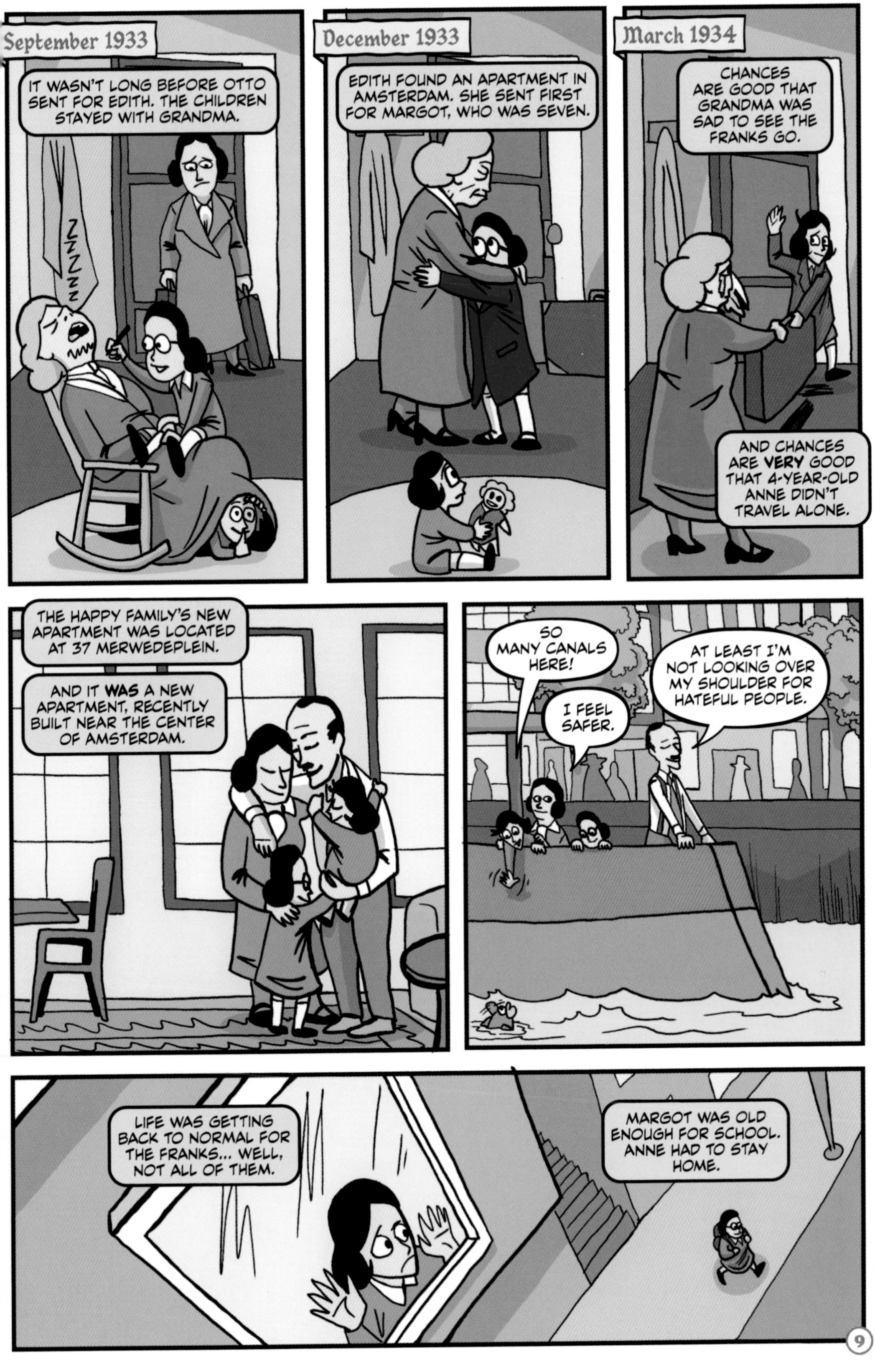

September 1933
IT WASN'T LONG BEFORE OTTO SENT FOR EDITH. THE CHILDREN STAYED WITH GRANDMA.
ZZZZZZ
December 1933
EDITH FOUND AN APARTMENT IN AMSTERDAM. SHE SENT FIRST FOR MARGOT, WHO WAS SEVEN.
March 1934
CHANCES ARE GOOD THAT GRANDMA WAS SAD TO SEE THE FRANKS GO.
AND CHANCES ARE **VERY** GOOD THAT 4-YEAR-OLD ANNE DIDN'T TRAVEL ALONE.
THE HAPPY FAMILY'S NEW APARTMENT WAS LOCATED AT 37 MERWEDEPLEIN.
AND IT **WAS** A NEW APARTMENT, RECENTLY BUILT NEAR THE CENTER OF AMSTERDAM.
SO MANY CANALS HERE!
I FEEL SAFER.
AT LEAST I'M NOT LOOKING OVER MY SHOULDER FOR HATEFUL PEOPLE.
LIFE WAS GETTING BACK TO NORMAL FOR THE FRANKS... WELL, NOT ALL OF THEM.
MARGOT WAS OLD ENOUGH FOR SCHOOL. ANNE HAD TO STAY HOME.

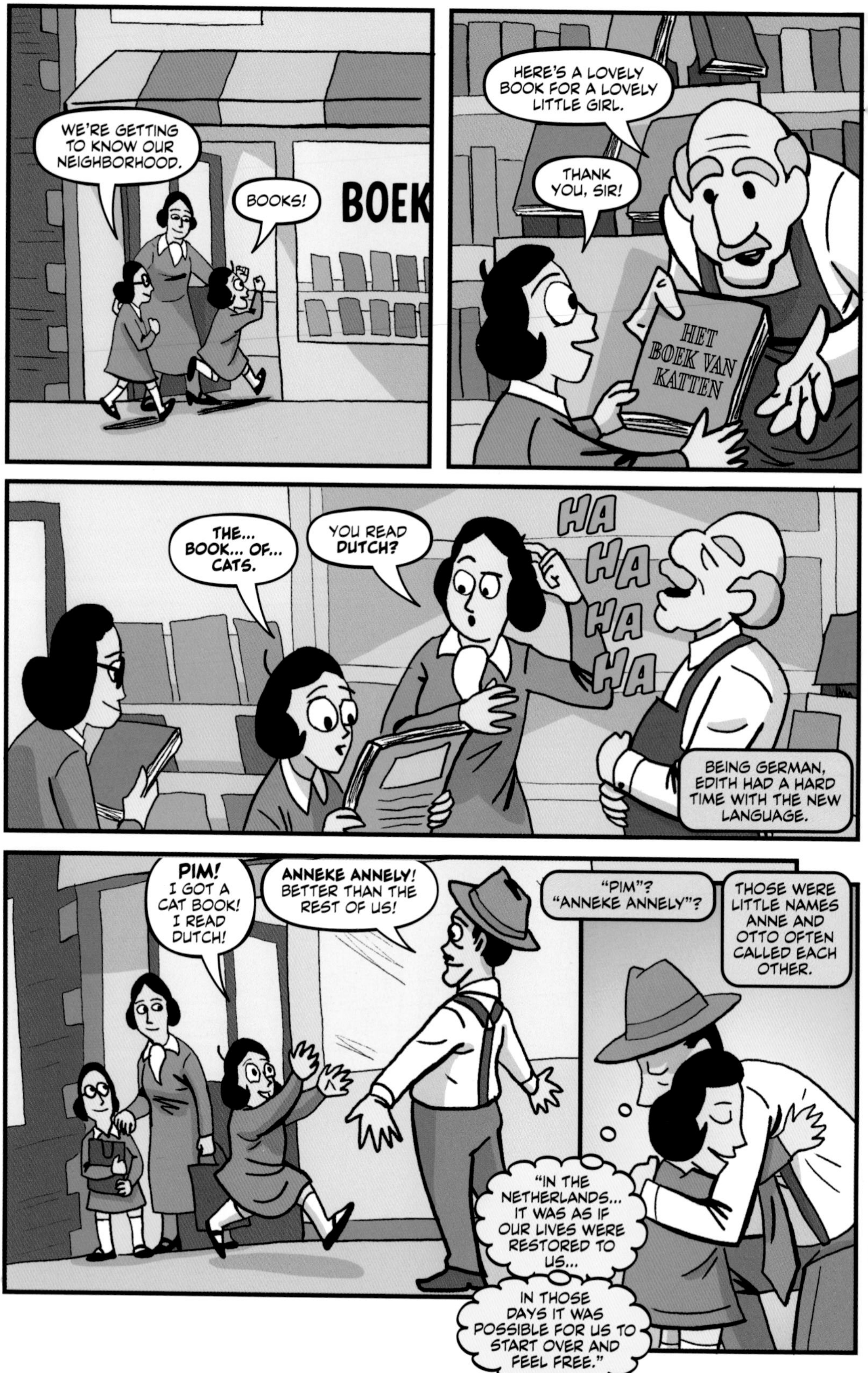
WE'RE GETTING TO KNOW OUR NEIGHBORHOOD.
BOOKS!
BOEK
HERE'S A LOVELY BOOK FOR A LOVELY LITTLE GIRL.
THANK YOU, SIR!
HET BOEK VAN KATTEN
THE... BOOK... OF... CATS.
YOU READ DUTCH?
HA HA HA HA HA
BEING GERMAN, EDITH HAD A HARD TIME WITH THE NEW LANGUAGE.
PIM! I GOT A CAT BOOK! I READ DUTCH!
ANNEKE ANNELY! BETTER THAN THE REST OF US!
"PIM"? "ANNEKE ANNELY"?
THOSE WERE LITTLE NAMES ANNE AND OTTO OFTEN CALLED EACH OTHER.
"IN THE NETHERLANDS... IT WAS AS IF OUR LIVES WERE RESTORED TO US...
IN THOSE DAYS IT WAS POSSIBLE FOR US TO START OVER AND FEEL FREE."

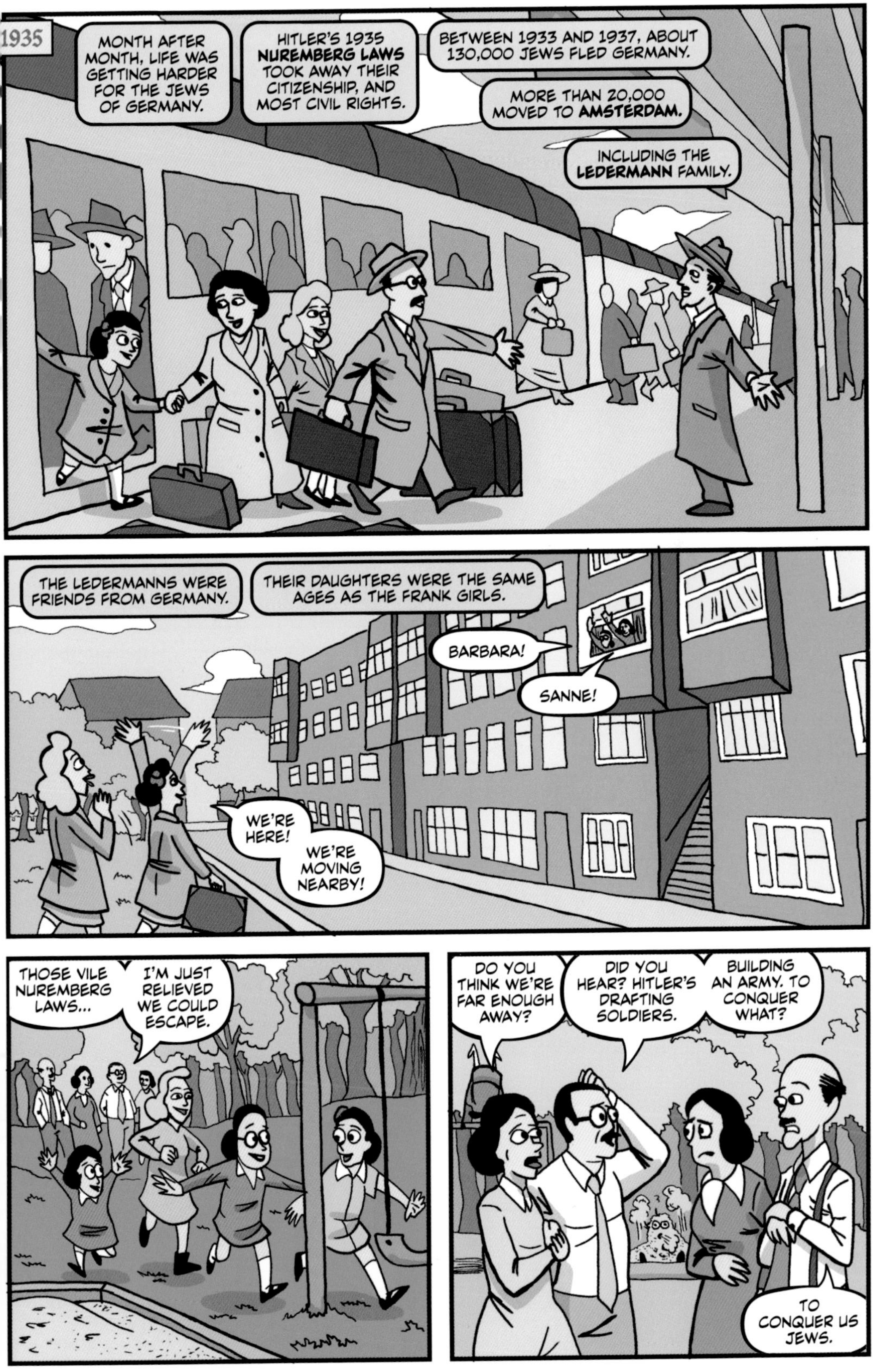
1935
MONTH AFTER MONTH, LIFE WAS GETTING HARDER FOR THE JEWS OF GERMANY.
HITLER'S 1935 **NUREMBERG LAWS** TOOK AWAY THEIR CITIZENSHIP, AND MOST CIVIL RIGHTS.
BETWEEN 1933 AND 1937, ABOUT 130,000 JEWS FLED GERMANY.
MORE THAN 20,000 MOVED TO **AMSTERDAM.**
INCLUDING THE **LEDERMANN** FAMILY.
THE LEDERMANNS WERE FRIENDS FROM GERMANY.
THEIR DAUGHTERS WERE THE SAME AGES AS THE FRANK GIRLS.
BARBARA!
SANNE!
WE'RE HERE!
WE'RE MOVING NEARBY!
THOSE VILE NUREMBERG LAWS...
I'M JUST RELIEVED WE COULD ESCAPE.
DO YOU THINK WE'RE FAR ENOUGH AWAY?
DID YOU HEAR? HITLER'S DRAFTING SOLDIERS.
BUILDING AN ARMY. TO CONQUER WHAT?
TO CONQUER US JEWS.

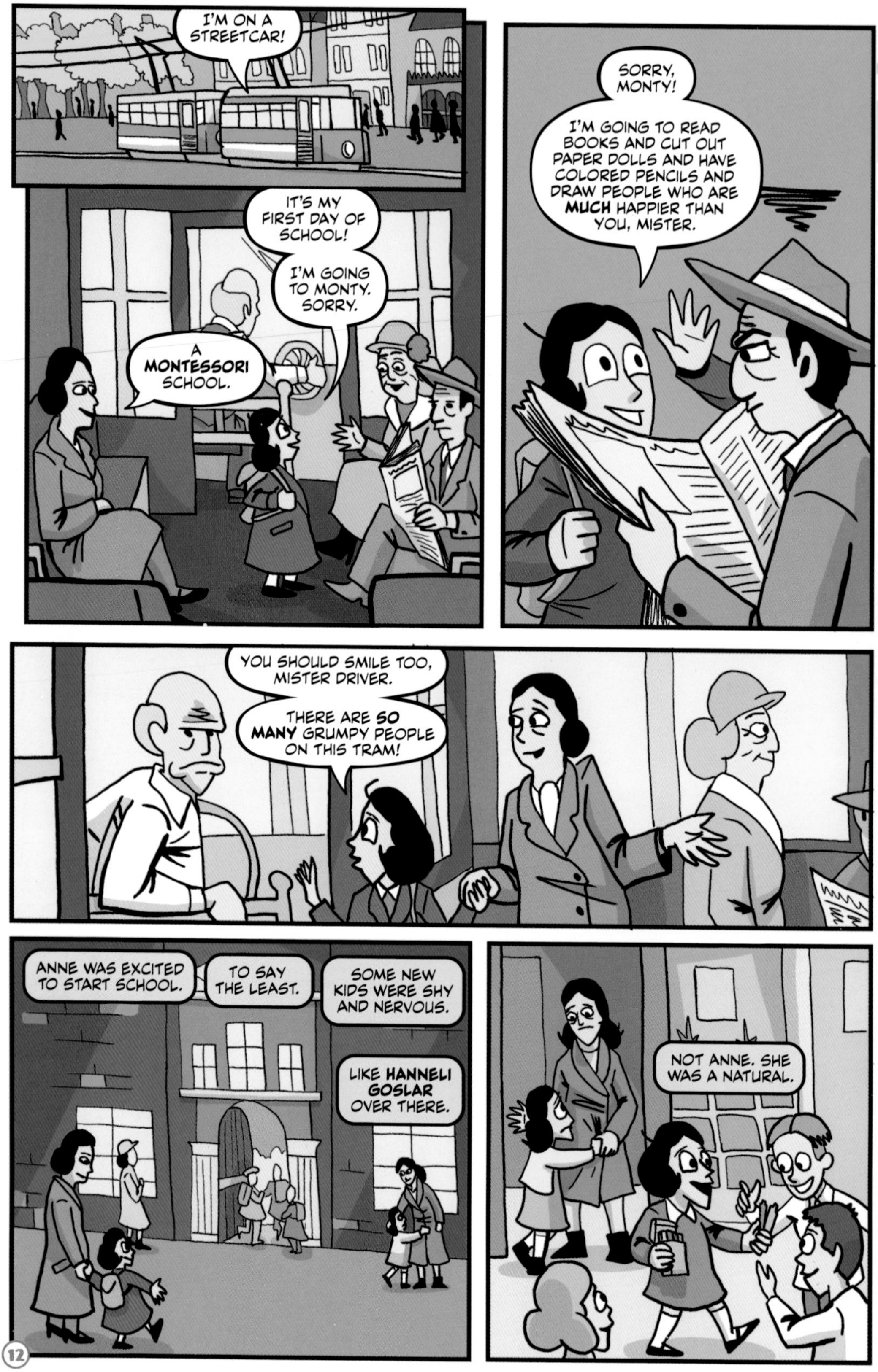

I'M ON A STREETCAR!
IT'S MY FIRST DAY OF SCHOOL!
I'M GOING TO MONTY. SORRY.
A MONTESSORI SCHOOL.
SORRY, MONTY!
I'M GOING TO READ BOOKS AND CUT OUT PAPER DOLLS AND HAVE COLORED PENCILS AND DRAW PEOPLE WHO ARE MUCH HAPPIER THAN YOU, MISTER.
YOU SHOULD SMILE TOO, MISTER DRIVER.
THERE ARE SO MANY GRUMPY PEOPLE ON THIS TRAM!
ANNE WAS EXCITED TO START SCHOOL.
TO SAY THE LEAST.
SOME NEW KIDS WERE SHY AND NERVOUS.
LIKE HANNELI GOSLAR OVER THERE.
NOT ANNE. SHE WAS A NATURAL.

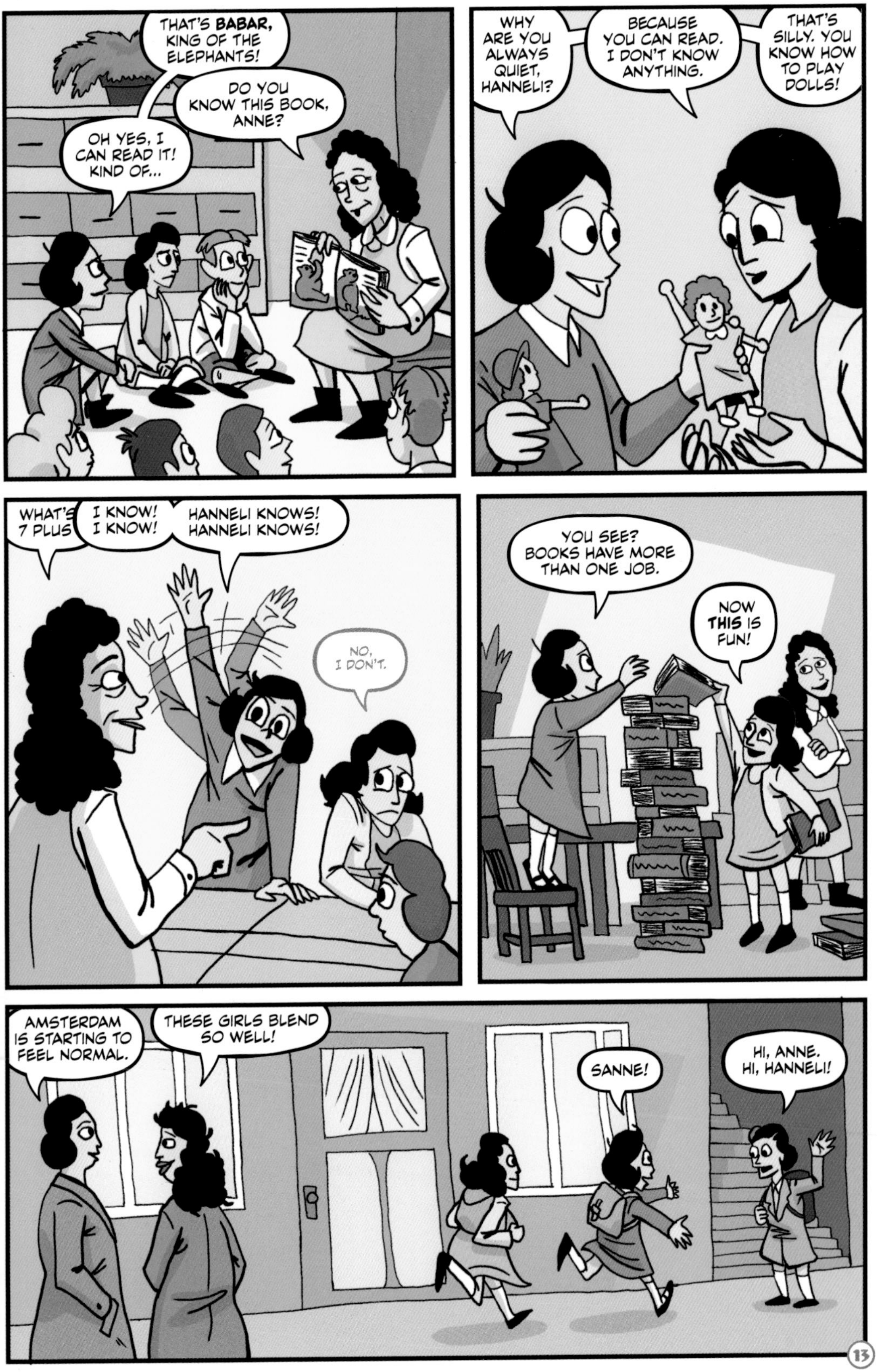
DO YOU KNOW THIS BOOK, ANNE?
OH YES, I CAN READ IT! KIND OF...
THAT'S **BABAR,** KING OF THE ELEPHANTS!
WHY ARE YOU ALWAYS QUIET, HANNELI?
BECAUSE YOU CAN READ. I DON'T KNOW ANYTHING.
THAT'S SILLY. YOU KNOW HOW TO PLAY DOLLS!
WHAT'S 7 PLUS
I KNOW! I KNOW!
HANNELI KNOWS! HANNELI KNOWS!
NO, I DON'T.
YOU SEE? BOOKS HAVE MORE THAN ONE JOB.
NOW **THIS** IS FUN!
AMSTERDAM IS STARTING TO FEEL NORMAL.
THESE GIRLS BLEND SO WELL!
SANNE!
HI, ANNE. HI, HANNELI!

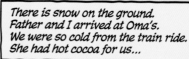
1936

Dear Anne, I'm so sorry you were too sick with the flu to come to see Grandma in Basel with father and me...

There is snow on the ground. Father and I arrived at Oma's. We were so cold from the train ride. She had hot cocoa for us...

Basel, Switzerland

We went ice skating on the Rhine river.

And I learned to ski!

I am not very good but I have not broken any bones. Your sister, Margot.

WELL, YOU COULD HAVE BROKEN AT LEAST **ONE** LITTLE BONE.

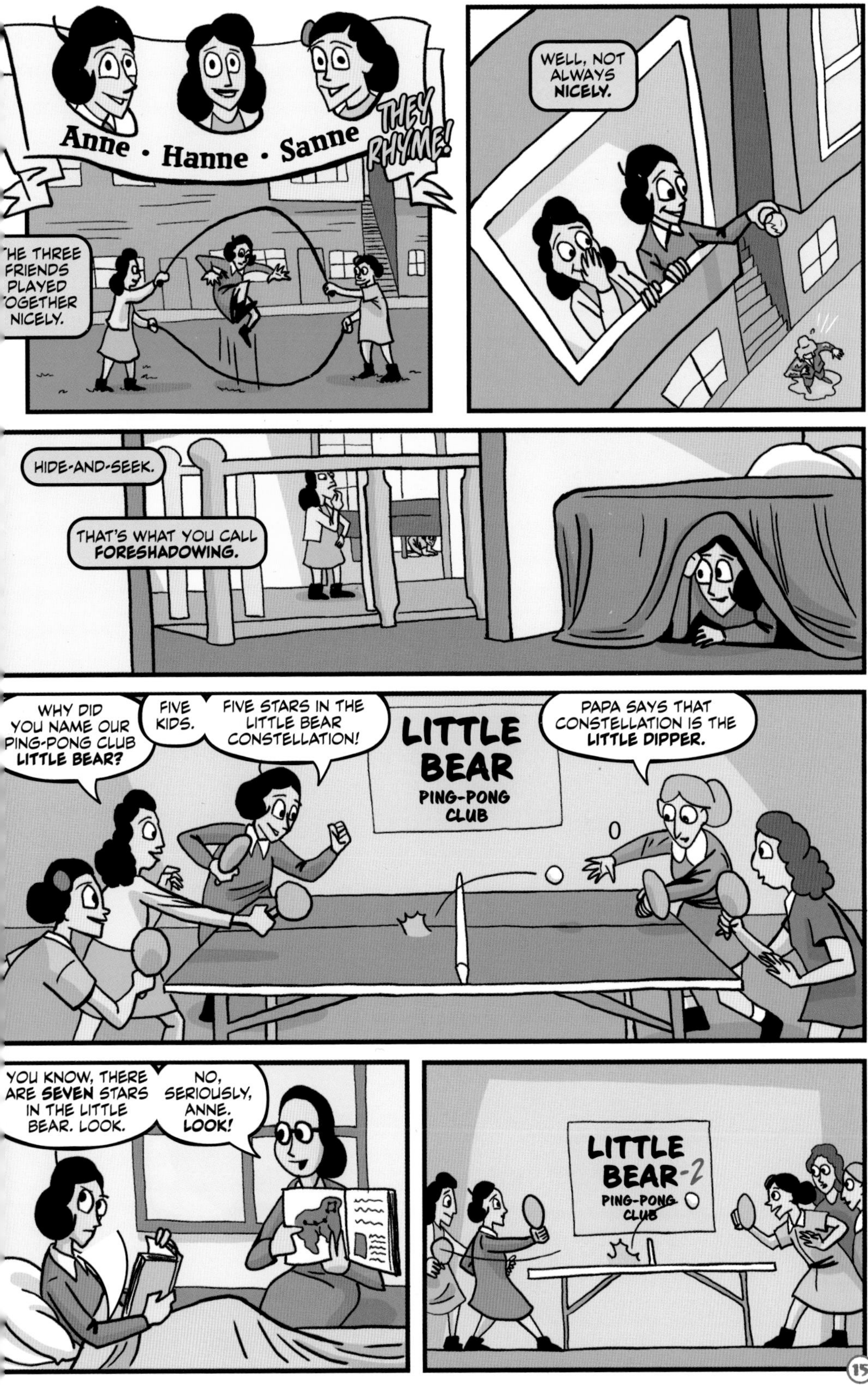
Anne · Hanne · Sanne
THEY RHYME!
THE THREE FRIENDS PLAYED TOGETHER NICELY.
WELL, NOT ALWAYS NICELY.
HIDE-AND-SEEK.
THAT'S WHAT YOU CALL FORESHADOWING.
WHY DID YOU NAME OUR PING-PONG CLUB LITTLE BEAR?
FIVE KIDS.
FIVE STARS IN THE LITTLE BEAR CONSTELLATION!
LITTLE BEAR PING-PONG CLUB
PAPA SAYS THAT CONSTELLATION IS THE LITTLE DIPPER.
YOU KNOW, THERE ARE SEVEN STARS IN THE LITTLE BEAR. LOOK.
NO, SERIOUSLY, ANNE. LOOK!
LITTLE BEAR-2 PING-PONG CLUB

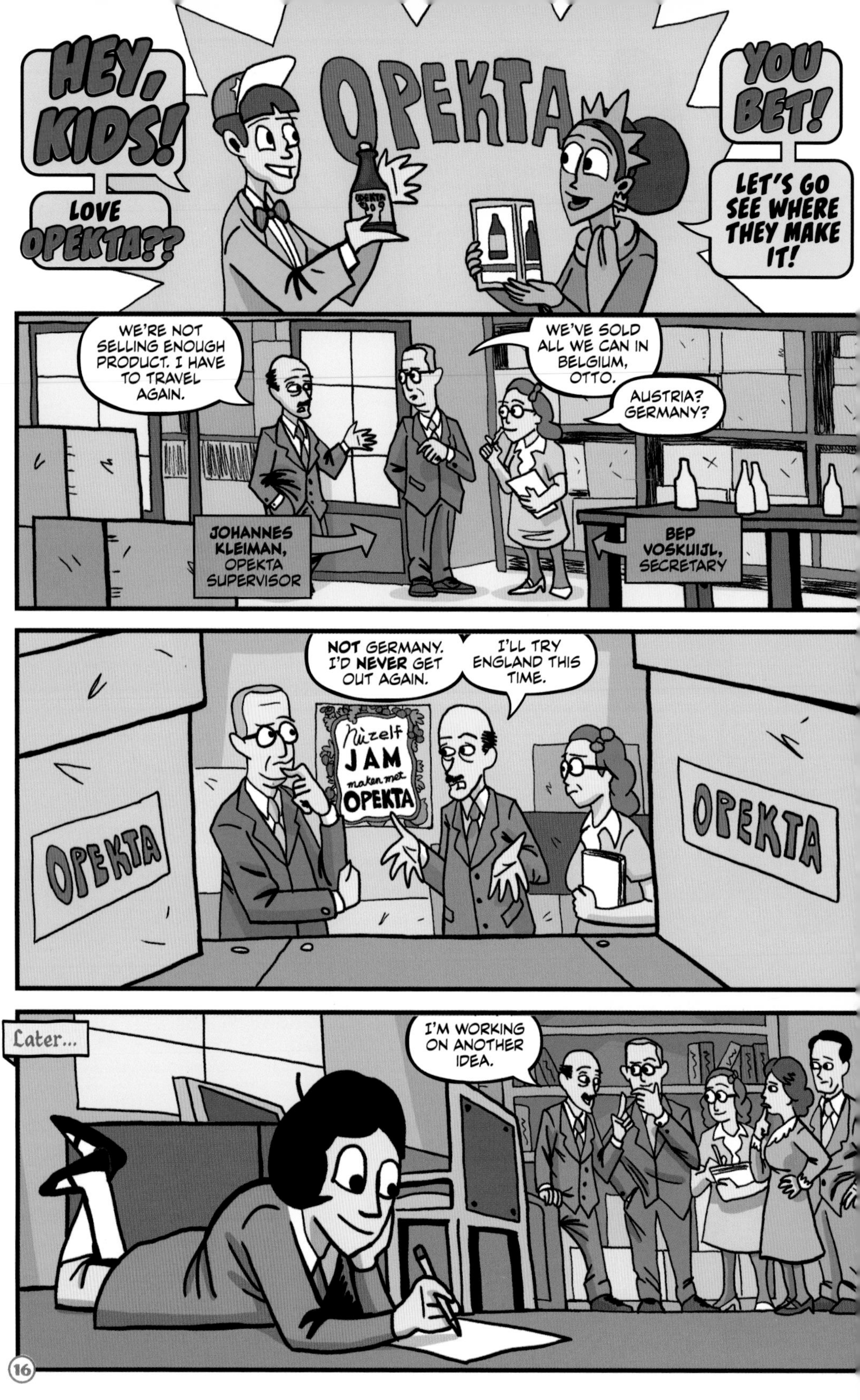
HEY, KIDS!
LOVE OPEKTA??
OPEKTA
YOU BET!
LET'S GO SEE WHERE THEY MAKE IT!
WE'RE NOT SELLING ENOUGH PRODUCT. I HAVE TO TRAVEL AGAIN.
WE'VE SOLD ALL WE CAN IN BELGIUM, OTTO.
AUSTRIA? GERMANY?
JOHANNES KLEIMAN, OPEKTA SUPERVISOR
BEP VOSKUIJL, SECRETARY
NOT GERMANY. I'D NEVER GET OUT AGAIN.
I'LL TRY ENGLAND THIS TIME.
Nu zelf JAM maken met OPEKTA
OPEKTA
OPEKTA
Later...
I'M WORKING ON ANOTHER IDEA.

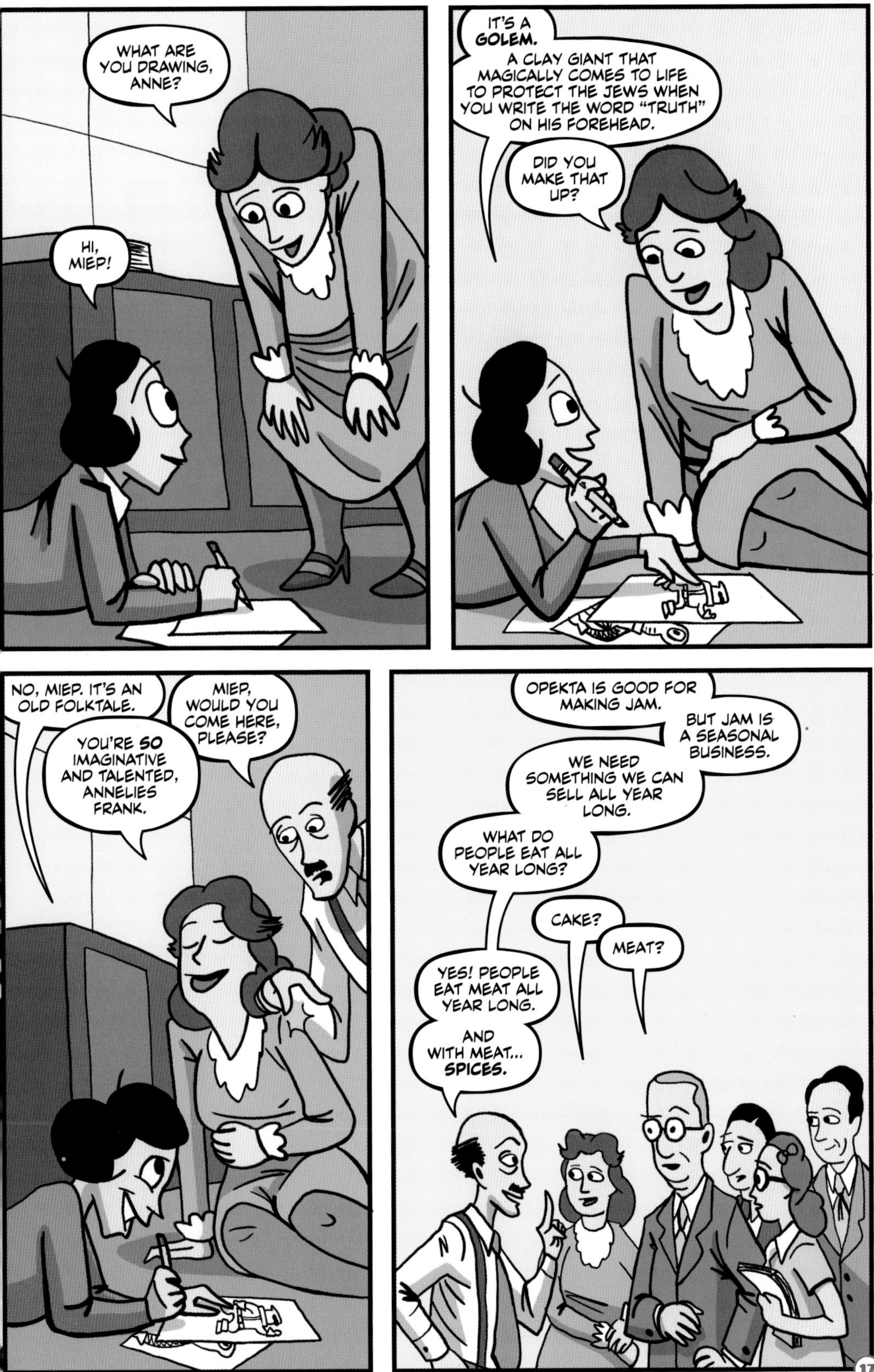
WHAT ARE YOU DRAWING, ANNE?
HI, MIEP!
IT'S A GOLEM.
A CLAY GIANT THAT MAGICALLY COMES TO LIFE TO PROTECT THE JEWS WHEN YOU WRITE THE WORD "TRUTH" ON HIS FOREHEAD.
DID YOU MAKE THAT UP?
NO, MIEP. IT'S AN OLD FOLKTALE.
YOU'RE SO IMAGINATIVE AND TALENTED, ANNELIES FRANK.
MIEP, WOULD YOU COME HERE, PLEASE?
OPEKTA IS GOOD FOR MAKING JAM.
BUT JAM IS A SEASONAL BUSINESS.
WE NEED SOMETHING WE CAN SELL ALL YEAR LONG.
WHAT DO PEOPLE EAT ALL YEAR LONG?
CAKE?
MEAT?
YES! PEOPLE EAT MEAT ALL YEAR LONG.
AND WITH MEAT... SPICES.

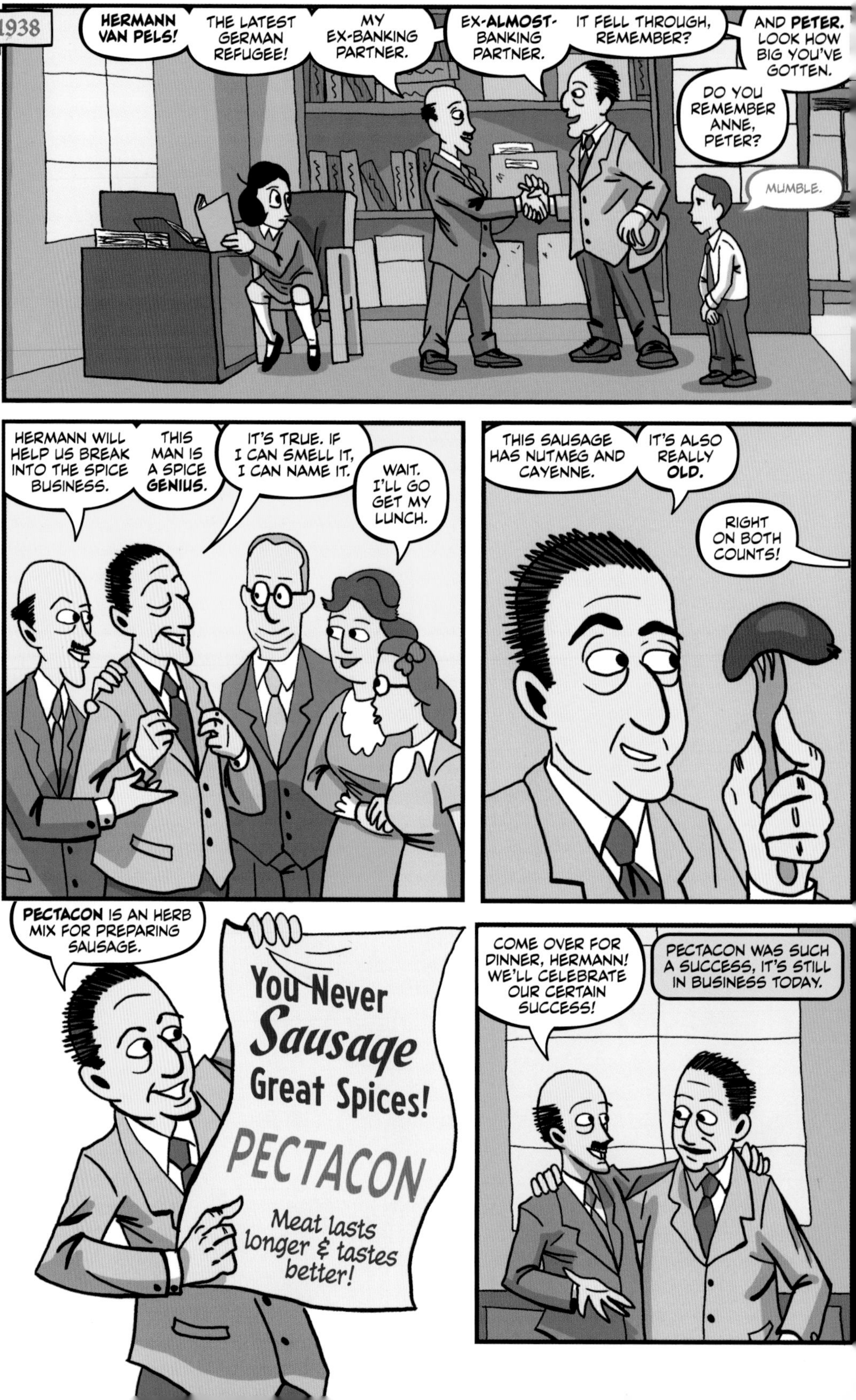
1938
HERMANN VAN PELS!
THE LATEST GERMAN REFUGEE!
MY EX-BANKING PARTNER.
EX-ALMOST-BANKING PARTNER.
IT FELL THROUGH, REMEMBER?
AND PETER. LOOK HOW BIG YOU'VE GOTTEN.
DO YOU REMEMBER ANNE, PETER?
MUMBLE.
HERMANN WILL HELP US BREAK INTO THE SPICE BUSINESS.
THIS MAN IS A SPICE GENIUS.
IT'S TRUE. IF I CAN SMELL IT, I CAN NAME IT.
WAIT. I'LL GO GET MY LUNCH.
THIS SAUSAGE HAS NUTMEG AND CAYENNE.
IT'S ALSO REALLY OLD.
RIGHT ON BOTH COUNTS!
PECTACON IS AN HERB MIX FOR PREPARING SAUSAGE.
You Never Sausage Great Spices!
PECTACON
Meat lasts longer & tastes better!
COME OVER FOR DINNER, HERMANN! WE'LL CELEBRATE OUR CERTAIN SUCCESS!
PECTACON WAS SUCH A SUCCESS, IT'S STILL IN BUSINESS TODAY.

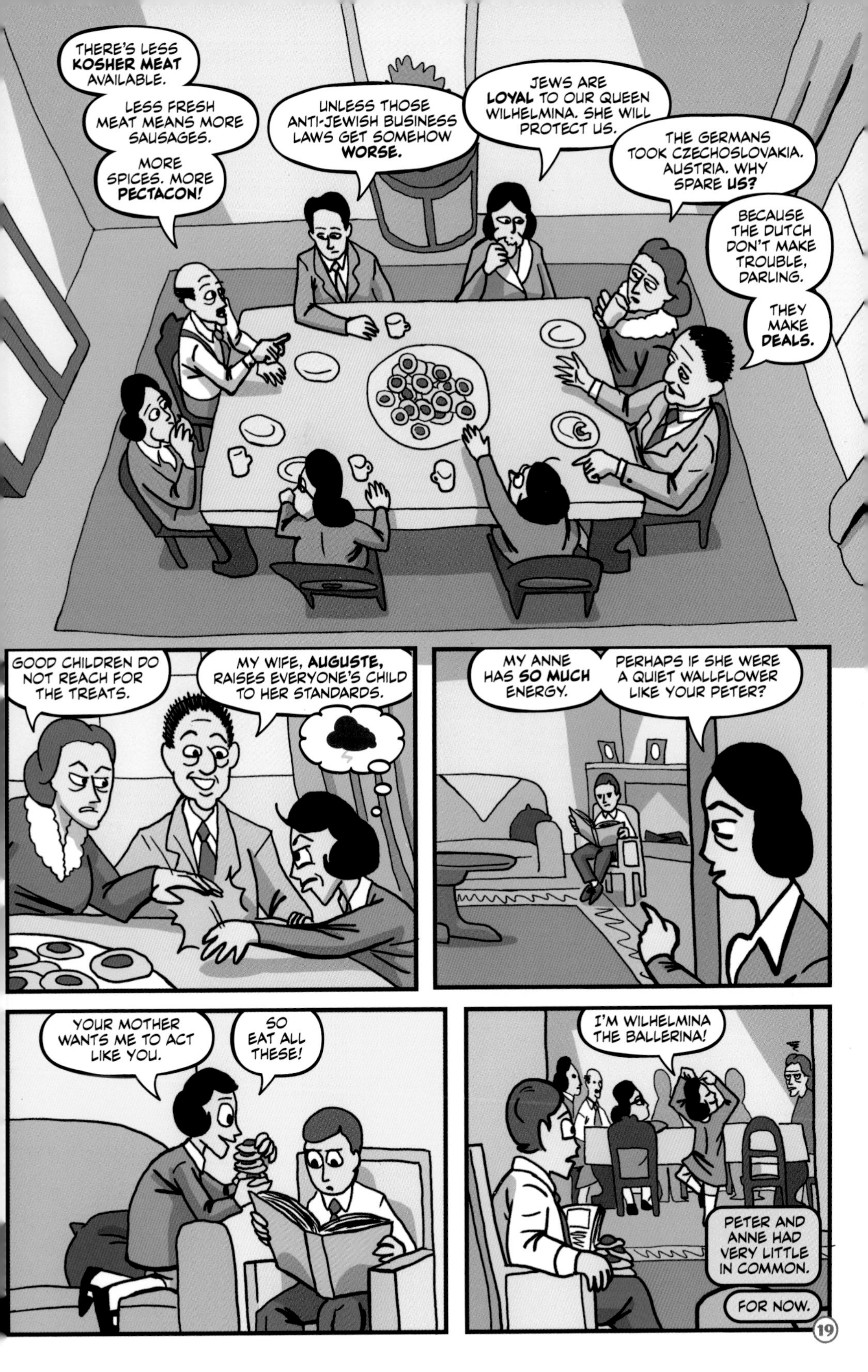
THERE'S LESS KOSHER MEAT AVAILABLE.
LESS FRESH MEAT MEANS MORE SAUSAGES.
MORE SPICES. MORE PECTACON!
UNLESS THOSE ANTI-JEWISH BUSINESS LAWS GET SOMEHOW WORSE.
JEWS ARE LOYAL TO OUR QUEEN WILHELMINA. SHE WILL PROTECT US.
THE GERMANS TOOK CZECHOSLOVAKIA. AUSTRIA. WHY SPARE US?
BECAUSE THE DUTCH DON'T MAKE TROUBLE, DARLING.
THEY MAKE DEALS.
GOOD CHILDREN DO NOT REACH FOR THE TREATS.
MY WIFE, AUGUSTE, RAISES EVERYONE'S CHILD TO HER STANDARDS.
MY ANNE HAS SO MUCH ENERGY.
PERHAPS IF SHE WERE A QUIET WALLFLOWER LIKE YOUR PETER?
YOUR MOTHER WANTS ME TO ACT LIKE YOU.
SO EAT ALL THESE!
I'M WILHELMINA THE BALLERINA!
PETER AND ANNE HAD VERY LITTLE IN COMMON.
FOR NOW.

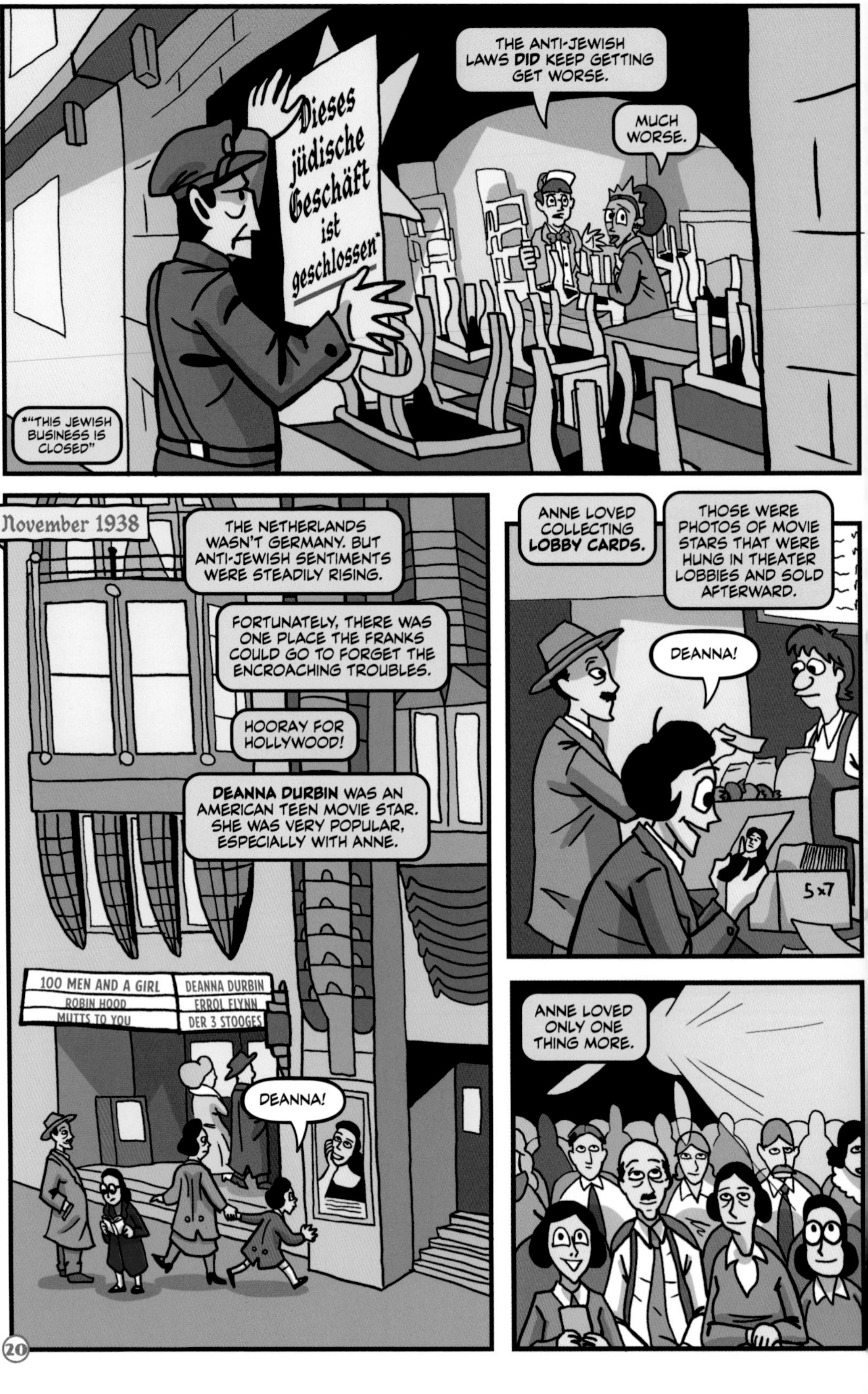
Dieses jüdische Geschäft ist geschlossen*
THE ANTI-JEWISH LAWS DID KEEP GETTING GET WORSE.
MUCH WORSE.
*"THIS JEWISH BUSINESS IS CLOSED"
November 1938
THE NETHERLANDS WASN'T GERMANY. BUT ANTI-JEWISH SENTIMENTS WERE STEADILY RISING.
FORTUNATELY, THERE WAS ONE PLACE THE FRANKS COULD GO TO FORGET THE ENCROACHING TROUBLES.
HOORAY FOR HOLLYWOOD!
DEANNA DURBIN WAS AN AMERICAN TEEN MOVIE STAR. SHE WAS VERY POPULAR, ESPECIALLY WITH ANNE.
100 MEN AND A GIRL
DEANNA DURBIN
ROBIN HOOD
ERROL FLYNN
MUTTS TO YOU
DER 3 STOOGES
DEANNA!
ANNE LOVED COLLECTING LOBBY CARDS.
THOSE WERE PHOTOS OF MOVIE STARS THAT WERE HUNG IN THEATER LOBBIES AND SOLD AFTERWARD.
DEANNA!
5x7
ANNE LOVED ONLY ONE THING MORE.

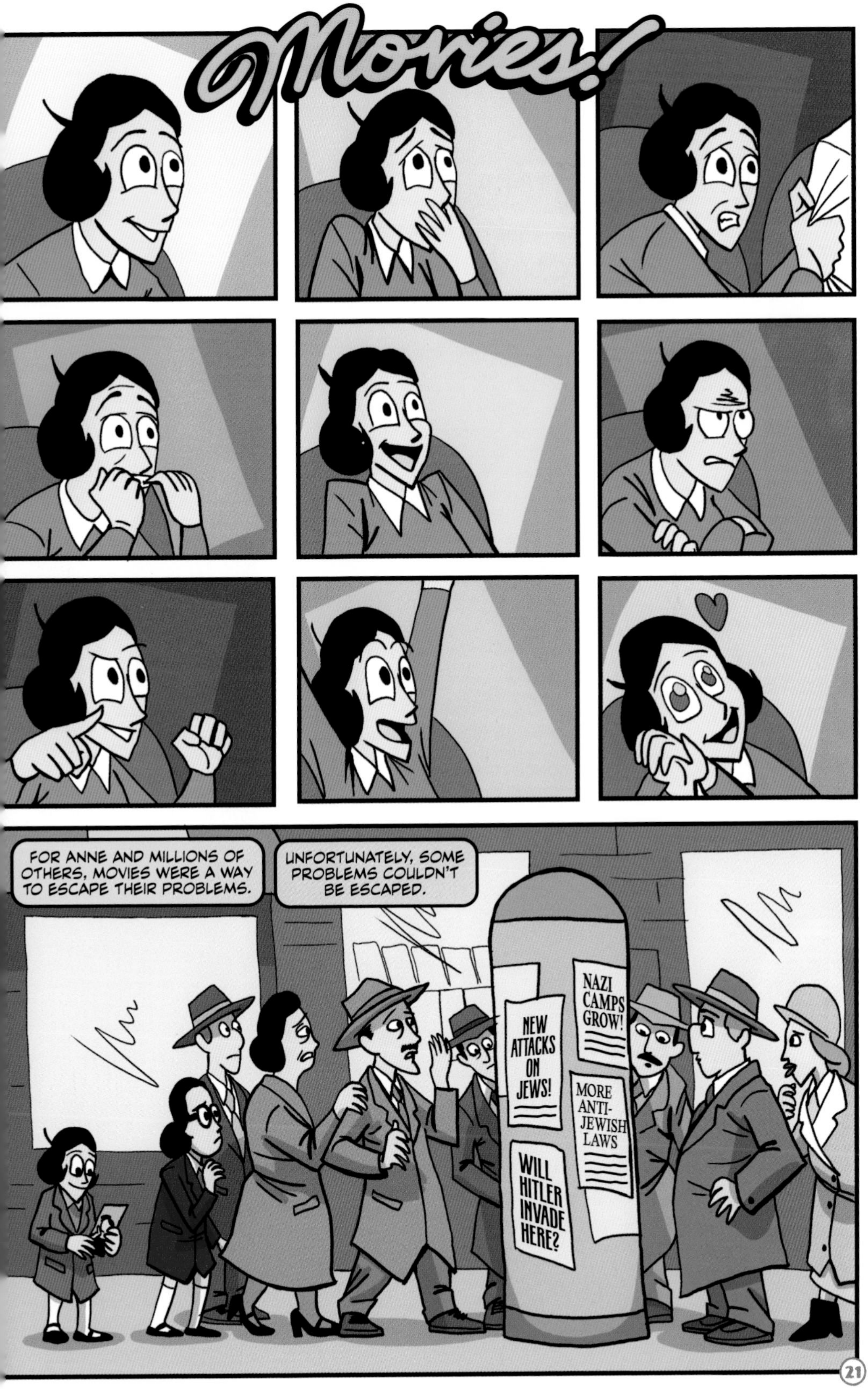
Movies!
FOR ANNE AND MILLIONS OF OTHERS, MOVIES WERE A WAY TO ESCAPE THEIR PROBLEMS.
UNFORTUNATELY, SOME PROBLEMS COULDN'T BE ESCAPED.
NEW ATTACKS ON JEWS!
NAZI CAMPS GROW!
MORE ANTI-JEWISH LAWS
WILL HITLER INVADE HERE?

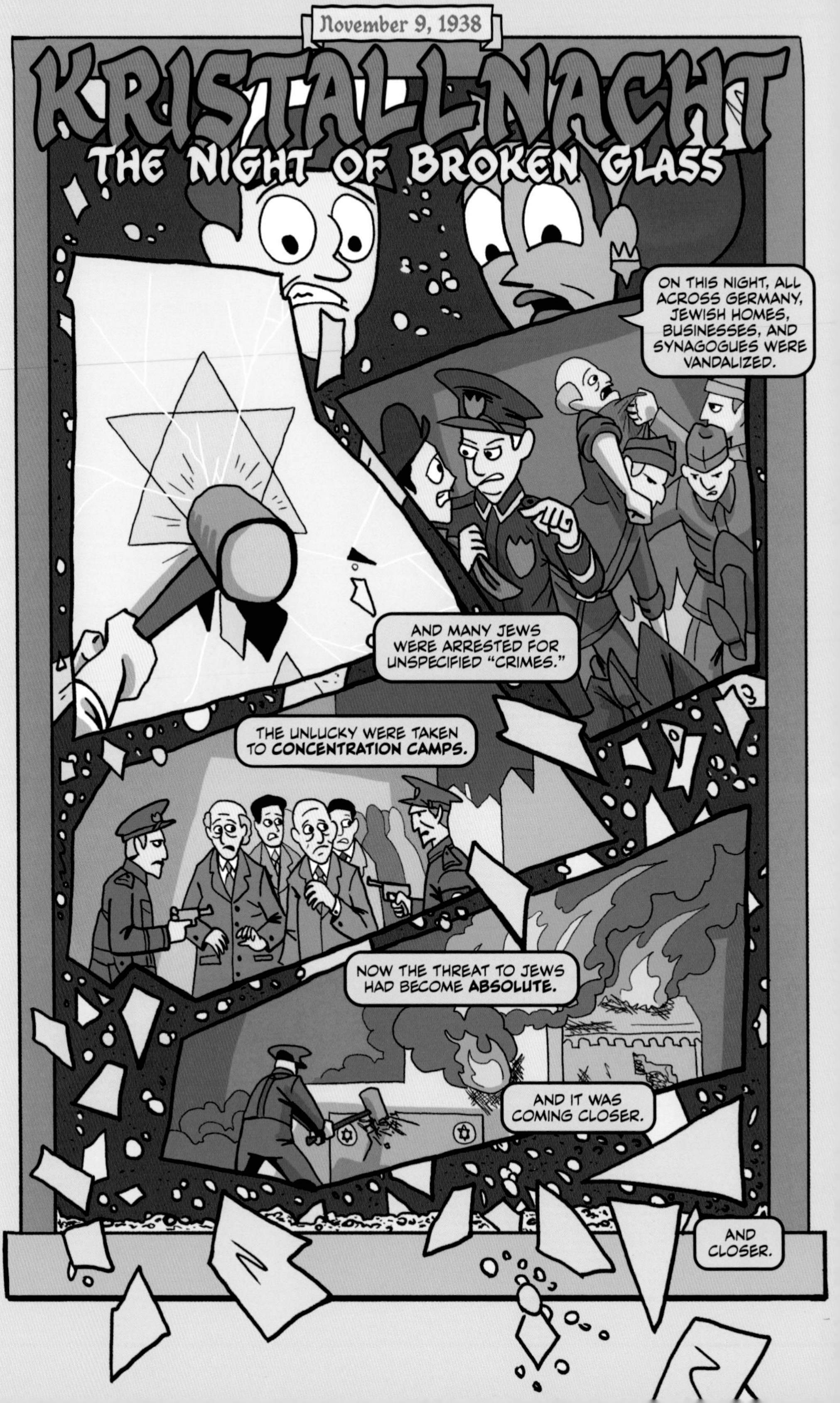
November 9, 1938
KRISTALLNACHT
THE NIGHT OF BROKEN GLASS
ON THIS NIGHT, ALL ACROSS GERMANY, JEWISH HOMES, BUSINESSES, AND SYNAGOGUES WERE VANDALIZED.
AND MANY JEWS WERE ARRESTED FOR UNSPECIFIED "CRIMES."
THE UNLUCKY WERE TAKEN TO CONCENTRATION CAMPS.
NOW THE THREAT TO JEWS HAD BECOME ABSOLUTE.
AND IT WAS COMING CLOSER.
AND CLOSER.

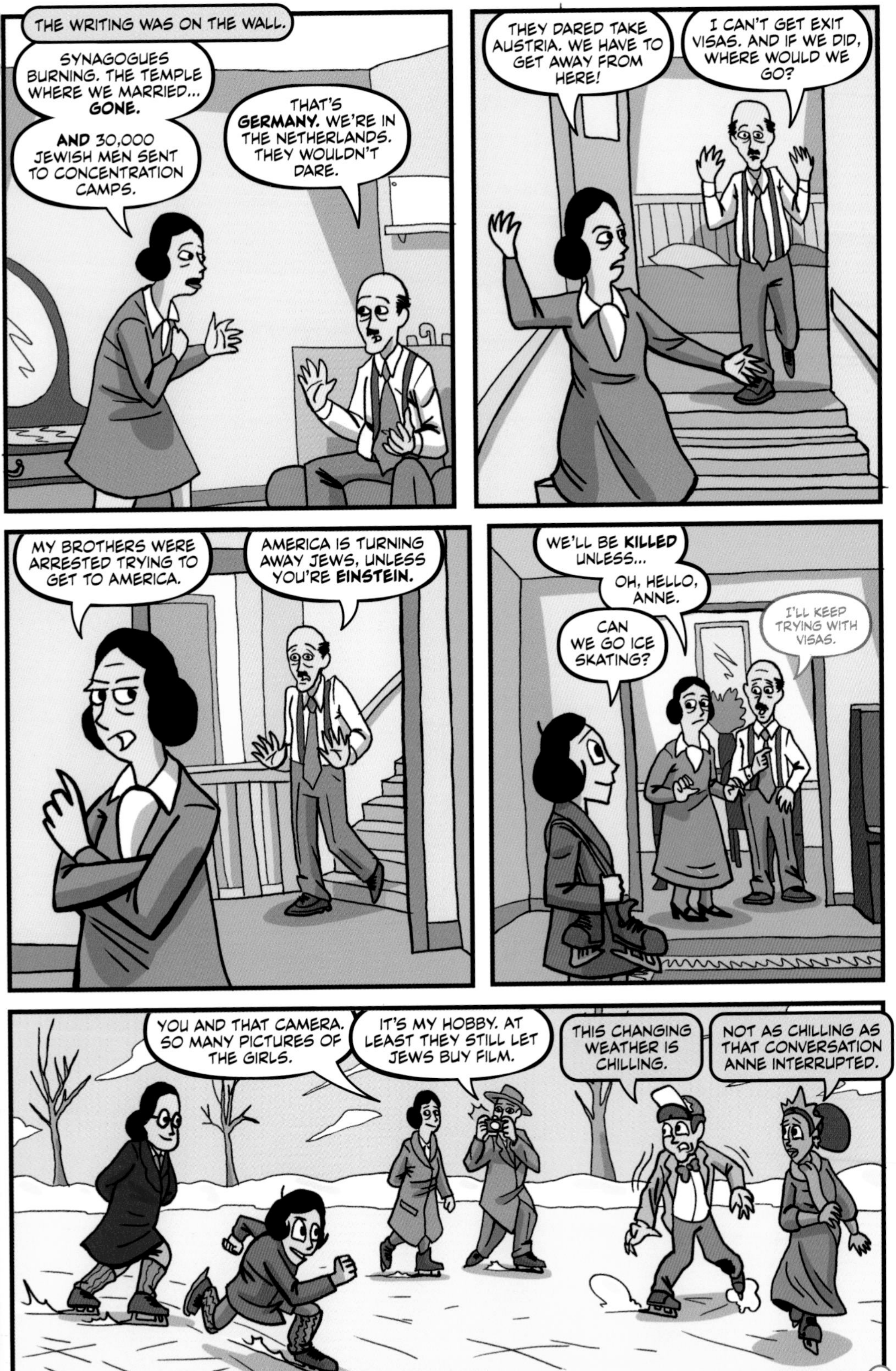
THE WRITING WAS ON THE WALL.
SYNAGOGUES BURNING. THE TEMPLE WHERE WE MARRIED... GONE.
AND 30,000 JEWISH MEN SENT TO CONCENTRATION CAMPS.
THAT'S GERMANY. WE'RE IN THE NETHERLANDS. THEY WOULDN'T DARE.
THEY DARED TAKE AUSTRIA. WE HAVE TO GET AWAY FROM HERE!
I CAN'T GET EXIT VISAS. AND IF WE DID, WHERE WOULD WE GO?
MY BROTHERS WERE ARRESTED TRYING TO GET TO AMERICA.
AMERICA IS TURNING AWAY JEWS, UNLESS YOU'RE EINSTEIN.
WE'LL BE KILLED UNLESS...
OH, HELLO, ANNE.
CAN WE GO ICE SKATING?
I'LL KEEP TRYING WITH VISAS.
YOU AND THAT CAMERA. SO MANY PICTURES OF THE GIRLS.
IT'S MY HOBBY. AT LEAST THEY STILL LET JEWS BUY FILM.
THIS CHANGING WEATHER IS CHILLING.
NOT AS CHILLING AS THAT CONVERSATION ANNE INTERRUPTED.

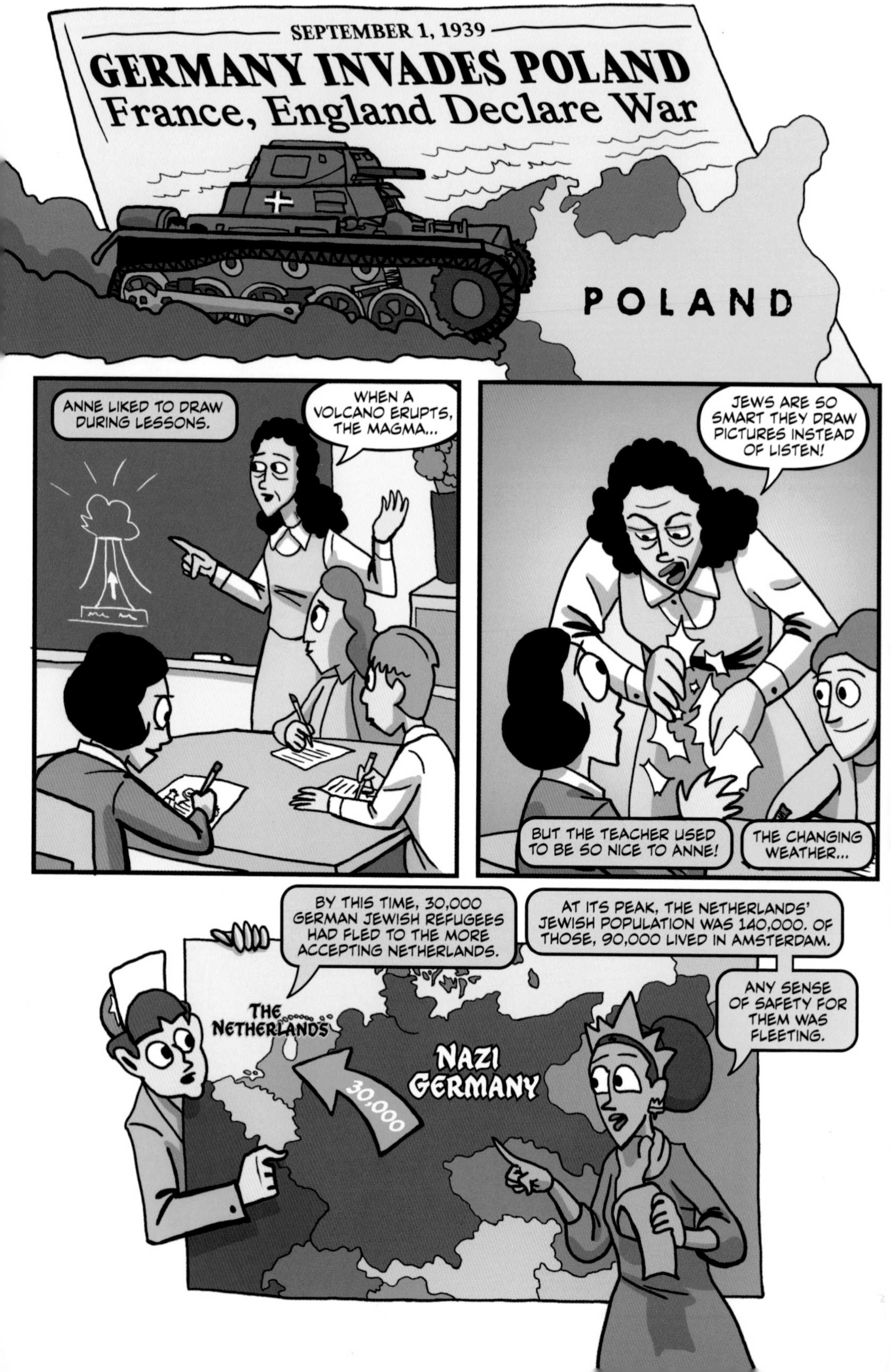
SEPTEMBER 1, 1939
GERMANY INVADES POLAND
France, England Declare War
POLAND
ANNE LIKED TO DRAW DURING LESSONS.
WHEN A VOLCANO ERUPTS, THE MAGMA...
JEWS ARE SO SMART THEY DRAW PICTURES INSTEAD OF LISTEN!
BUT THE TEACHER USED TO BE SO NICE TO ANNE!
THE CHANGING WEATHER...
BY THIS TIME, 30,000 GERMAN JEWISH REFUGEES HAD FLED TO THE MORE ACCEPTING NETHERLANDS.
AT ITS PEAK, THE NETHERLANDS' JEWISH POPULATION WAS 140,000. OF THOSE, 90,000 LIVED IN AMSTERDAM.
ANY SENSE OF SAFETY FOR THEM WAS FLEETING.
THE NETHERLANDS
NAZI GERMANY
30,000

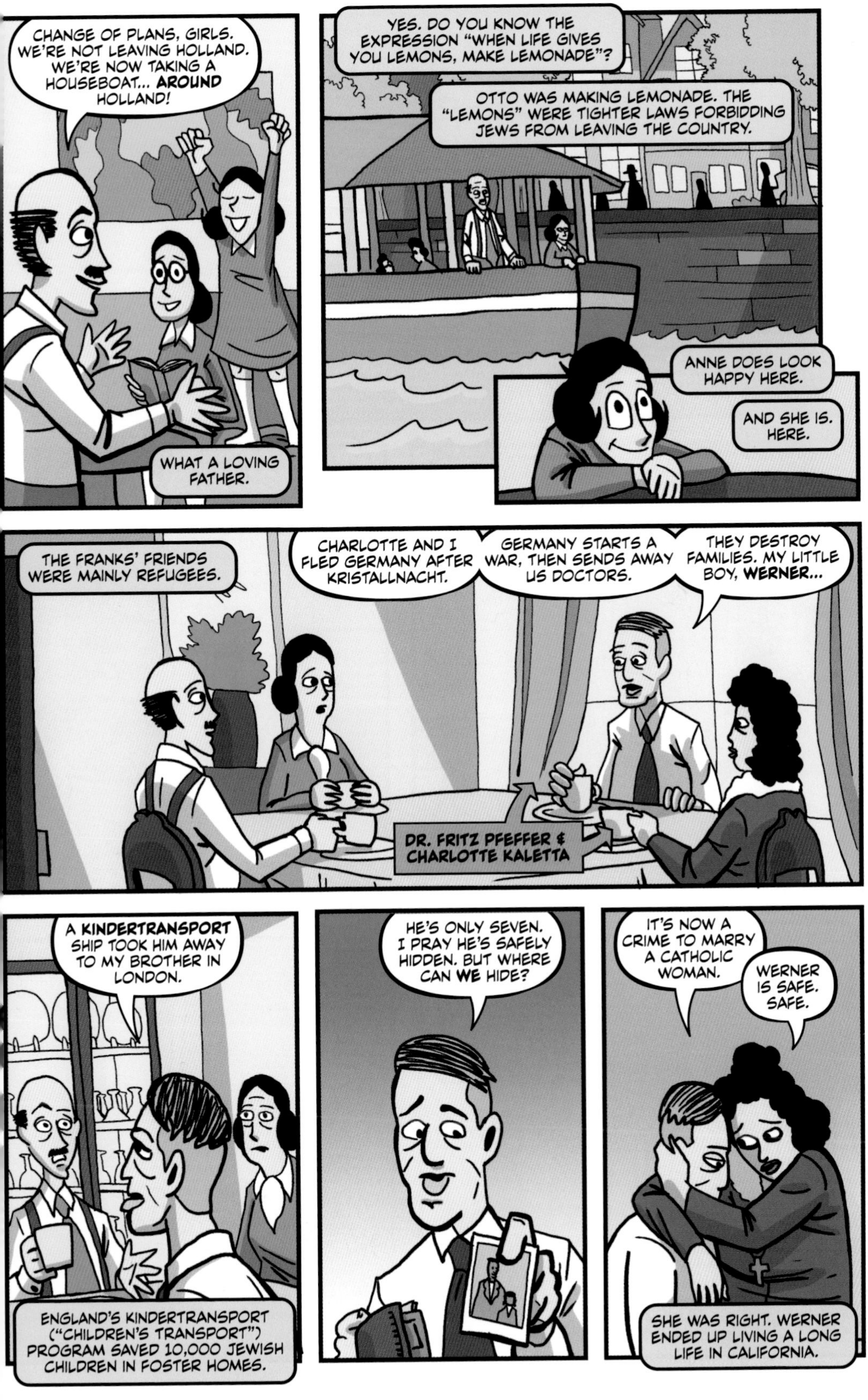
CHANGE OF PLANS, GIRLS. WE'RE NOT LEAVING HOLLAND. WE'RE NOW TAKING A HOUSEBOAT... **AROUND** HOLLAND!
WHAT A LOVING FATHER.
YES. DO YOU KNOW THE EXPRESSION "WHEN LIFE GIVES YOU LEMONS, MAKE LEMONADE"?
OTTO WAS MAKING LEMONADE. THE "LEMONS" WERE TIGHTER LAWS FORBIDDING JEWS FROM LEAVING THE COUNTRY.
ANNE DOES LOOK HAPPY HERE.
AND SHE IS. HERE.
THE FRANKS' FRIENDS WERE MAINLY REFUGEES.
CHARLOTTE AND I FLED GERMANY AFTER KRISTALLNACHT.
GERMANY STARTS A WAR, THEN SENDS AWAY US DOCTORS.
THEY DESTROY FAMILIES. MY LITTLE BOY, **WERNER...**
DR. FRITZ PFEFFER & CHARLOTTE KALETTA
A **KINDERTRANSPORT** SHIP TOOK HIM AWAY TO MY BROTHER IN LONDON.
ENGLAND'S KINDERTRANSPORT ("CHILDREN'S TRANSPORT") PROGRAM SAVED 10,000 JEWISH CHILDREN IN FOSTER HOMES.
HE'S ONLY SEVEN. I PRAY HE'S SAFELY HIDDEN. BUT WHERE CAN **WE** HIDE?
IT'S NOW A CRIME TO MARRY A CATHOLIC WOMAN.
WERNER IS SAFE. SAFE.
SHE WAS RIGHT. WERNER ENDED UP LIVING A LONG LIFE IN CALIFORNIA.

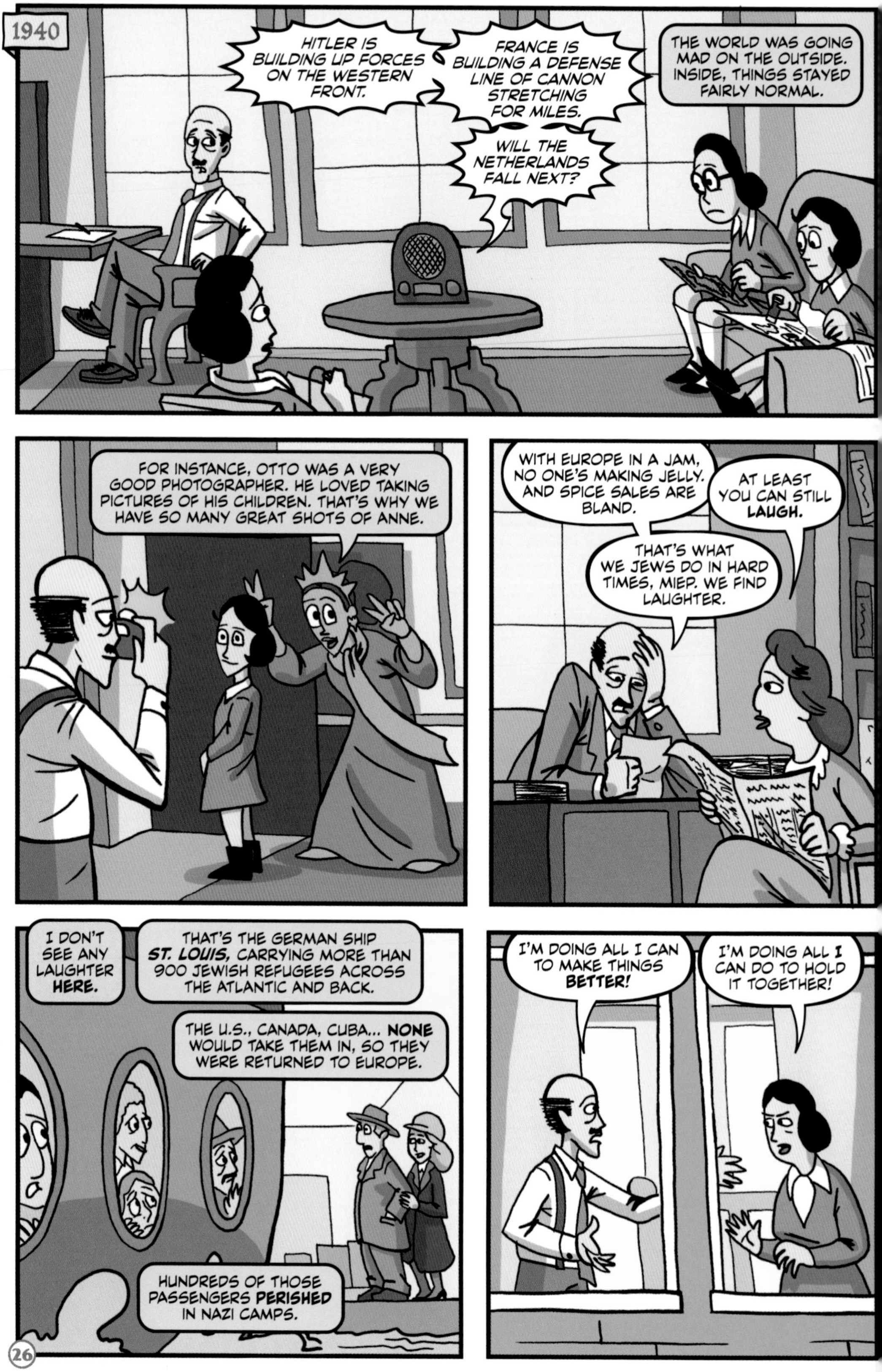
1940
HITLER IS BUILDING UP FORCES ON THE WESTERN FRONT.
FRANCE IS BUILDING A DEFENSE LINE OF CANNON STRETCHING FOR MILES.
WILL THE NETHERLANDS FALL NEXT?
THE WORLD WAS GOING MAD ON THE OUTSIDE. INSIDE, THINGS STAYED FAIRLY NORMAL.
FOR INSTANCE, OTTO WAS A VERY GOOD PHOTOGRAPHER. HE LOVED TAKING PICTURES OF HIS CHILDREN. THAT'S WHY WE HAVE SO MANY GREAT SHOTS OF ANNE.
WITH EUROPE IN A JAM, NO ONE'S MAKING JELLY. AND SPICE SALES ARE BLAND.
AT LEAST YOU CAN STILL **LAUGH.**
THAT'S WHAT WE JEWS DO IN HARD TIMES, MIEP. WE FIND LAUGHTER.
I DON'T SEE ANY LAUGHTER **HERE.**
THAT'S THE GERMAN SHIP ***ST. LOUIS,*** CARRYING MORE THAN 900 JEWISH REFUGEES ACROSS THE ATLANTIC AND BACK.
THE U.S., CANADA, CUBA... **NONE** WOULD TAKE THEM IN, SO THEY WERE RETURNED TO EUROPE.
HUNDREDS OF THOSE PASSENGERS **PERISHED** IN NAZI CAMPS.
I'M DOING ALL I CAN TO MAKE THINGS **BETTER!**
I'M DOING ALL **I** CAN DO TO HOLD IT TOGETHER!

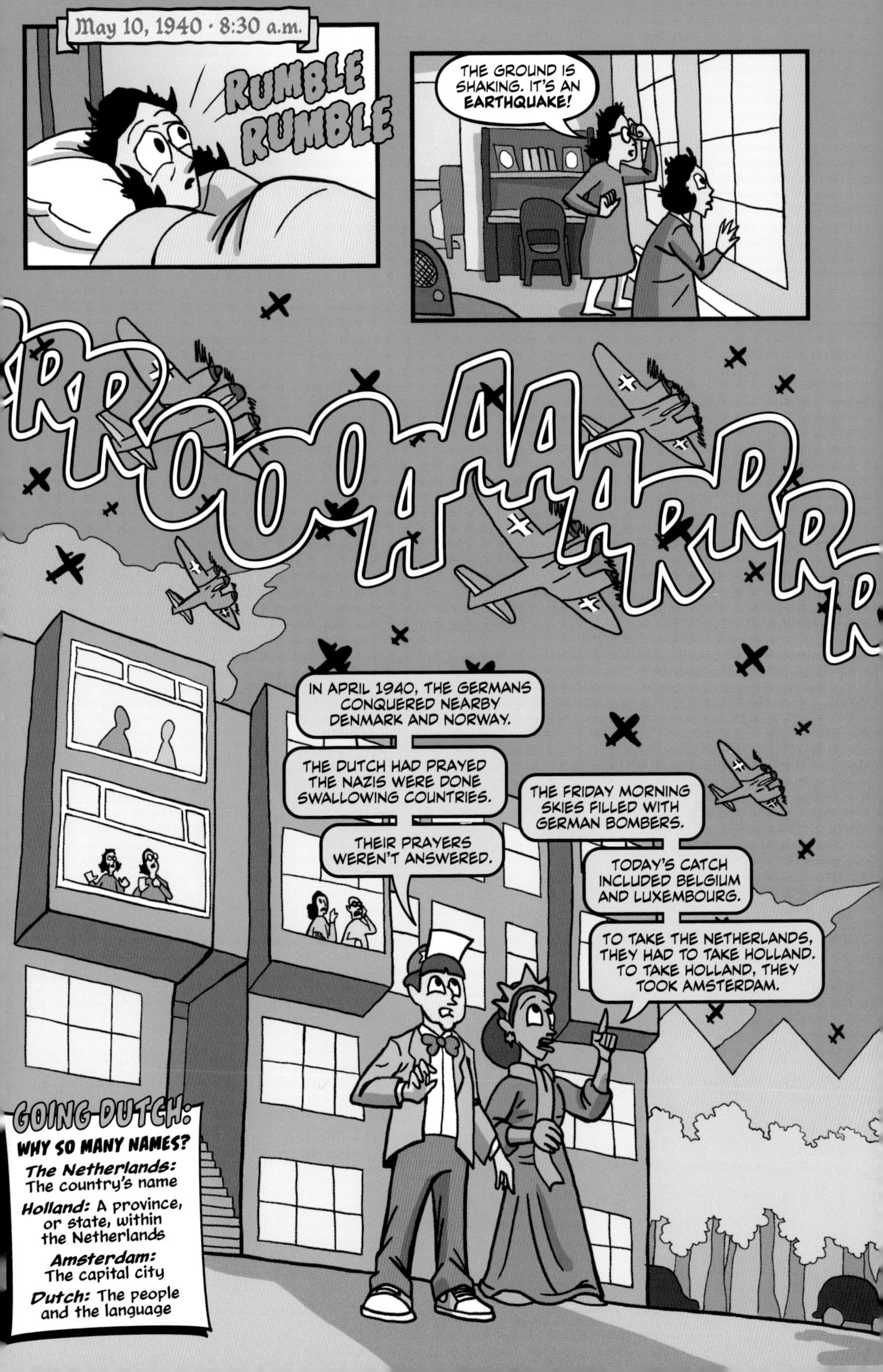
May 10, 1940 · 8:30 a.m.
RUMBLE RUMBLE
THE GROUND IS SHAKING. IT'S AN EARTHQUAKE!
RROOAAARRR
IN APRIL 1940, THE GERMANS CONQUERED NEARBY DENMARK AND NORWAY.
THE DUTCH HAD PRAYED THE NAZIS WERE DONE SWALLOWING COUNTRIES.
THEIR PRAYERS WEREN'T ANSWERED.
THE FRIDAY MORNING SKIES FILLED WITH GERMAN BOMBERS.
TODAY'S CATCH INCLUDED BELGIUM AND LUXEMBOURG.
TO TAKE THE NETHERLANDS, THEY HAD TO TAKE HOLLAND. TO TAKE HOLLAND, THEY TOOK AMSTERDAM.
GOING DUTCH:
WHY SO MANY NAMES?
The Netherlands: The country's name
Holland: A province, or state, within the Netherlands
Amsterdam: The capital city
Dutch: The people and the language

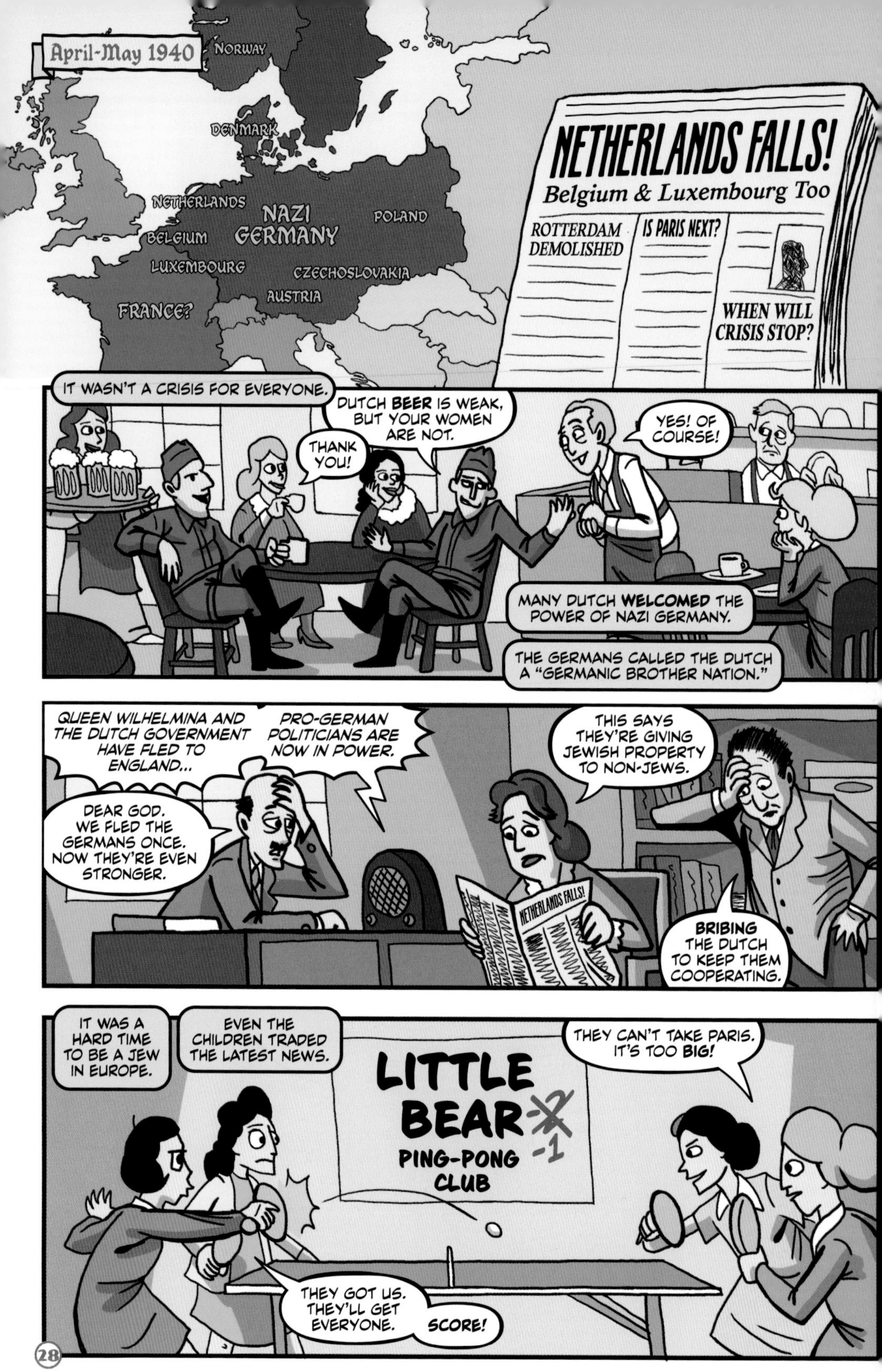

April-May 1940
NORWAY
DENMARK
NETHERLANDS
NAZI GERMANY
POLAND
BELGIUM
LUXEMBOURG
CZECHOSLOVAKIA
AUSTRIA
FRANCE?
NETHERLANDS FALLS!
Belgium & Luxembourg Too
ROTTERDAM DEMOLISHED
IS PARIS NEXT?
WHEN WILL CRISIS STOP?
IT WASN'T A CRISIS FOR EVERYONE.
DUTCH BEER IS WEAK, BUT YOUR WOMEN ARE NOT.
THANK YOU!
YES! OF COURSE!
MANY DUTCH WELCOMED THE POWER OF NAZI GERMANY.
THE GERMANS CALLED THE DUTCH A "GERMANIC BROTHER NATION."
QUEEN WILHELMINA AND THE DUTCH GOVERNMENT HAVE FLED TO ENGLAND...
PRO-GERMAN POLITICIANS ARE NOW IN POWER.
DEAR GOD. WE FLED THE GERMANS ONCE. NOW THEY'RE EVEN STRONGER.
THIS SAYS THEY'RE GIVING JEWISH PROPERTY TO NON-JEWS.
NETHERLANDS FALLS!
BRIBING THE DUTCH TO KEEP THEM COOPERATING.
IT WAS A HARD TIME TO BE A JEW IN EUROPE.
EVEN THE CHILDREN TRADED THE LATEST NEWS.
LITTLE BEAR PING-PONG CLUB
-2 -1
THEY CAN'T TAKE PARIS. IT'S TOO BIG!
THEY GOT US. THEY'LL GET EVERYONE.
SCORE!

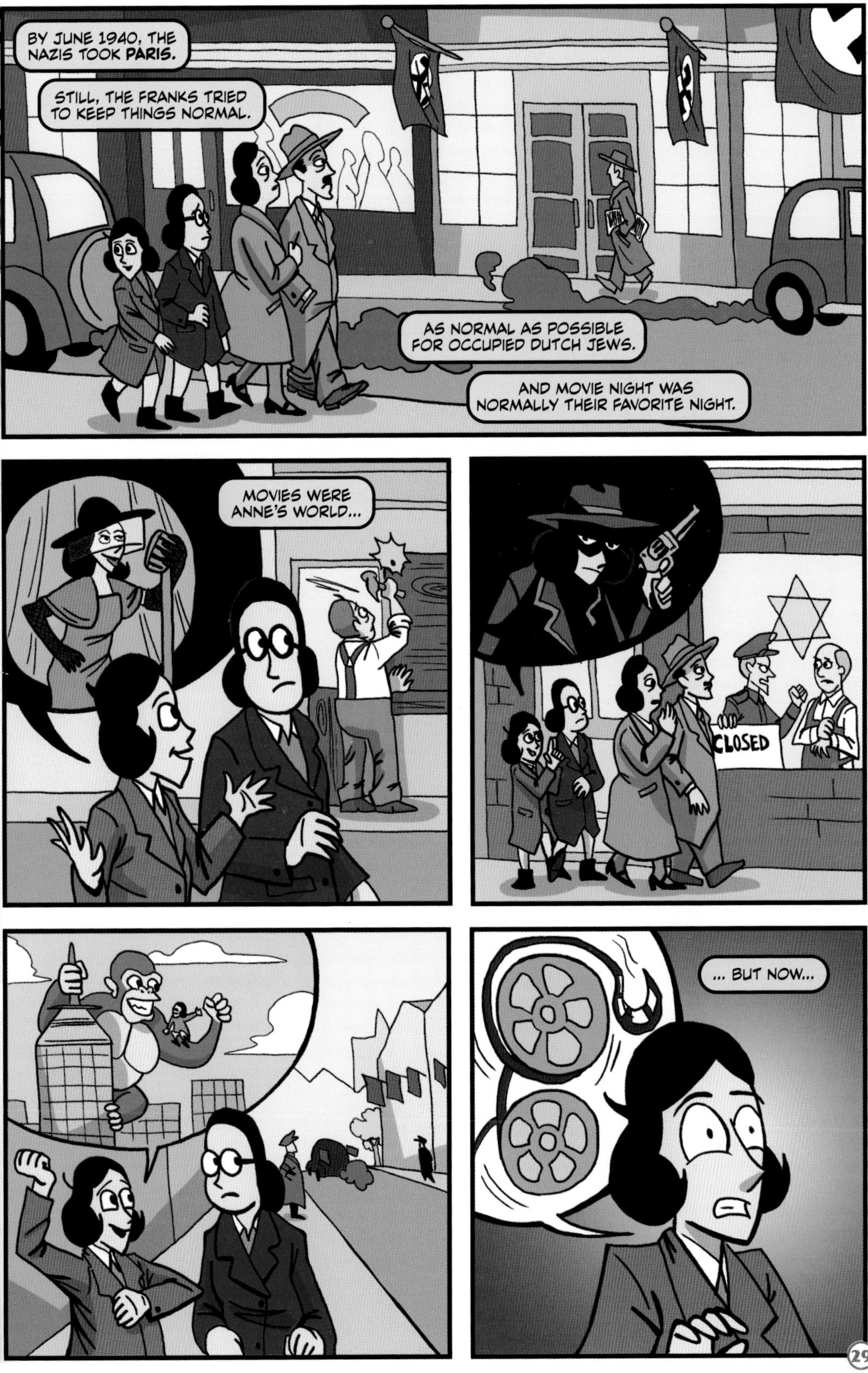
BY JUNE 1940, THE NAZIS TOOK **PARIS.**
STILL, THE FRANKS TRIED TO KEEP THINGS NORMAL.
AS NORMAL AS POSSIBLE FOR OCCUPIED DUTCH JEWS.
AND MOVIE NIGHT WAS NORMALLY THEIR FAVORITE NIGHT.
MOVIES WERE ANNE'S WORLD...
CLOSED
... BUT NOW...

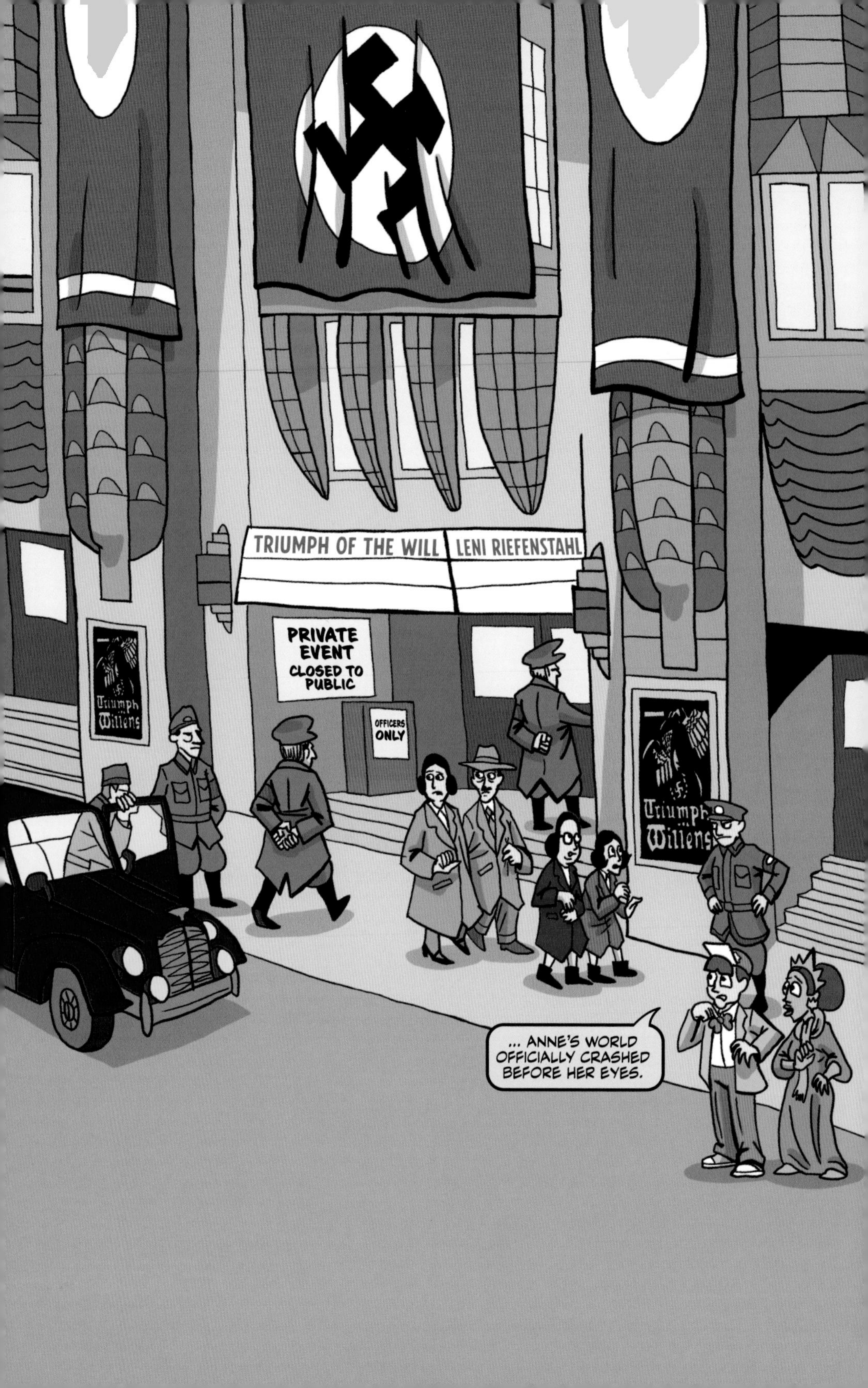
TRIUMPH OF THE WILL
LENI RIEFENSTAHL
PRIVATE EVENT CLOSED TO PUBLIC
OFFICERS ONLY
Triumph des Willens
Triumph des Willens
... ANNE'S WORLD OFFICIALLY CRASHED BEFORE HER EYES.

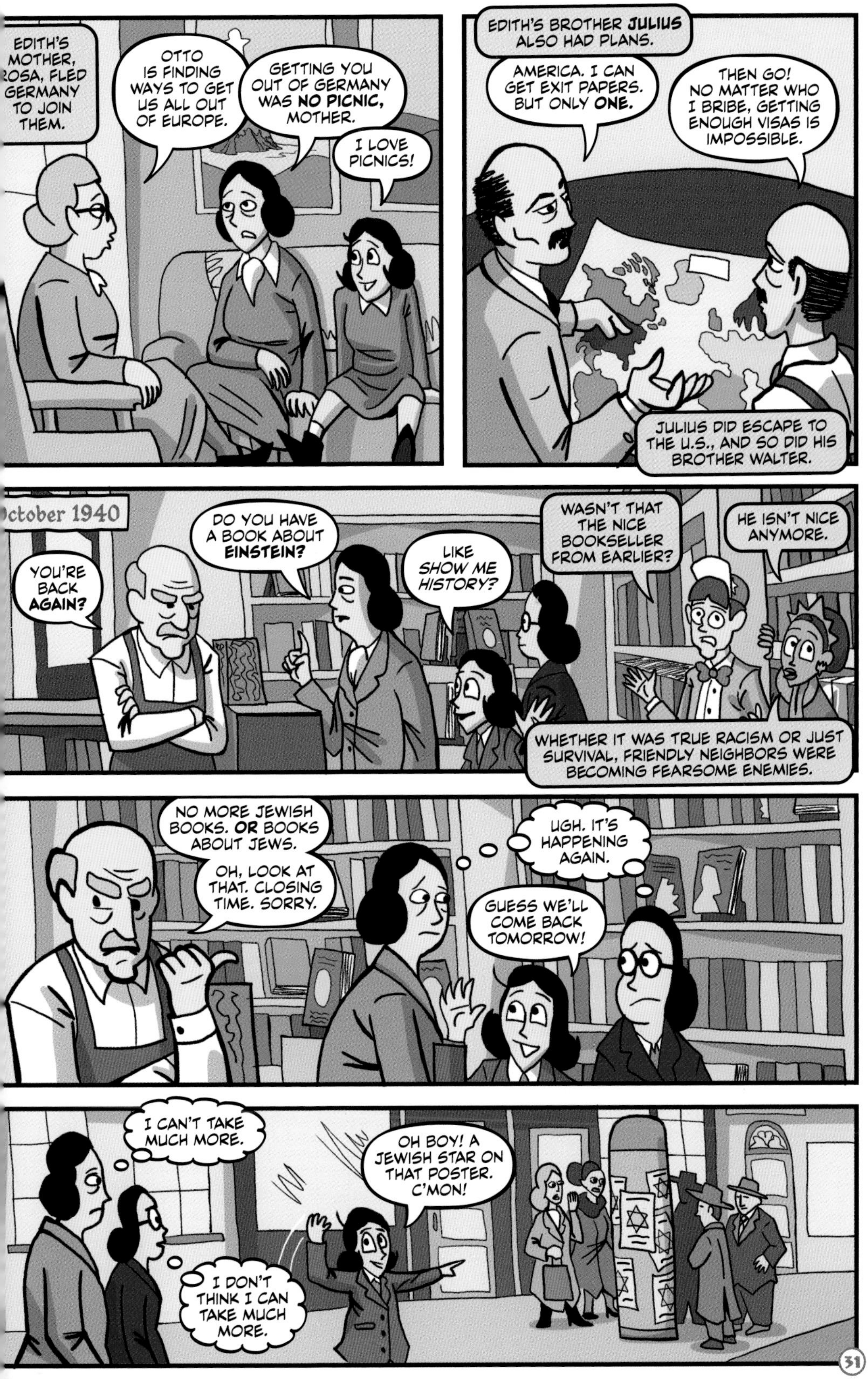
EDITH'S MOTHER, ROSA, FLED GERMANY TO JOIN THEM.
OTTO IS FINDING WAYS TO GET US ALL OUT OF EUROPE.
GETTING YOU OUT OF GERMANY WAS NO PICNIC, MOTHER.
I LOVE PICNICS!
EDITH'S BROTHER JULIUS ALSO HAD PLANS.
AMERICA. I CAN GET EXIT PAPERS. BUT ONLY ONE.
THEN GO! NO MATTER WHO I BRIBE, GETTING ENOUGH VISAS IS IMPOSSIBLE.
JULIUS DID ESCAPE TO THE U.S., AND SO DID HIS BROTHER WALTER.
October 1940
YOU'RE BACK AGAIN?
DO YOU HAVE A BOOK ABOUT EINSTEIN?
LIKE SHOW ME HISTORY?
WASN'T THAT THE NICE BOOKSELLER FROM EARLIER?
HE ISN'T NICE ANYMORE.
WHETHER IT WAS TRUE RACISM OR JUST SURVIVAL, FRIENDLY NEIGHBORS WERE BECOMING FEARSOME ENEMIES.
NO MORE JEWISH BOOKS. OR BOOKS ABOUT JEWS.
OH, LOOK AT THAT. CLOSING TIME. SORRY.
UGH. IT'S HAPPENING AGAIN.
GUESS WE'LL COME BACK TOMORROW!
I CAN'T TAKE MUCH MORE.
I DON'T THINK I CAN TAKE MUCH MORE.
OH BOY! A JEWISH STAR ON THAT POSTER. C'MON!

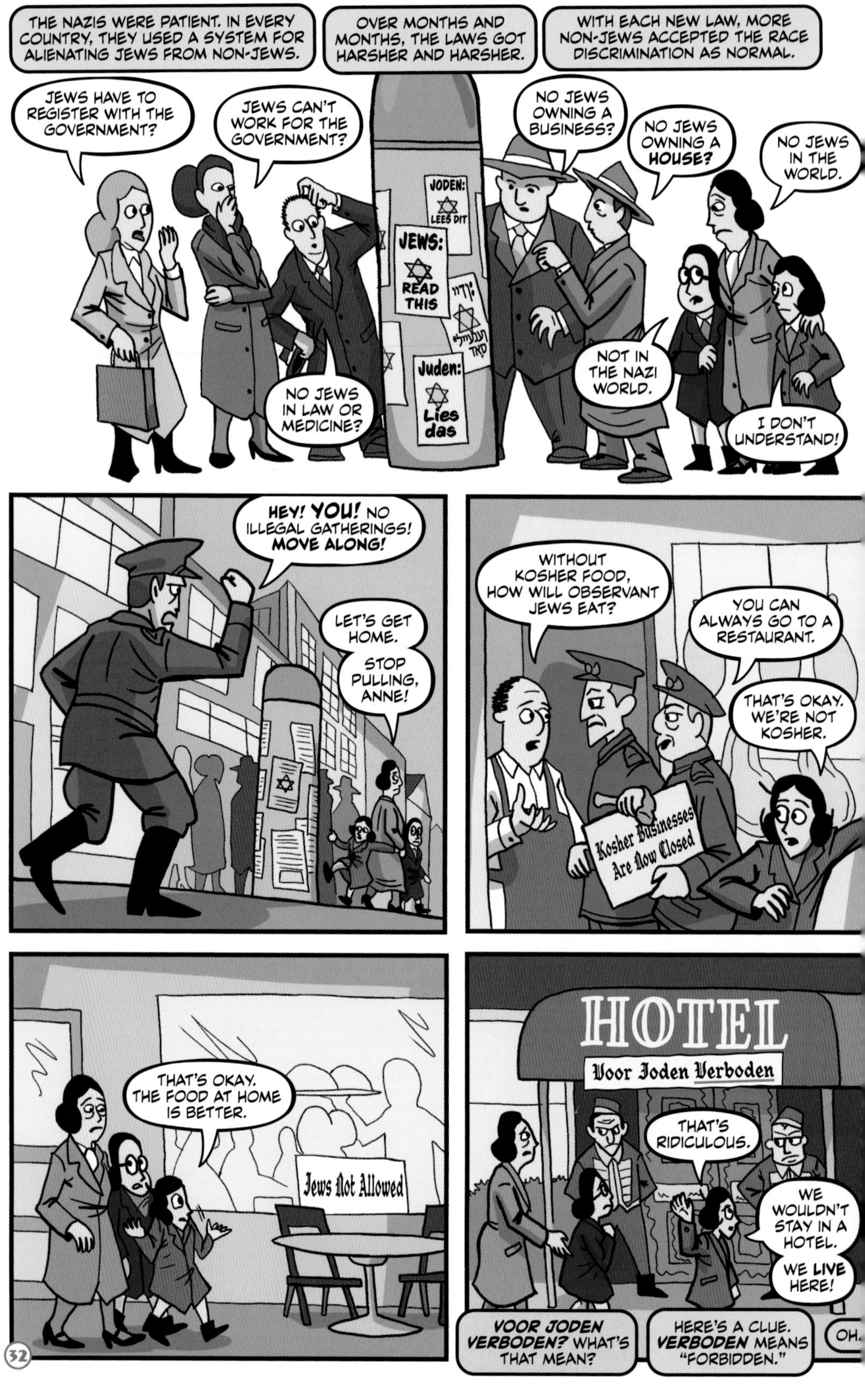
THE NAZIS WERE PATIENT. IN EVERY COUNTRY, THEY USED A SYSTEM FOR ALIENATING JEWS FROM NON-JEWS.
OVER MONTHS AND MONTHS, THE LAWS GOT HARSHER AND HARSHER.
WITH EACH NEW LAW, MORE NON-JEWS ACCEPTED THE RACE DISCRIMINATION AS NORMAL.
JEWS HAVE TO REGISTER WITH THE GOVERNMENT?
JEWS CAN'T WORK FOR THE GOVERNMENT?
NO JEWS IN LAW OR MEDICINE?
JODEN: LEES DIT
JEWS: READ THIS
Juden: Lies das
NO JEWS OWNING A BUSINESS?
NO JEWS OWNING A **HOUSE?**
NO JEWS IN THE WORLD.
NOT IN THE NAZI WORLD.
I DON'T UNDERSTAND!
HEY! YOU! NO ILLEGAL GATHERINGS! **MOVE ALONG!**
LET'S GET HOME.
STOP PULLING, ANNE!
WITHOUT KOSHER FOOD, HOW WILL OBSERVANT JEWS EAT?
YOU CAN ALWAYS GO TO A RESTAURANT.
Kosher Businesses Are Now Closed
THAT'S OKAY. WE'RE NOT KOSHER.
THAT'S OKAY. THE FOOD AT HOME IS BETTER.
Jews Not Allowed
HOTEL
Voor Joden Verboden
THAT'S RIDICULOUS.
WE WOULDN'T STAY IN A HOTEL.
WE **LIVE** HERE!
VOOR JODEN VERBODEN? WHAT'S THAT MEAN?
HERE'S A CLUE. ***VERBODEN*** MEANS "FORBIDDEN."
OH.

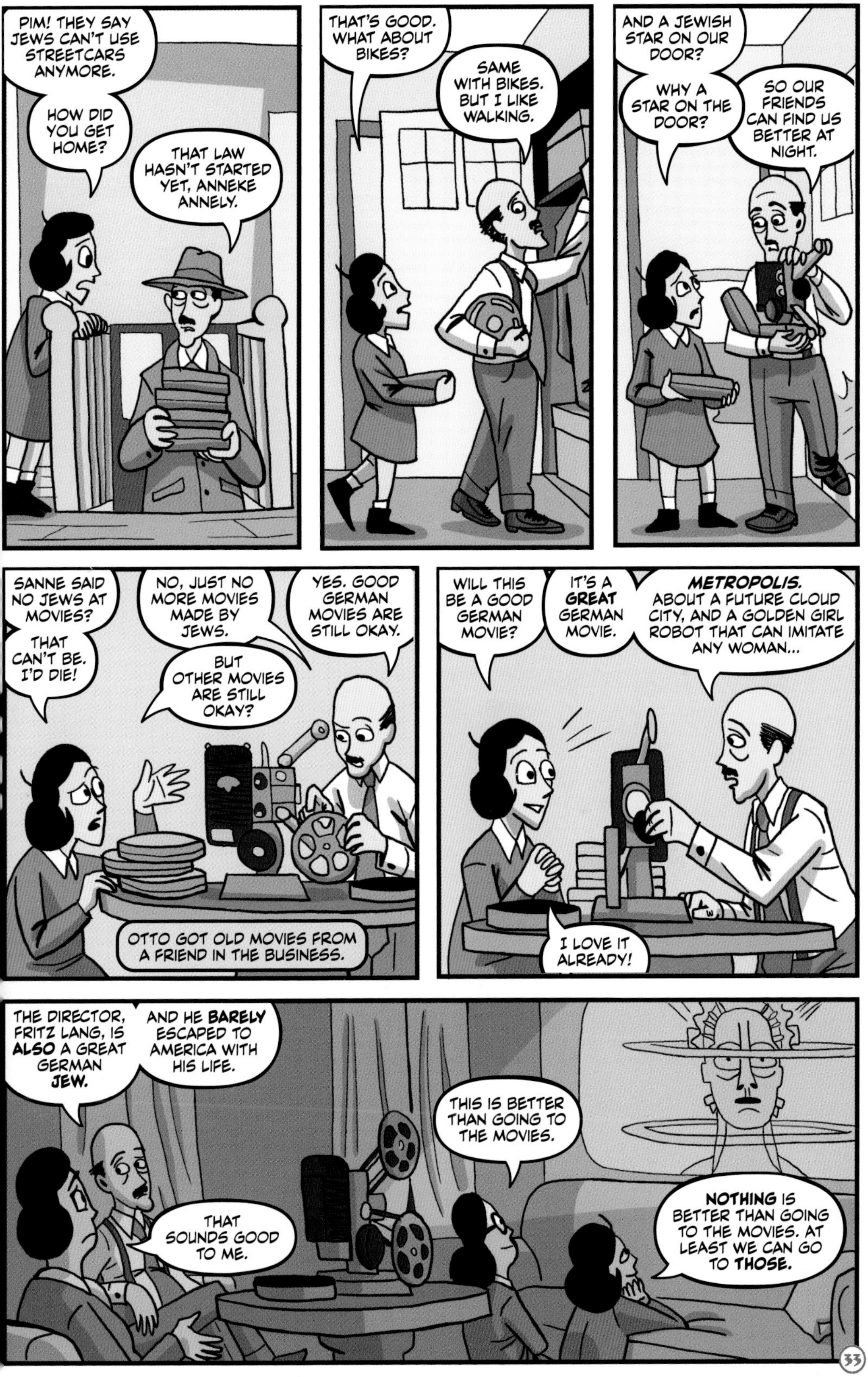
PIM! THEY SAY JEWS CAN'T USE STREETCARS ANYMORE.
HOW DID YOU GET HOME?
THAT LAW HASN'T STARTED YET, ANNEKE ANNELY.
THAT'S GOOD. WHAT ABOUT BIKES?
SAME WITH BIKES. BUT I LIKE WALKING.
AND A JEWISH STAR ON OUR DOOR?
WHY A STAR ON THE DOOR?
SO OUR FRIENDS CAN FIND US BETTER AT NIGHT.
SANNE SAID NO JEWS AT MOVIES?
THAT CAN'T BE. I'D DIE!
NO, JUST NO MORE MOVIES MADE BY JEWS.
BUT OTHER MOVIES ARE STILL OKAY?
YES. GOOD GERMAN MOVIES ARE STILL OKAY.
OTTO GOT OLD MOVIES FROM A FRIEND IN THE BUSINESS.
WILL THIS BE A GOOD GERMAN MOVIE?
IT'S A **GREAT** GERMAN MOVIE.
METROPOLIS. ABOUT A FUTURE CLOUD CITY, AND A GOLDEN GIRL ROBOT THAT CAN IMITATE ANY WOMAN...
I LOVE IT ALREADY!
THE DIRECTOR, FRITZ LANG, IS **ALSO** A GREAT GERMAN **JEW.**
AND HE **BARELY** ESCAPED TO AMERICA WITH HIS LIFE.
THAT SOUNDS GOOD TO ME.
THIS IS BETTER THAN GOING TO THE MOVIES.
NOTHING IS BETTER THAN GOING TO THE MOVIES. AT LEAST WE CAN GO TO **THOSE.**

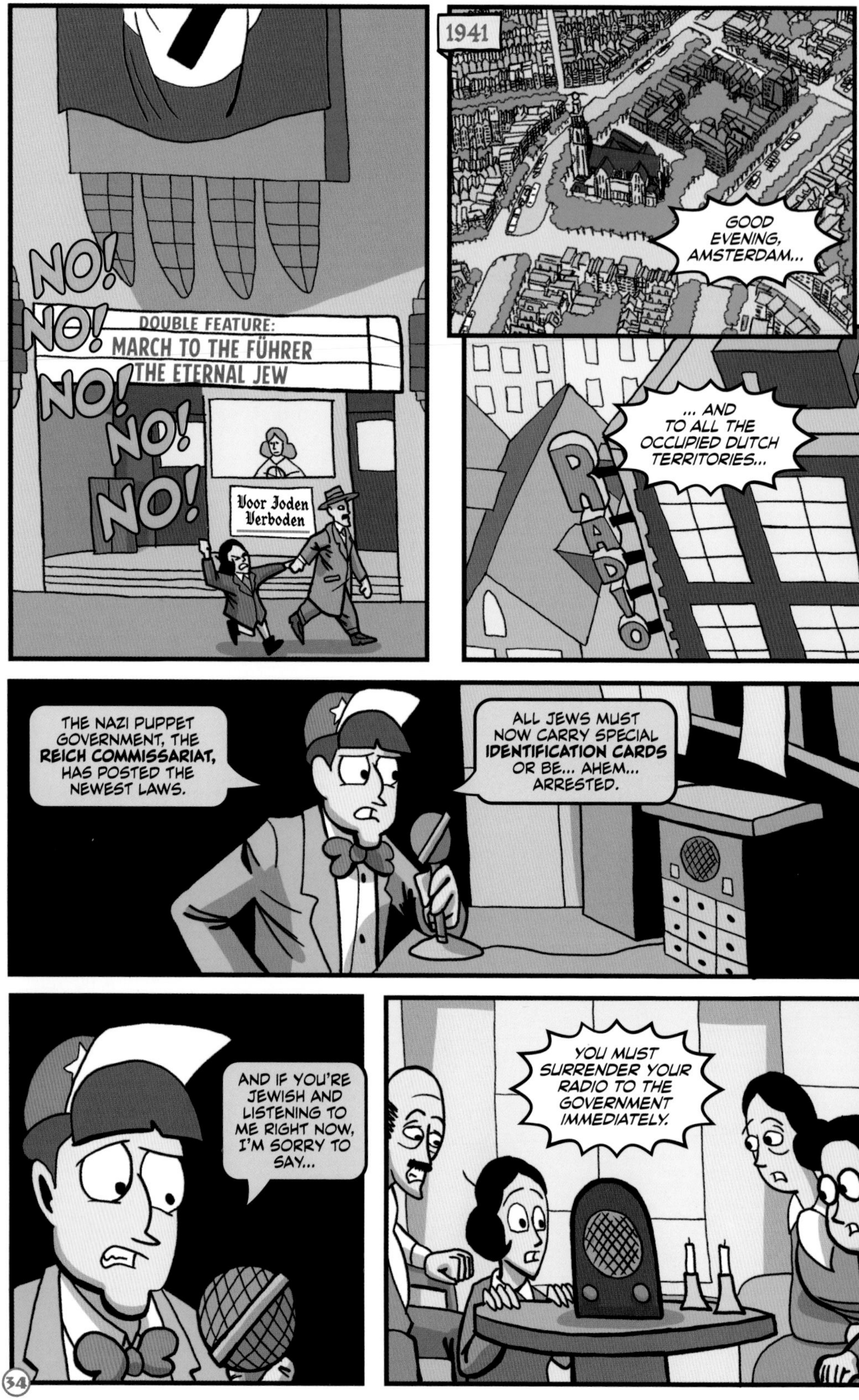
NO!
NO!
DOUBLE FEATURE:
MARCH TO THE FÜHRER
THE ETERNAL JEW
NO!
NO!
NO!
Voor Joden Verboden
1941
GOOD EVENING, AMSTERDAM...
... AND TO ALL THE OCCUPIED DUTCH TERRITORIES...
RADIO
THE NAZI PUPPET GOVERNMENT, THE **REICH COMMISSARIAT,** HAS POSTED THE NEWEST LAWS.
ALL JEWS MUST NOW CARRY SPECIAL **IDENTIFICATION CARDS** OR BE... AHEM... ARRESTED.
AND IF YOU'RE JEWISH AND LISTENING TO ME RIGHT NOW, I'M SORRY TO SAY...
YOU MUST SURRENDER YOUR RADIO TO THE GOVERNMENT IMMEDIATELY.

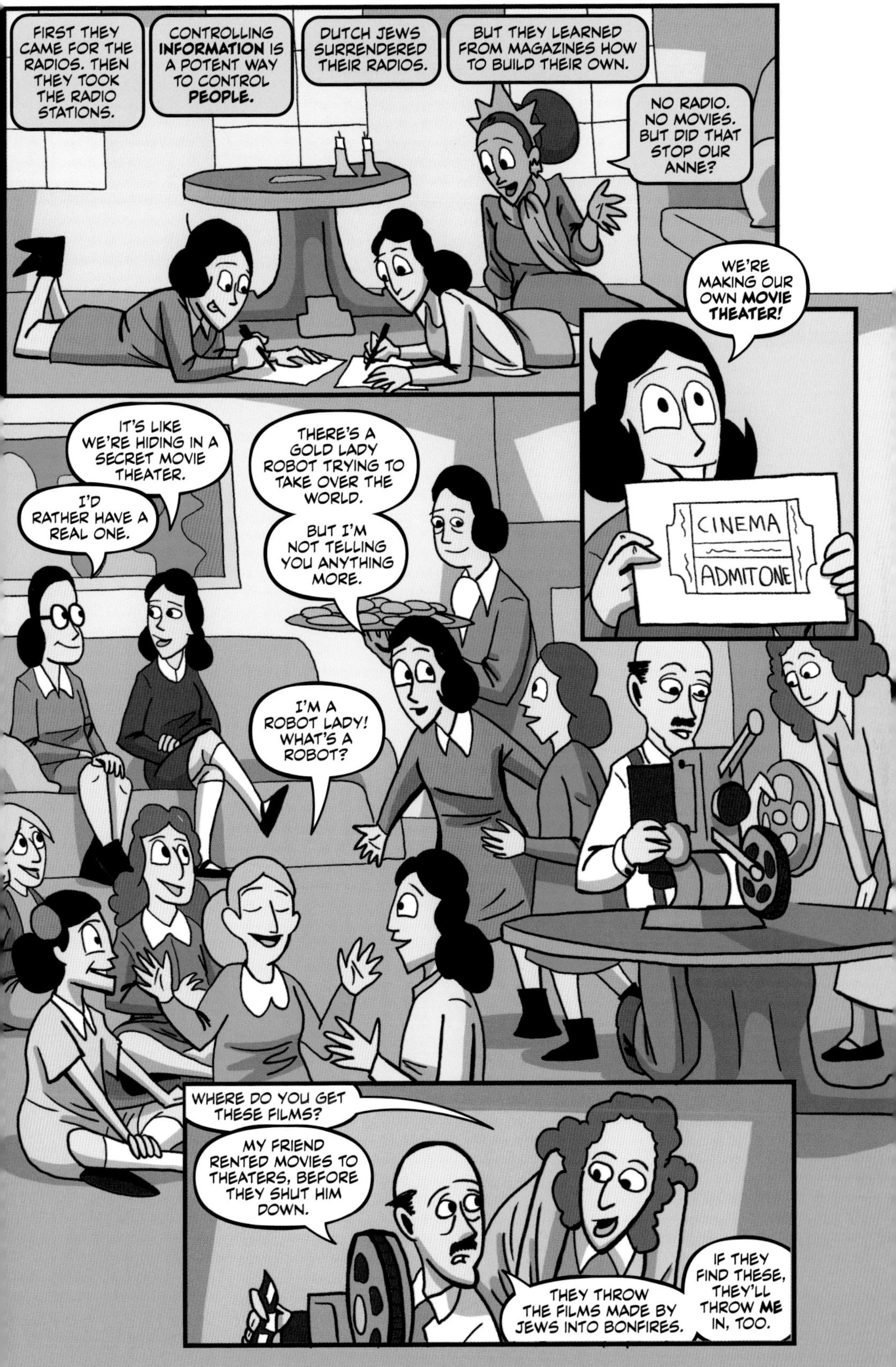

FIRST THEY CAME FOR THE RADIOS. THEN THEY TOOK THE RADIO STATIONS.
CONTROLLING **INFORMATION** IS A POTENT WAY TO CONTROL **PEOPLE.**
DUTCH JEWS SURRENDERED THEIR RADIOS.
BUT THEY LEARNED FROM MAGAZINES HOW TO BUILD THEIR OWN.
NO RADIO. NO MOVIES. BUT DID THAT STOP OUR ANNE?
WE'RE MAKING OUR OWN **MOVIE THEATER!**
CINEMA
ADMIT ONE
IT'S LIKE WE'RE HIDING IN A SECRET MOVIE THEATER.
I'D RATHER HAVE A REAL ONE.
THERE'S A GOLD LADY ROBOT TRYING TO TAKE OVER THE WORLD.
BUT I'M NOT TELLING YOU ANYTHING MORE.
I'M A ROBOT LADY! WHAT'S A ROBOT?
WHERE DO YOU GET THESE FILMS?
MY FRIEND RENTED MOVIES TO THEATERS, BEFORE THEY SHUT HIM DOWN.
THEY THROW THE FILMS MADE BY JEWS INTO BONFIRES.
IF THEY FIND THESE, THEY'LL THROW **ME** IN, TOO.

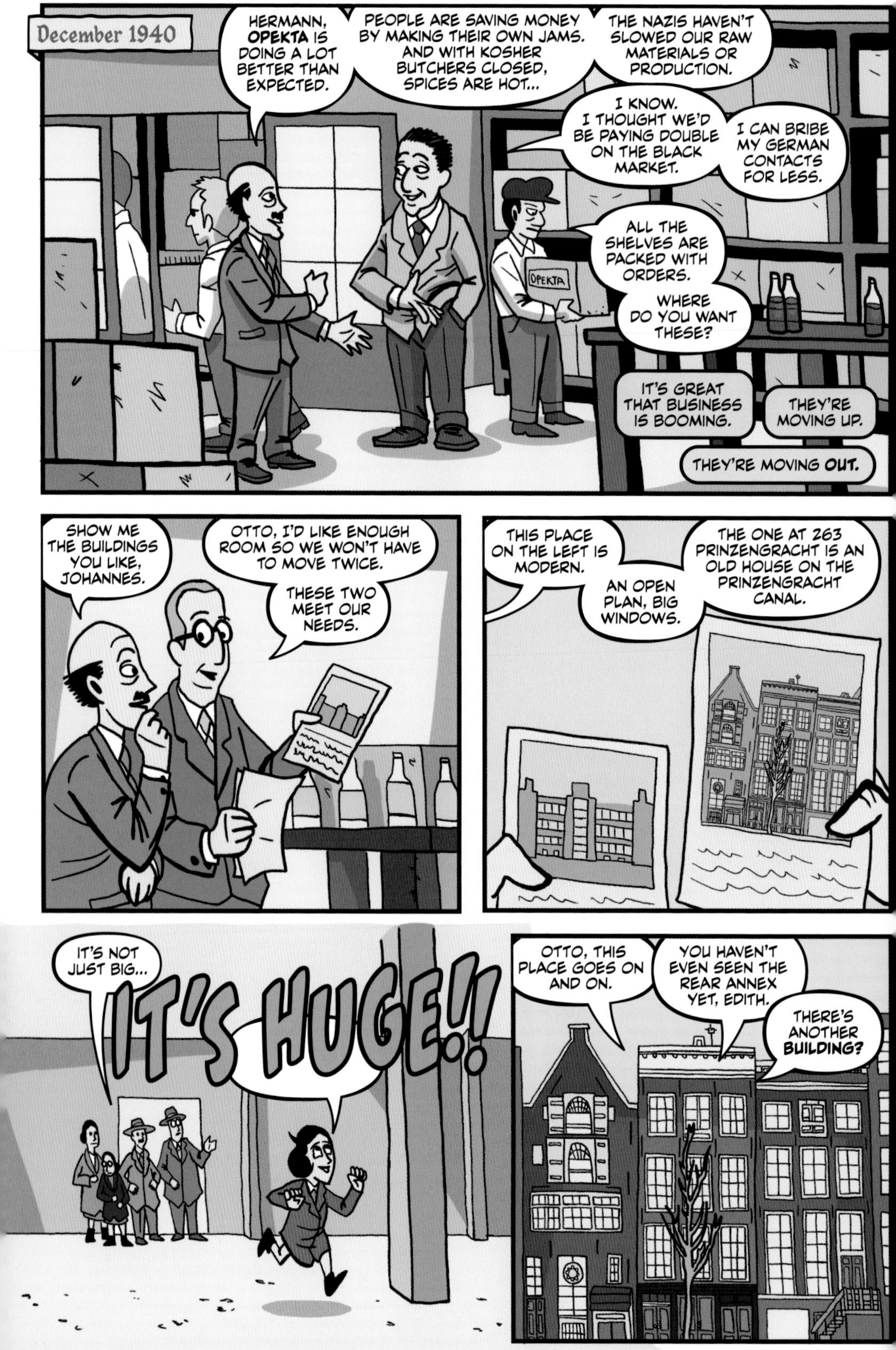
December 1940
HERMANN, OPEKTA IS DOING A LOT BETTER THAN EXPECTED.
PEOPLE ARE SAVING MONEY BY MAKING THEIR OWN JAMS. AND WITH KOSHER BUTCHERS CLOSED, SPICES ARE HOT...
THE NAZIS HAVEN'T SLOWED OUR RAW MATERIALS OR PRODUCTION.
I KNOW. I THOUGHT WE'D BE PAYING DOUBLE ON THE BLACK MARKET.
I CAN BRIBE MY GERMAN CONTACTS FOR LESS.
ALL THE SHELVES ARE PACKED WITH ORDERS.
WHERE DO YOU WANT THESE?
OPEKTA
IT'S GREAT THAT BUSINESS IS BOOMING.
THEY'RE MOVING UP.
THEY'RE MOVING OUT.
SHOW ME THE BUILDINGS YOU LIKE, JOHANNES.
OTTO, I'D LIKE ENOUGH ROOM SO WE WON'T HAVE TO MOVE TWICE.
THESE TWO MEET OUR NEEDS.
THIS PLACE ON THE LEFT IS MODERN.
AN OPEN PLAN, BIG WINDOWS.
THE ONE AT 263 PRINZENGRACHT IS AN OLD HOUSE ON THE PRINZENGRACHT CANAL.
IT'S NOT JUST BIG...
IT'S HUGE!!
OTTO, THIS PLACE GOES ON AND ON.
YOU HAVEN'T EVEN SEEN THE REAR ANNEX YET, EDITH.
THERE'S ANOTHER BUILDING?

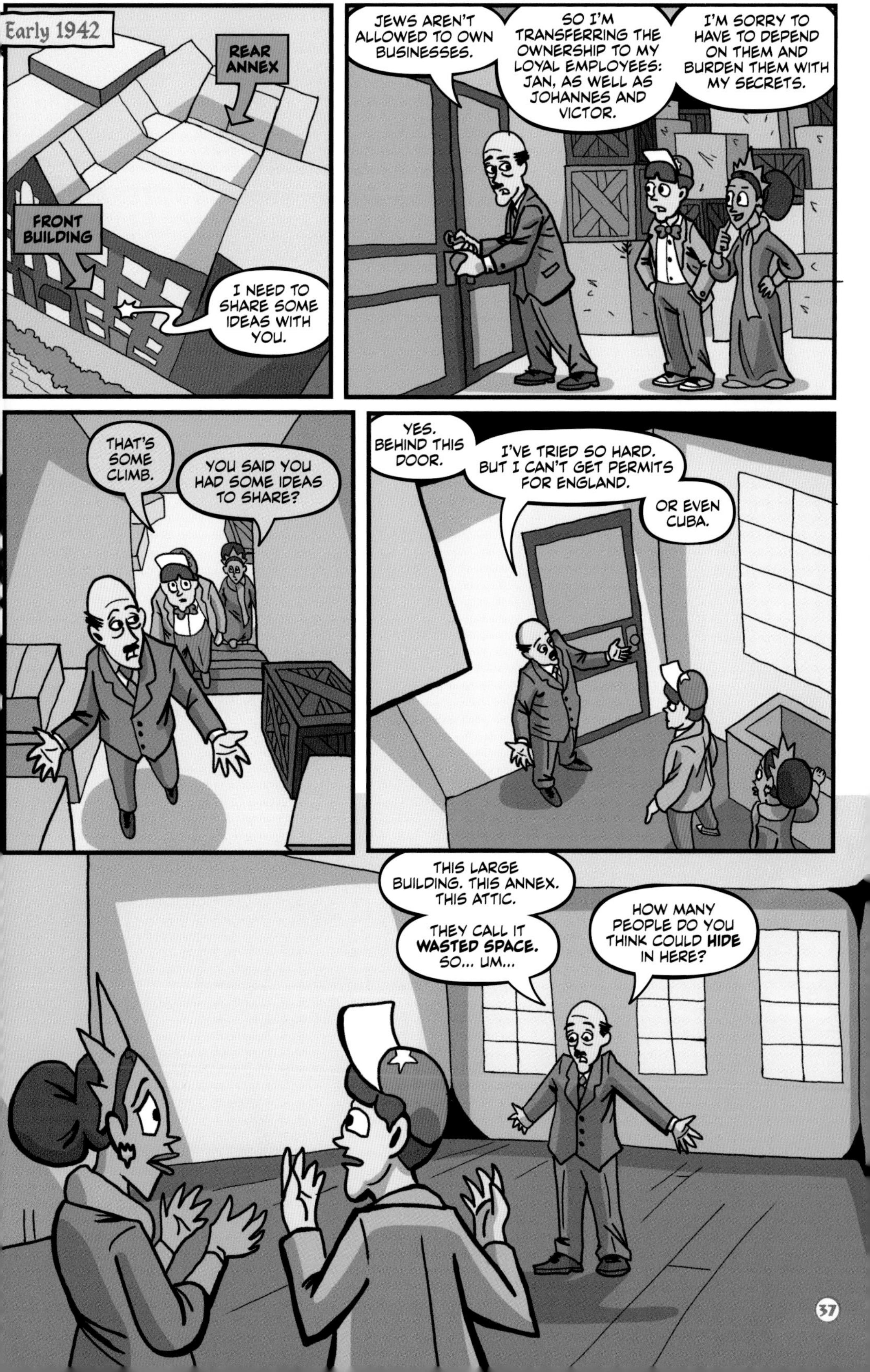

Early 1942
REAR ANNEX
FRONT BUILDING
I NEED TO SHARE SOME IDEAS WITH YOU.
JEWS AREN'T ALLOWED TO OWN BUSINESSES.
SO I'M TRANSFERRING THE OWNERSHIP TO MY LOYAL EMPLOYEES: JAN, AS WELL AS JOHANNES AND VICTOR.
I'M SORRY TO HAVE TO DEPEND ON THEM AND BURDEN THEM WITH MY SECRETS.
THAT'S SOME CLIMB.
YOU SAID YOU HAD SOME IDEAS TO SHARE?
YES. BEHIND THIS DOOR.
I'VE TRIED SO HARD. BUT I CAN'T GET PERMITS FOR ENGLAND.
OR EVEN CUBA.
THIS LARGE BUILDING. THIS ANNEX. THIS ATTIC.
THEY CALL IT **WASTED SPACE.** SO... UM...
HOW MANY PEOPLE DO YOU THINK COULD **HIDE** IN HERE?

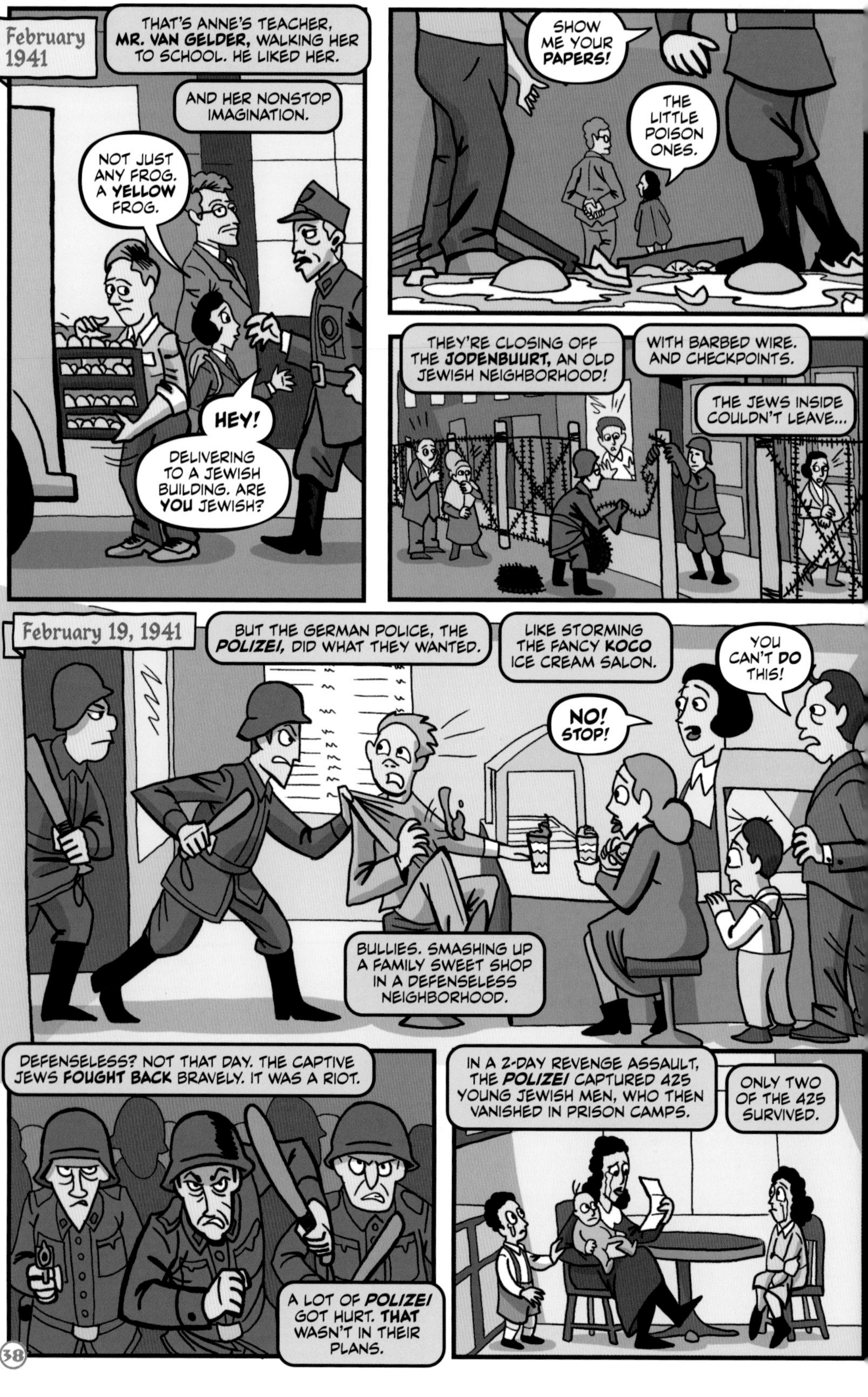
February 1941
THAT'S ANNE'S TEACHER, MR. VAN GELDER, WALKING HER TO SCHOOL. HE LIKED HER.
AND HER NONSTOP IMAGINATION.
NOT JUST ANY FROG. A YELLOW FROG.
HEY!
DELIVERING TO A JEWISH BUILDING. ARE YOU JEWISH?
SHOW ME YOUR PAPERS!
THE LITTLE POISON ONES.
THEY'RE CLOSING OFF THE JODENBUURT, AN OLD JEWISH NEIGHBORHOOD!
WITH BARBED WIRE. AND CHECKPOINTS.
THE JEWS INSIDE COULDN'T LEAVE...
February 19, 1941
BUT THE GERMAN POLICE, THE POLIZEI, DID WHAT THEY WANTED.
LIKE STORMING THE FANCY KOCO ICE CREAM SALON.
YOU CAN'T DO THIS!
NO! STOP!
BULLIES. SMASHING UP A FAMILY SWEET SHOP IN A DEFENSELESS NEIGHBORHOOD.
DEFENSELESS? NOT THAT DAY. THE CAPTIVE JEWS FOUGHT BACK BRAVELY. IT WAS A RIOT.
A LOT OF POLIZEI GOT HURT. THAT WASN'T IN THEIR PLANS.
IN A 2-DAY REVENGE ASSAULT, THE POLIZEI CAPTURED 425 YOUNG JEWISH MEN, WHO THEN VANISHED IN PRISON CAMPS.
ONLY TWO OF THE 425 SURVIVED.

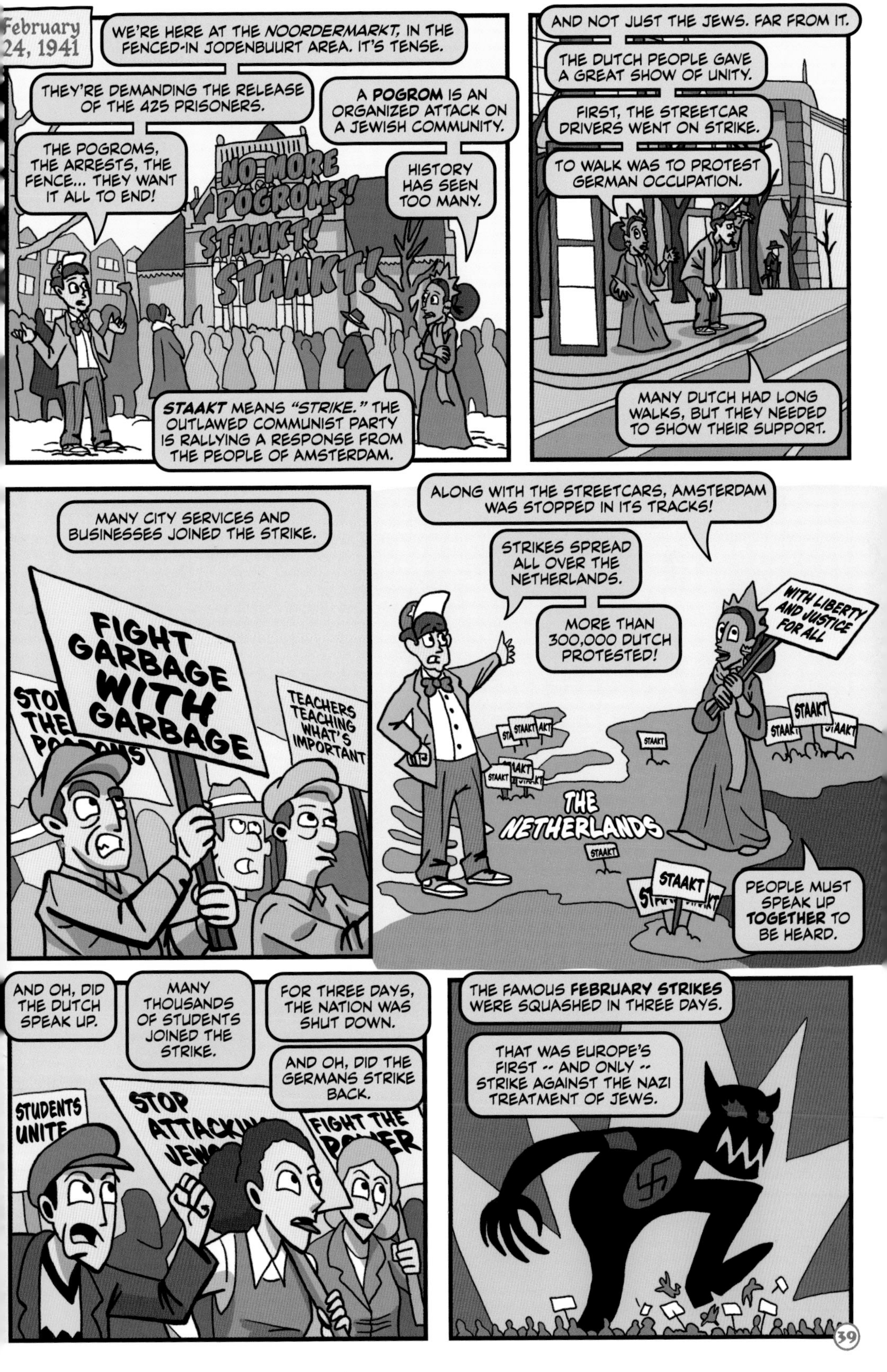
February 24, 1941
WE'RE HERE AT THE *NOORDERMARKT*, IN THE FENCED-IN JODENBUURT AREA. IT'S TENSE.
THEY'RE DEMANDING THE RELEASE OF THE 425 PRISONERS.
THE POGROMS, THE ARRESTS, THE FENCE... THEY WANT IT ALL TO END!
A **POGROM** IS AN ORGANIZED ATTACK ON A JEWISH COMMUNITY.
HISTORY HAS SEEN TOO MANY.
NO MORE POGROMS!
STAAKT!
STAAKT!
STAAKT MEANS *"STRIKE."* THE OUTLAWED COMMUNIST PARTY IS RALLYING A RESPONSE FROM THE PEOPLE OF AMSTERDAM.
AND NOT JUST THE JEWS. FAR FROM IT.
THE DUTCH PEOPLE GAVE A GREAT SHOW OF UNITY.
FIRST, THE STREETCAR DRIVERS WENT ON STRIKE.
TO WALK WAS TO PROTEST GERMAN OCCUPATION.
MANY DUTCH HAD LONG WALKS, BUT THEY NEEDED TO SHOW THEIR SUPPORT.
MANY CITY SERVICES AND BUSINESSES JOINED THE STRIKE.
FIGHT GARBAGE WITH GARBAGE
TEACHERS TEACHING WHAT'S IMPORTANT
ALONG WITH THE STREETCARS, AMSTERDAM WAS STOPPED IN ITS TRACKS!
STRIKES SPREAD ALL OVER THE NETHERLANDS.
MORE THAN 300,000 DUTCH PROTESTED!
WITH LIBERTY AND JUSTICE FOR ALL
THE NETHERLANDS
STAAKT
PEOPLE MUST SPEAK UP **TOGETHER** TO BE HEARD.
AND OH, DID THE DUTCH SPEAK UP.
MANY THOUSANDS OF STUDENTS JOINED THE STRIKE.
FOR THREE DAYS, THE NATION WAS SHUT DOWN.
AND OH, DID THE GERMANS STRIKE BACK.
STUDENTS UNITE
STOP
THE FAMOUS **FEBRUARY STRIKES** WERE SQUASHED IN THREE DAYS.
THAT WAS EUROPE'S FIRST -- AND ONLY -- STRIKE AGAINST THE NAZI TREATMENT OF JEWS.

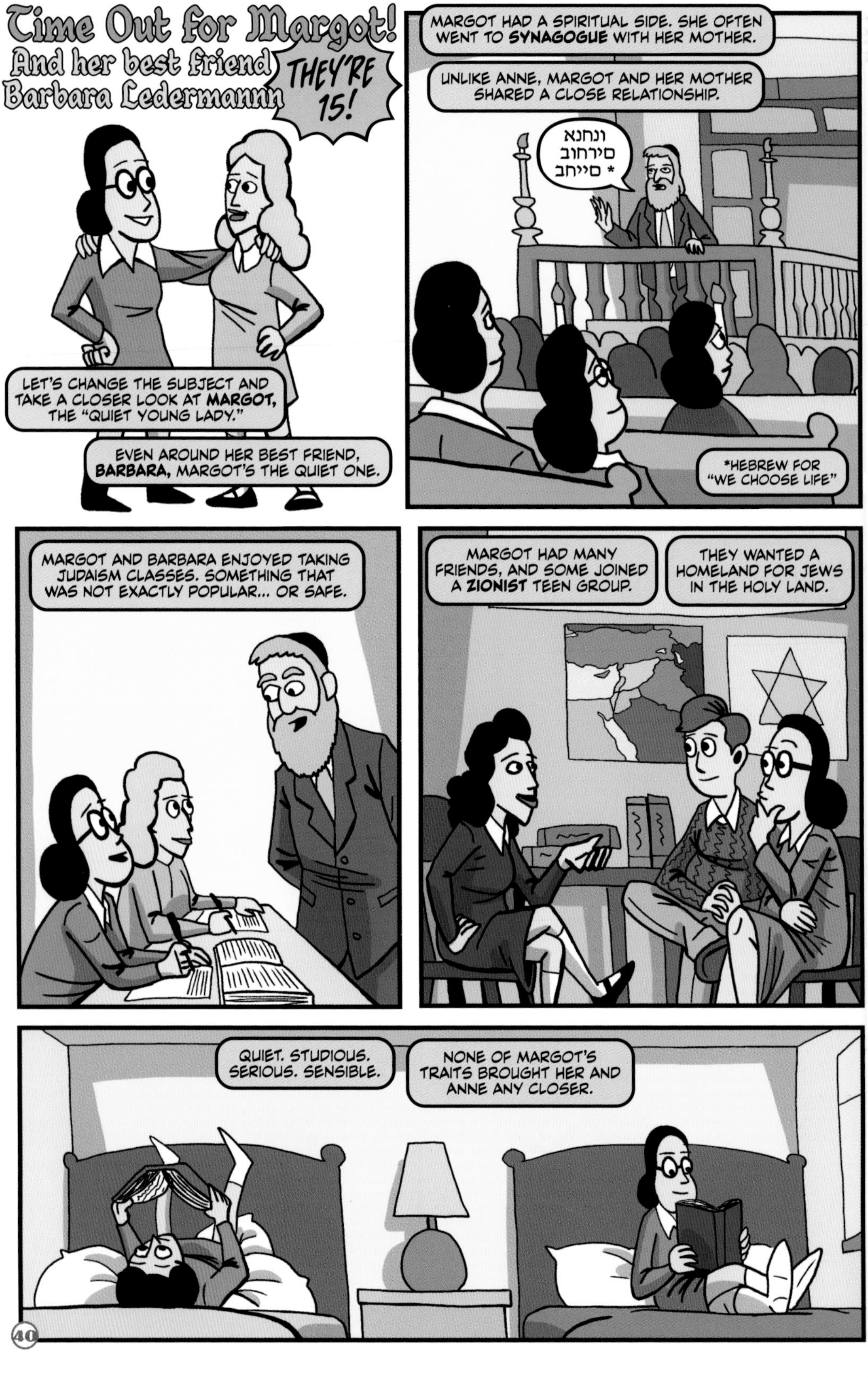
Time Out for Margot!
And her best friend Barbara Ledermannn
THEY'RE 15!
LET'S CHANGE THE SUBJECT AND TAKE A CLOSER LOOK AT MARGOT, THE "QUIET YOUNG LADY."
EVEN AROUND HER BEST FRIEND, BARBARA, MARGOT'S THE QUIET ONE.
MARGOT HAD A SPIRITUAL SIDE. SHE OFTEN WENT TO SYNAGOGUE WITH HER MOTHER.
UNLIKE ANNE, MARGOT AND HER MOTHER SHARED A CLOSE RELATIONSHIP.
ונתנא סירחוב סייחב *
*HEBREW FOR "WE CHOOSE LIFE"
MARGOT AND BARBARA ENJOYED TAKING JUDAISM CLASSES. SOMETHING THAT WAS NOT EXACTLY POPULAR... OR SAFE.
MARGOT HAD MANY FRIENDS, AND SOME JOINED A ZIONIST TEEN GROUP.
THEY WANTED A HOMELAND FOR JEWS IN THE HOLY LAND.
QUIET. STUDIOUS. SERIOUS. SENSIBLE.
NONE OF MARGOT'S TRAITS BROUGHT HER AND ANNE ANY CLOSER.

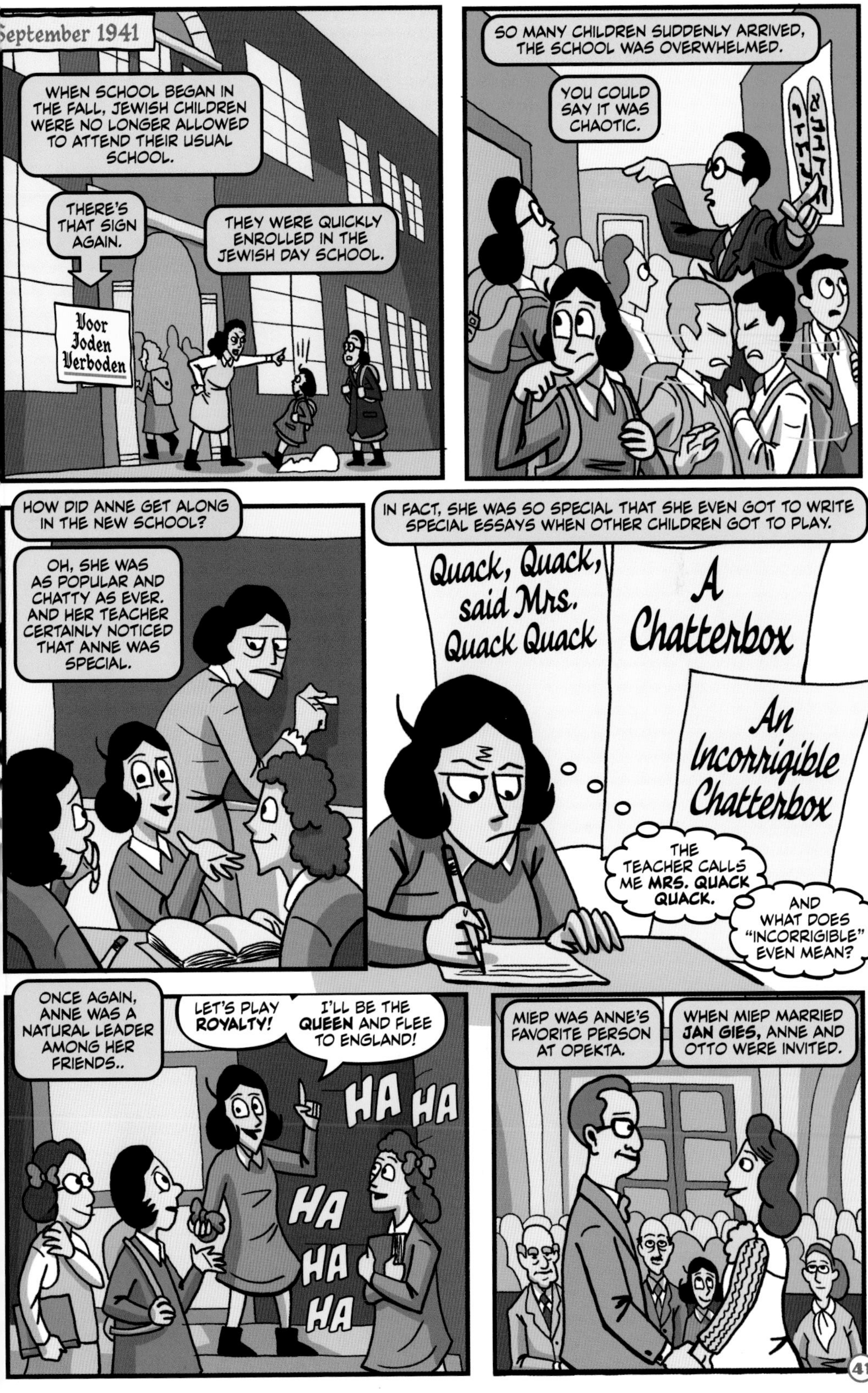
September 1941
WHEN SCHOOL BEGAN IN THE FALL, JEWISH CHILDREN WERE NO LONGER ALLOWED TO ATTEND THEIR USUAL SCHOOL.
THERE'S THAT SIGN AGAIN.
THEY WERE QUICKLY ENROLLED IN THE JEWISH DAY SCHOOL.
Voor Joden Verboden
SO MANY CHILDREN SUDDENLY ARRIVED, THE SCHOOL WAS OVERWHELMED.
YOU COULD SAY IT WAS CHAOTIC.
HOW DID ANNE GET ALONG IN THE NEW SCHOOL?
OH, SHE WAS AS POPULAR AND CHATTY AS EVER. AND HER TEACHER CERTAINLY NOTICED THAT ANNE WAS SPECIAL.
IN FACT, SHE WAS SO SPECIAL THAT SHE EVEN GOT TO WRITE SPECIAL ESSAYS WHEN OTHER CHILDREN GOT TO PLAY.
Quack, Quack, said Mrs. Quack Quack
A Chatterbox
An Incorrigible Chatterbox
THE TEACHER CALLS ME MRS. QUACK QUACK.
AND WHAT DOES "INCORRIGIBLE" EVEN MEAN?
ONCE AGAIN, ANNE WAS A NATURAL LEADER AMONG HER FRIENDS..
LET'S PLAY ROYALTY!
I'LL BE THE QUEEN AND FLEE TO ENGLAND!
HA HA
HA HA HA
MIEP WAS ANNE'S FAVORITE PERSON AT OPEKTA.
WHEN MIEP MARRIED JAN GIES, ANNE AND OTTO WERE INVITED.

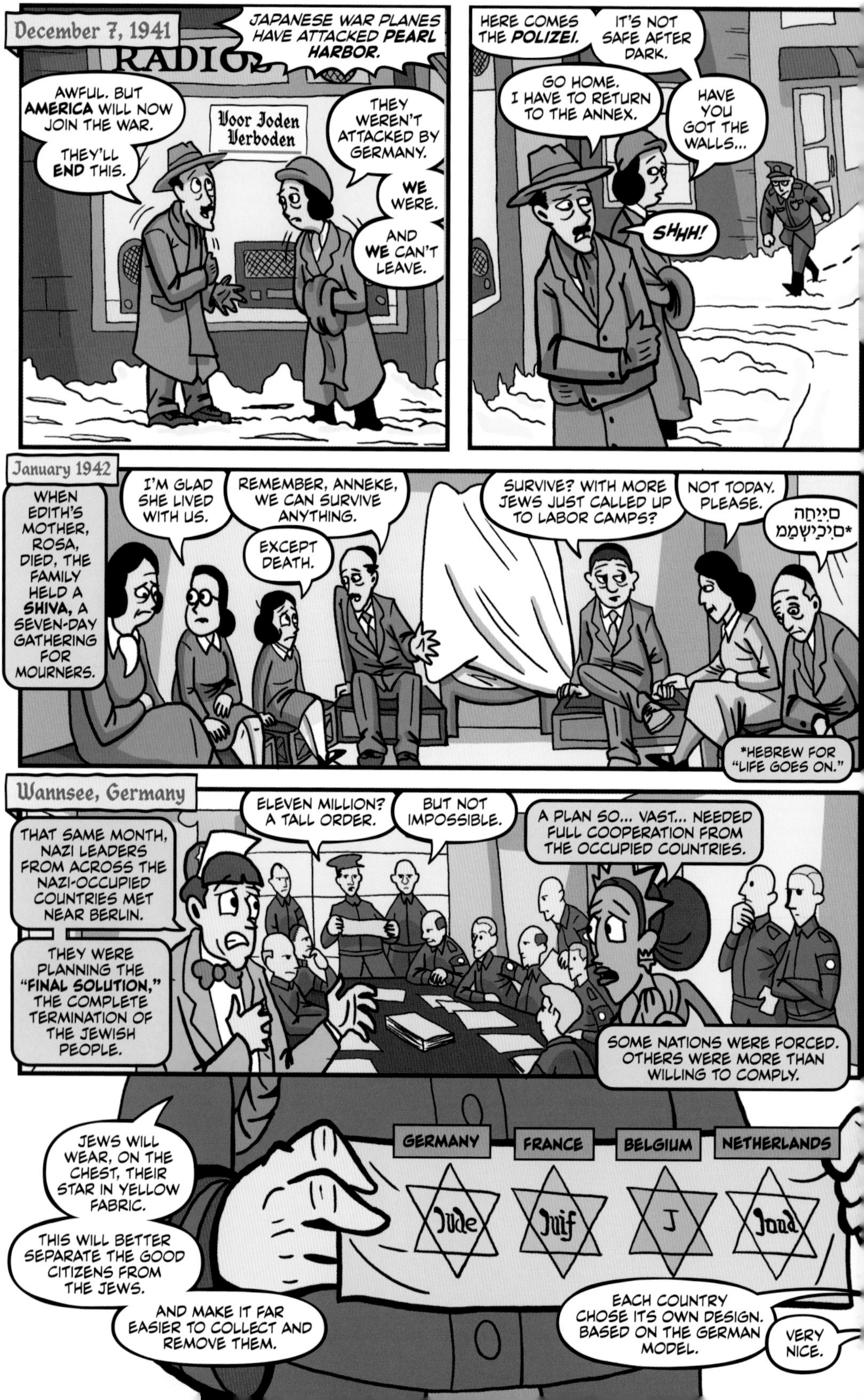

December 7, 1941
JAPANESE WAR PLANES HAVE ATTACKED PEARL HARBOR.
RADIO
AWFUL. BUT AMERICA WILL NOW JOIN THE WAR.
THEY'LL END THIS.
Voor Joden Verboden
THEY WEREN'T ATTACKED BY GERMANY.
WE WERE.
AND WE CAN'T LEAVE.
HERE COMES THE POLIZEI.
IT'S NOT SAFE AFTER DARK.
GO HOME. I HAVE TO RETURN TO THE ANNEX.
HAVE YOU GOT THE WALLS...
SHHH!
January 1942
WHEN EDITH'S MOTHER, ROSA, DIED, THE FAMILY HELD A SHIVA, A SEVEN-DAY GATHERING FOR MOURNERS.
I'M GLAD SHE LIVED WITH US.
REMEMBER, ANNEKE, WE CAN SURVIVE ANYTHING.
EXCEPT DEATH.
SURVIVE? WITH MORE JEWS JUST CALLED UP TO LABOR CAMPS?
NOT TODAY. PLEASE.
החיים
*םיכישממ
*HEBREW FOR "LIFE GOES ON."
Wannsee, Germany
THAT SAME MONTH, NAZI LEADERS FROM ACROSS THE NAZI-OCCUPIED COUNTRIES MET NEAR BERLIN.
THEY WERE PLANNING THE "FINAL SOLUTION," THE COMPLETE TERMINATION OF THE JEWISH PEOPLE.
ELEVEN MILLION? A TALL ORDER.
BUT NOT IMPOSSIBLE.
A PLAN SO... VAST... NEEDED FULL COOPERATION FROM THE OCCUPIED COUNTRIES.
SOME NATIONS WERE FORCED. OTHERS WERE MORE THAN WILLING TO COMPLY.
JEWS WILL WEAR, ON THE CHEST, THEIR STAR IN YELLOW FABRIC.
THIS WILL BETTER SEPARATE THE GOOD CITIZENS FROM THE JEWS.
AND MAKE IT FAR EASIER TO COLLECT AND REMOVE THEM.
GERMANY
FRANCE
BELGIUM
NETHERLANDS
Jude
Juif
J
Jood
EACH COUNTRY CHOSE ITS OWN DESIGN. BASED ON THE GERMAN MODEL.
VERY NICE.

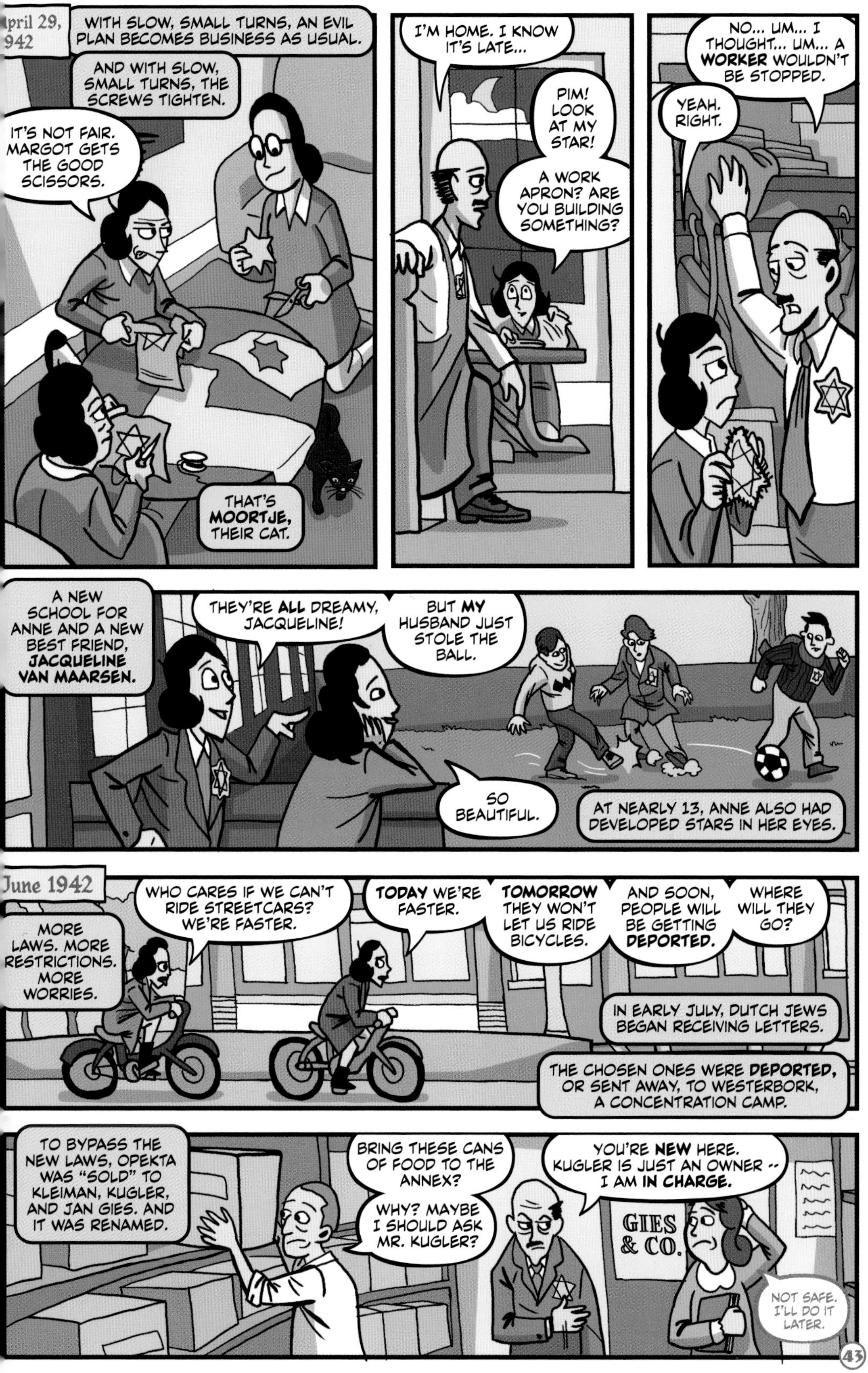
April 29, 1942
WITH SLOW, SMALL TURNS, AN EVIL PLAN BECOMES BUSINESS AS USUAL.
AND WITH SLOW, SMALL TURNS, THE SCREWS TIGHTEN.
IT'S NOT FAIR. MARGOT GETS THE GOOD SCISSORS.
THAT'S MOORTJE, THEIR CAT.
I'M HOME. I KNOW IT'S LATE...
PIM! LOOK AT MY STAR!
A WORK APRON? ARE YOU BUILDING SOMETHING?
NO... UM... I THOUGHT... UM... A WORKER WOULDN'T BE STOPPED.
YEAH. RIGHT.
A NEW SCHOOL FOR ANNE AND A NEW BEST FRIEND, JACQUELINE VAN MAARSEN.
THEY'RE ALL DREAMY, JACQUELINE!
BUT MY HUSBAND JUST STOLE THE BALL.
SO BEAUTIFUL.
AT NEARLY 13, ANNE ALSO HAD DEVELOPED STARS IN HER EYES.
June 1942
MORE LAWS. MORE RESTRICTIONS. MORE WORRIES.
WHO CARES IF WE CAN'T RIDE STREETCARS? WE'RE FASTER.
TODAY WE'RE FASTER.
TOMORROW THEY WON'T LET US RIDE BICYCLES.
AND SOON, PEOPLE WILL BE GETTING DEPORTED.
WHERE WILL THEY GO?
IN EARLY JULY, DUTCH JEWS BEGAN RECEIVING LETTERS.
THE CHOSEN ONES WERE DEPORTED, OR SENT AWAY, TO WESTERBORK, A CONCENTRATION CAMP.
TO BYPASS THE NEW LAWS, OPEKTA WAS "SOLD" TO KLEIMAN, KUGLER, AND JAN GIES. AND IT WAS RENAMED.
BRING THESE CANS OF FOOD TO THE ANNEX?
WHY? MAYBE I SHOULD ASK MR. KUGLER?
YOU'RE NEW HERE. KUGLER IS JUST AN OWNER -- I AM IN CHARGE.
GIES & CO.
NOT SAFE. I'LL DO IT LATER.

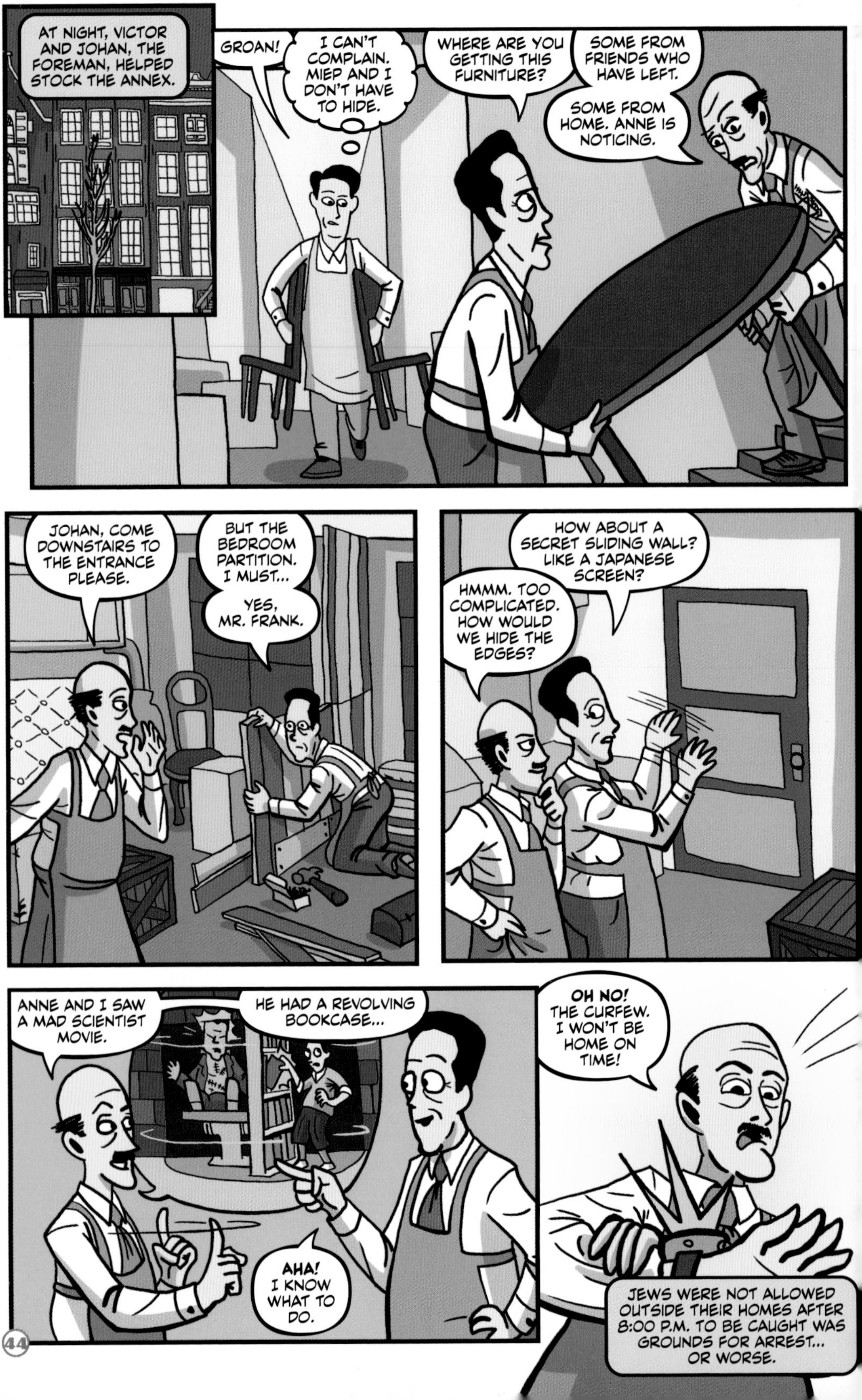
AT NIGHT, VICTOR AND JOHAN, THE FOREMAN, HELPED STOCK THE ANNEX.
GROAN!
I CAN'T COMPLAIN. MIEP AND I DON'T HAVE TO HIDE.
WHERE ARE YOU GETTING THIS FURNITURE?
SOME FROM FRIENDS WHO HAVE LEFT.
SOME FROM HOME. ANNE IS NOTICING.
JOHAN, COME DOWNSTAIRS TO THE ENTRANCE PLEASE.
BUT THE BEDROOM PARTITION. I MUST...
YES, MR. FRANK.
HOW ABOUT A SECRET SLIDING WALL? LIKE A JAPANESE SCREEN?
HMMM. TOO COMPLICATED. HOW WOULD WE HIDE THE EDGES?
ANNE AND I SAW A MAD SCIENTIST MOVIE.
HE HAD A REVOLVING BOOKCASE...
AHA! I KNOW WHAT TO DO.
OH NO! THE CURFEW. I WON'T BE HOME ON TIME!
JEWS WERE NOT ALLOWED OUTSIDE THEIR HOMES AFTER 8:00 P.M. TO BE CAUGHT WAS GROUNDS FOR ARREST... OR WORSE.

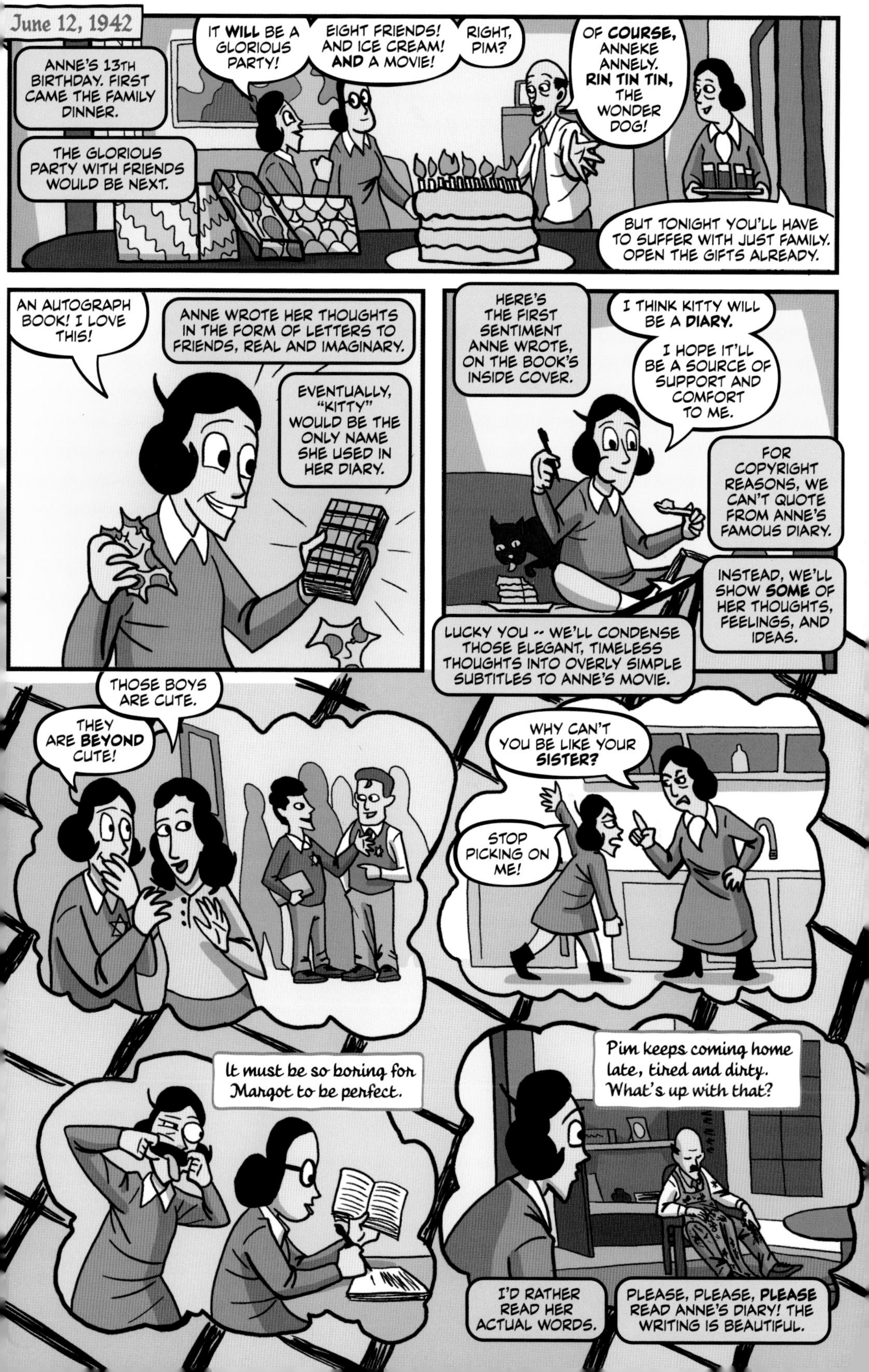
June 12, 1942
ANNE'S 13TH BIRTHDAY. FIRST CAME THE FAMILY DINNER.
THE GLORIOUS PARTY WITH FRIENDS WOULD BE NEXT.
IT WILL BE A GLORIOUS PARTY!
EIGHT FRIENDS! AND ICE CREAM! AND A MOVIE!
RIGHT, PIM?
OF COURSE, ANNEKE ANNELY. RIN TIN TIN, THE WONDER DOG!
BUT TONIGHT YOU'LL HAVE TO SUFFER WITH JUST FAMILY. OPEN THE GIFTS ALREADY.
AN AUTOGRAPH BOOK! I LOVE THIS!
ANNE WROTE HER THOUGHTS IN THE FORM OF LETTERS TO FRIENDS, REAL AND IMAGINARY.
EVENTUALLY, "KITTY" WOULD BE THE ONLY NAME SHE USED IN HER DIARY.
HERE'S THE FIRST SENTIMENT ANNE WROTE, ON THE BOOK'S INSIDE COVER.
I THINK KITTY WILL BE A DIARY.
I HOPE IT'LL BE A SOURCE OF SUPPORT AND COMFORT TO ME.
FOR COPYRIGHT REASONS, WE CAN'T QUOTE FROM ANNE'S FAMOUS DIARY.
INSTEAD, WE'LL SHOW SOME OF HER THOUGHTS, FEELINGS, AND IDEAS.
LUCKY YOU -- WE'LL CONDENSE THOSE ELEGANT, TIMELESS THOUGHTS INTO OVERLY SIMPLE SUBTITLES TO ANNE'S MOVIE.
THOSE BOYS ARE CUTE.
THEY ARE BEYOND CUTE!
WHY CAN'T YOU BE LIKE YOUR SISTER?
STOP PICKING ON ME!
It must be so boring for Margot to be perfect.
Pim keeps coming home late, tired and dirty. What's up with that?
I'D RATHER READ HER ACTUAL WORDS.
PLEASE, PLEASE, PLEASE READ ANNE'S DIARY! THE WRITING IS BEAUTIFUL.

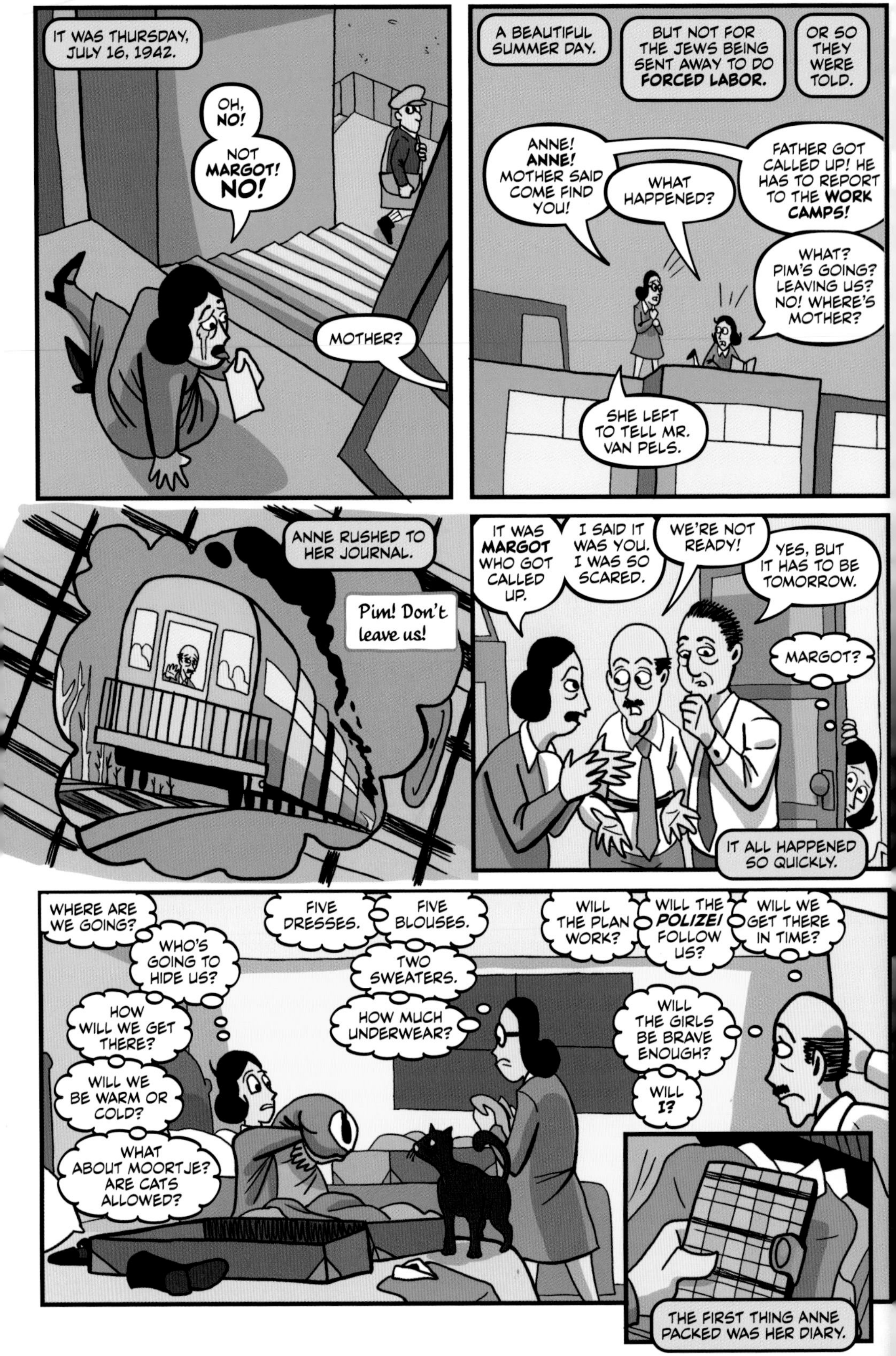
IT WAS THURSDAY, JULY 16, 1942.
OH, NO!
NOT MARGOT! NO!
MOTHER?
A BEAUTIFUL SUMMER DAY.
BUT NOT FOR THE JEWS BEING SENT AWAY TO DO FORCED LABOR.
OR SO THEY WERE TOLD.
ANNE! ANNE! MOTHER SAID COME FIND YOU!
WHAT HAPPENED?
FATHER GOT CALLED UP! HE HAS TO REPORT TO THE WORK CAMPS!
WHAT? PIM'S GOING? LEAVING US? NO! WHERE'S MOTHER?
SHE LEFT TO TELL MR. VAN PELS.
ANNE RUSHED TO HER JOURNAL.
Pim! Don't leave us!
IT WAS MARGOT WHO GOT CALLED UP.
I SAID IT WAS YOU. I WAS SO SCARED.
WE'RE NOT READY!
YES, BUT IT HAS TO BE TOMORROW.
MARGOT?
IT ALL HAPPENED SO QUICKLY.
WHERE ARE WE GOING?
WHO'S GOING TO HIDE US?
HOW WILL WE GET THERE?
WILL WE BE WARM OR COLD?
WHAT ABOUT MOORTJE? ARE CATS ALLOWED?
FIVE DRESSES.
FIVE BLOUSES.
TWO SWEATERS.
HOW MUCH UNDERWEAR?
WILL THE PLAN WORK?
WILL THE POLIZEI FOLLOW US?
WILL WE GET THERE IN TIME?
WILL THE GIRLS BE BRAVE ENOUGH?
WILL I?
THE FIRST THING ANNE PACKED WAS HER DIARY.

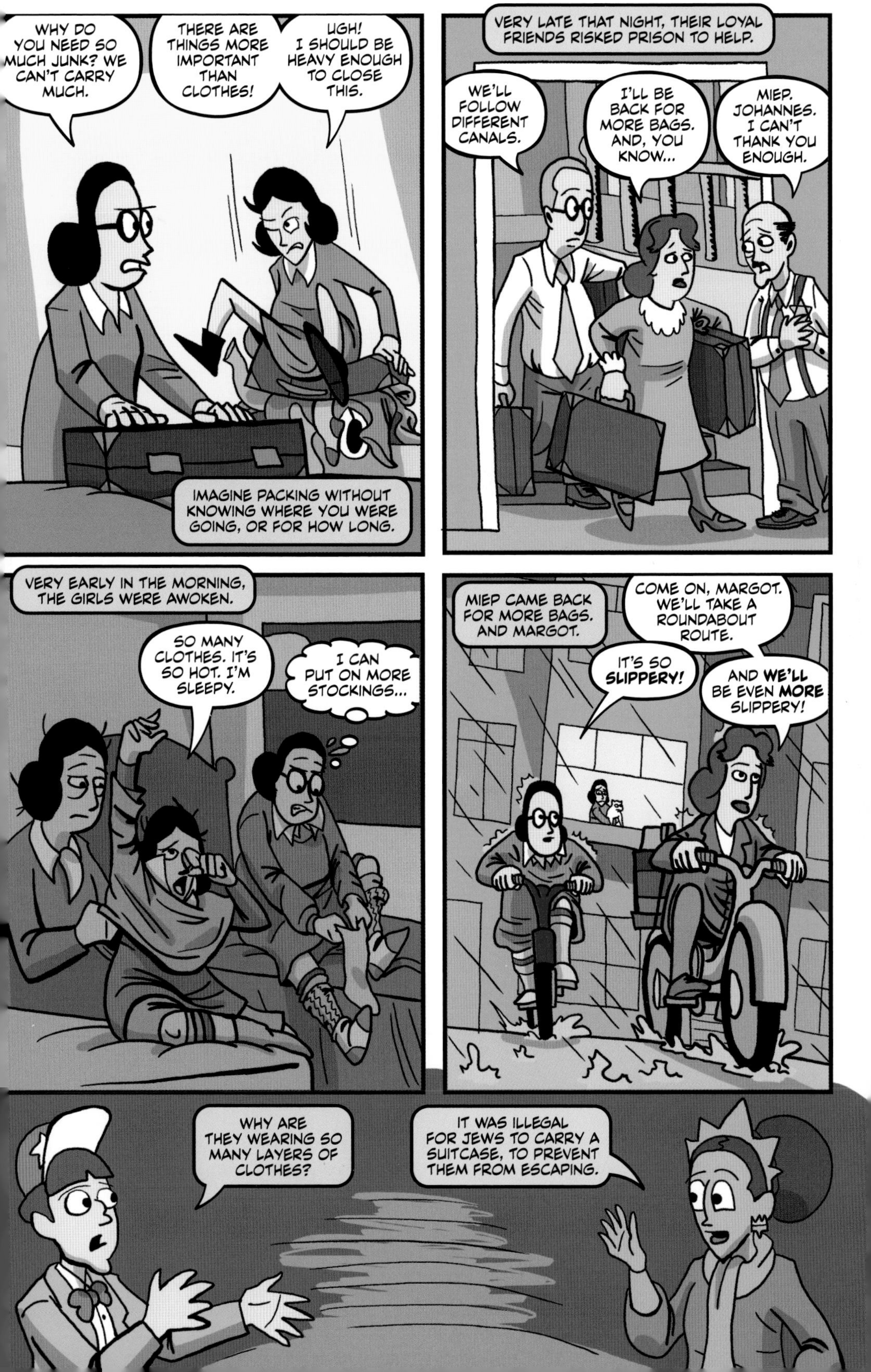
WHY DO YOU NEED SO MUCH JUNK? WE CAN'T CARRY MUCH.
THERE ARE THINGS MORE IMPORTANT THAN CLOTHES!
UGH! I SHOULD BE HEAVY ENOUGH TO CLOSE THIS.
IMAGINE PACKING WITHOUT KNOWING WHERE YOU WERE GOING, OR FOR HOW LONG.
VERY LATE THAT NIGHT, THEIR LOYAL FRIENDS RISKED PRISON TO HELP.
WE'LL FOLLOW DIFFERENT CANALS.
I'LL BE BACK FOR MORE BAGS. AND, YOU KNOW...
MIEP. JOHANNES. I CAN'T THANK YOU ENOUGH.
VERY EARLY IN THE MORNING, THE GIRLS WERE AWOKEN.
SO MANY CLOTHES. IT'S SO HOT. I'M SLEEPY.
I CAN PUT ON MORE STOCKINGS...
MIEP CAME BACK FOR MORE BAGS. AND MARGOT.
COME ON, MARGOT. WE'LL TAKE A ROUNDABOUT ROUTE.
IT'S SO **SLIPPERY!**
AND **WE'LL** BE EVEN **MORE** SLIPPERY!
WHY ARE THEY WEARING SO MANY LAYERS OF CLOTHES?
IT WAS ILLEGAL FOR JEWS TO CARRY A SUITCASE, TO PREVENT THEM FROM ESCAPING.

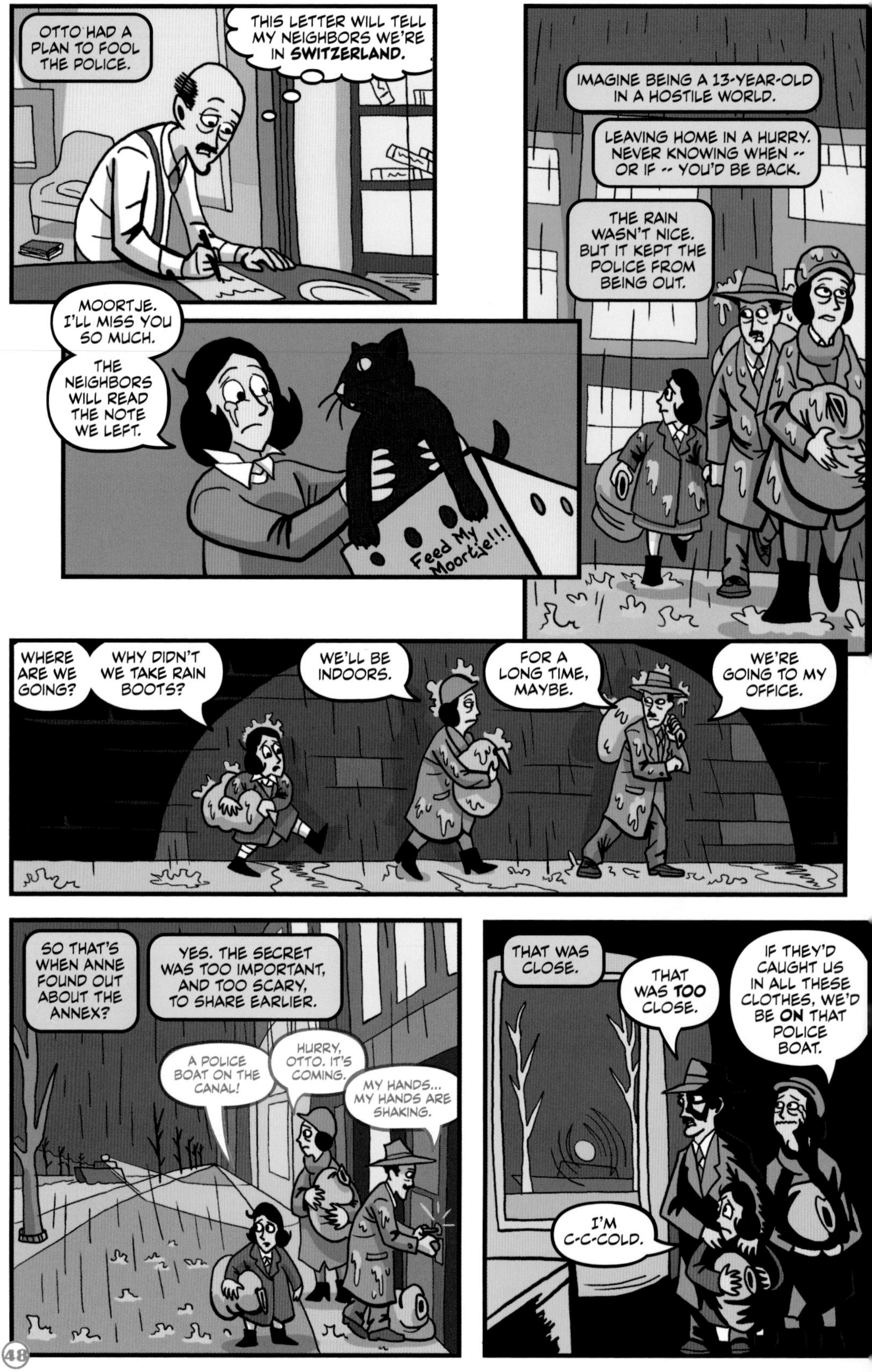
OTTO HAD A PLAN TO FOOL THE POLICE.
THIS LETTER WILL TELL MY NEIGHBORS WE'RE IN **SWITZERLAND.**
IMAGINE BEING A 13-YEAR-OLD IN A HOSTILE WORLD.
LEAVING HOME IN A HURRY. NEVER KNOWING WHEN -- OR IF -- YOU'D BE BACK.
THE RAIN WASN'T NICE. BUT IT KEPT THE POLICE FROM BEING OUT.
MOORTJE. I'LL MISS YOU SO MUCH.
THE NEIGHBORS WILL READ THE NOTE WE LEFT.
Feed My Moortje!!!
WHERE ARE WE GOING?
WHY DIDN'T WE TAKE RAIN BOOTS?
WE'LL BE INDOORS.
FOR A LONG TIME, MAYBE.
WE'RE GOING TO MY OFFICE.
SO THAT'S WHEN ANNE FOUND OUT ABOUT THE ANNEX?
YES. THE SECRET WAS TOO IMPORTANT, AND TOO SCARY, TO SHARE EARLIER.
A POLICE BOAT ON THE CANAL!
HURRY, OTTO. IT'S COMING.
MY HANDS... MY HANDS ARE SHAKING.
THAT WAS CLOSE.
THAT WAS **TOO** CLOSE.
IF THEY'D CAUGHT US IN ALL THESE CLOTHES, WE'D BE **ON** THAT POLICE BOAT.
I'M C-C-COLD.

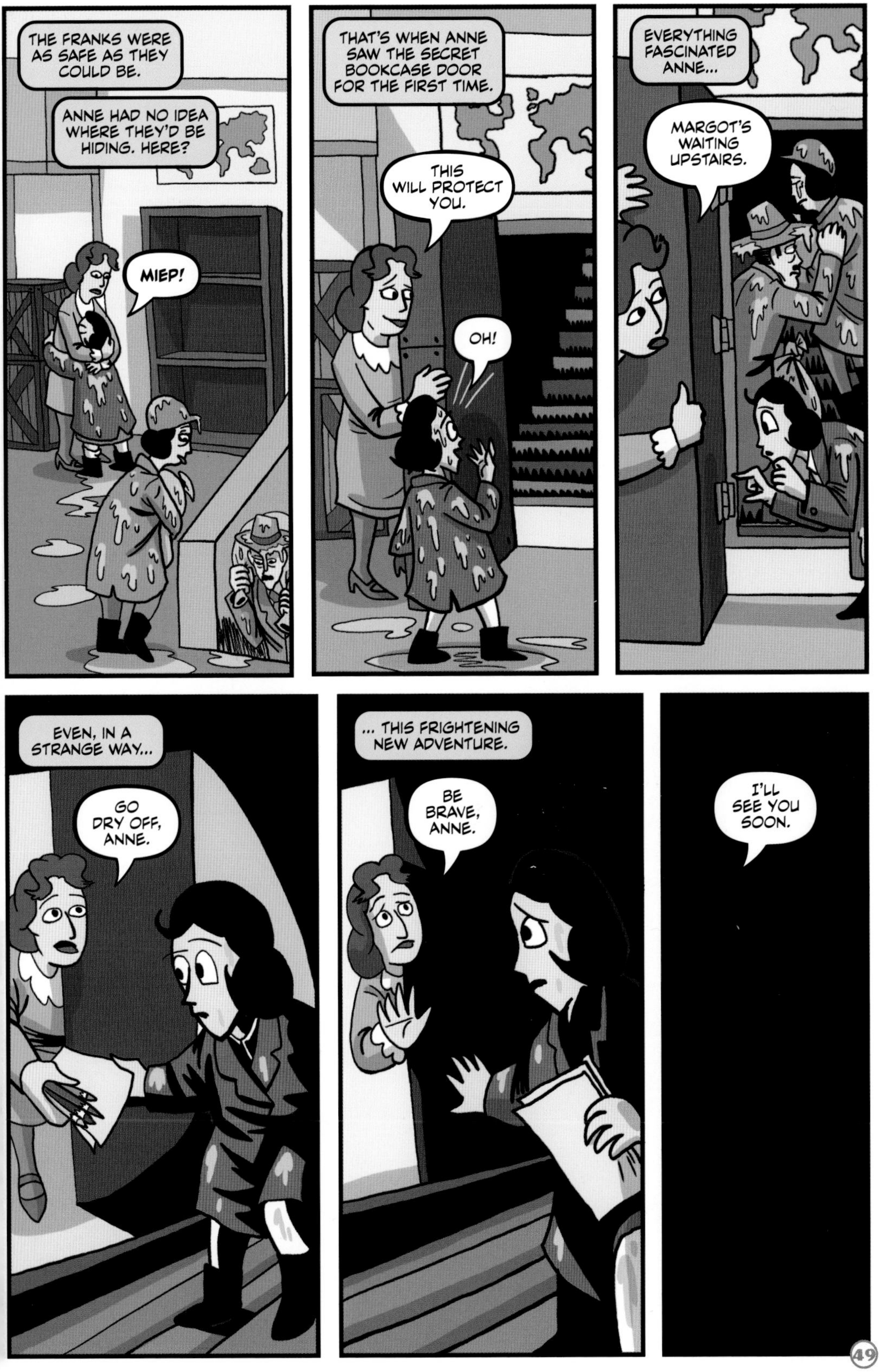
THE FRANKS WERE AS SAFE AS THEY COULD BE.
ANNE HAD NO IDEA WHERE THEY'D BE HIDING. HERE?
MIEP!
THAT'S WHEN ANNE SAW THE SECRET BOOKCASE DOOR FOR THE FIRST TIME.
THIS WILL PROTECT YOU.
OH!
EVERYTHING FASCINATED ANNE...
MARGOT'S WAITING UPSTAIRS.
EVEN, IN A STRANGE WAY...
GO DRY OFF, ANNE.
... THIS FRIGHTENING NEW ADVENTURE.
BE BRAVE, ANNE.
I'LL SEE YOU SOON.

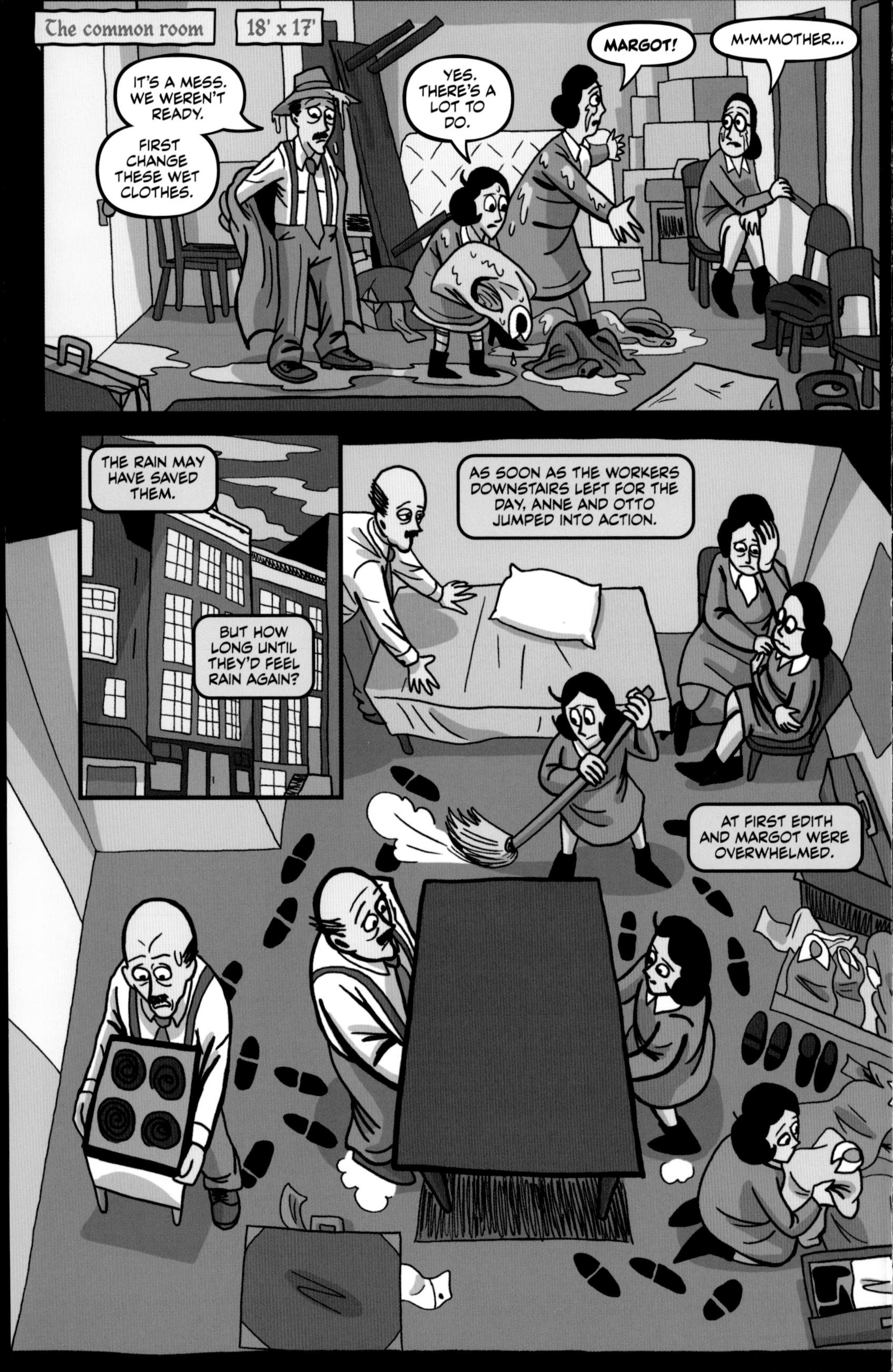
The common room
18' x 17'
IT'S A MESS. WE WEREN'T READY.
FIRST CHANGE THESE WET CLOTHES.
YES. THERE'S A LOT TO DO.
MARGOT!
M-M-MOTHER...
THE RAIN MAY HAVE SAVED THEM.
BUT HOW LONG UNTIL THEY'D FEEL RAIN AGAIN?
AS SOON AS THE WORKERS DOWNSTAIRS LEFT FOR THE DAY, ANNE AND OTTO JUMPED INTO ACTION.
AT FIRST EDITH AND MARGOT WERE OVERWHELMED.

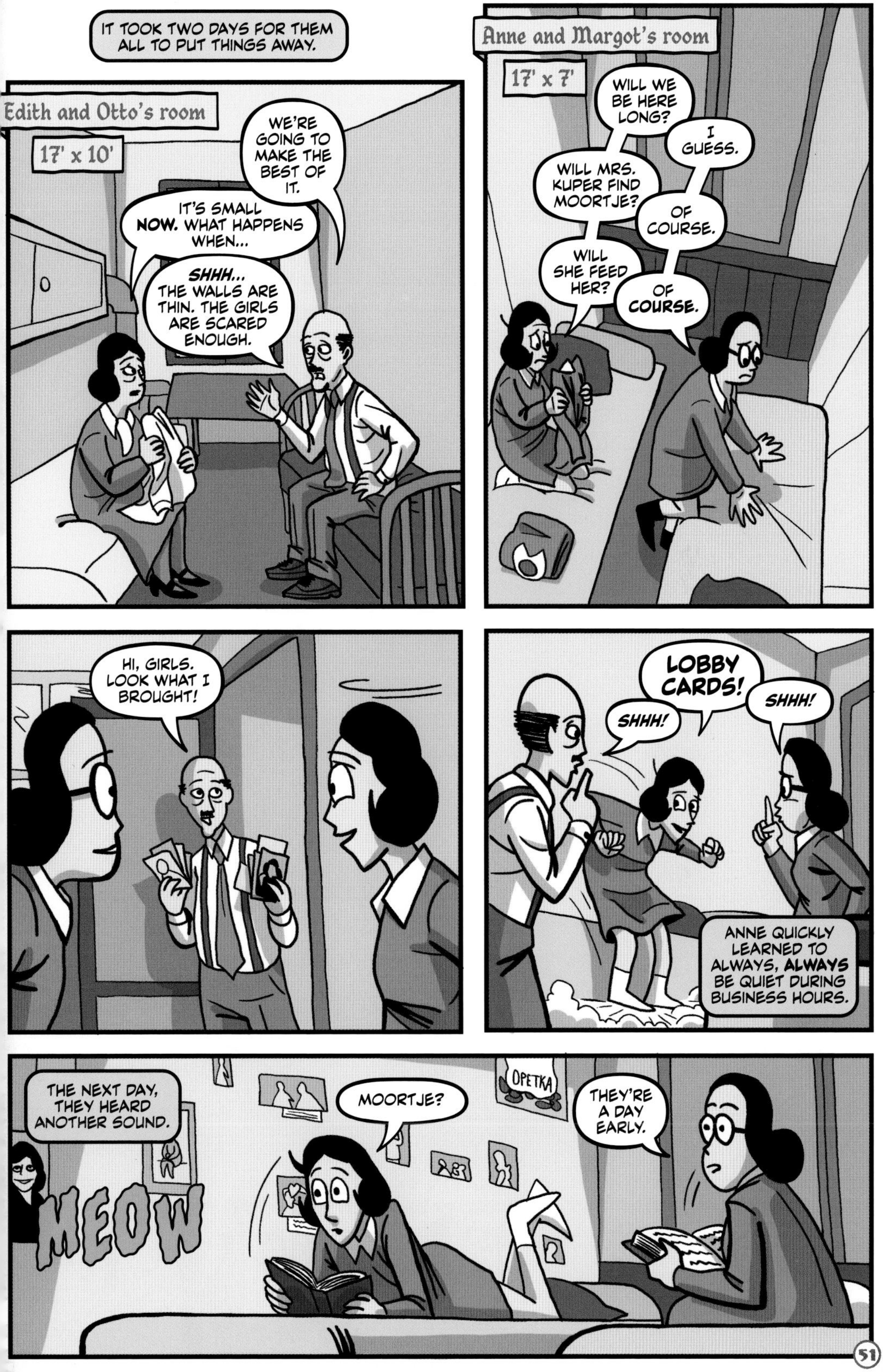
IT TOOK TWO DAYS FOR THEM ALL TO PUT THINGS AWAY.
Edith and Otto's room
17' x 10'
IT'S SMALL NOW. WHAT HAPPENS WHEN...
WE'RE GOING TO MAKE THE BEST OF IT.
SHHH... THE WALLS ARE THIN. THE GIRLS ARE SCARED ENOUGH.
Anne and Margot's room
17' x 7'
WILL WE BE HERE LONG?
I GUESS.
WILL MRS. KUPER FIND MOORTJE?
OF COURSE.
WILL SHE FEED HER?
OF COURSE.
HI, GIRLS. LOOK WHAT I BROUGHT!
LOBBY CARDS!
SHHH!
SHHH!
ANNE QUICKLY LEARNED TO ALWAYS, ALWAYS BE QUIET DURING BUSINESS HOURS.
THE NEXT DAY, THEY HEARD ANOTHER SOUND.
MEOW
MOORTJE?
OPETKA
THEY'RE A DAY EARLY.

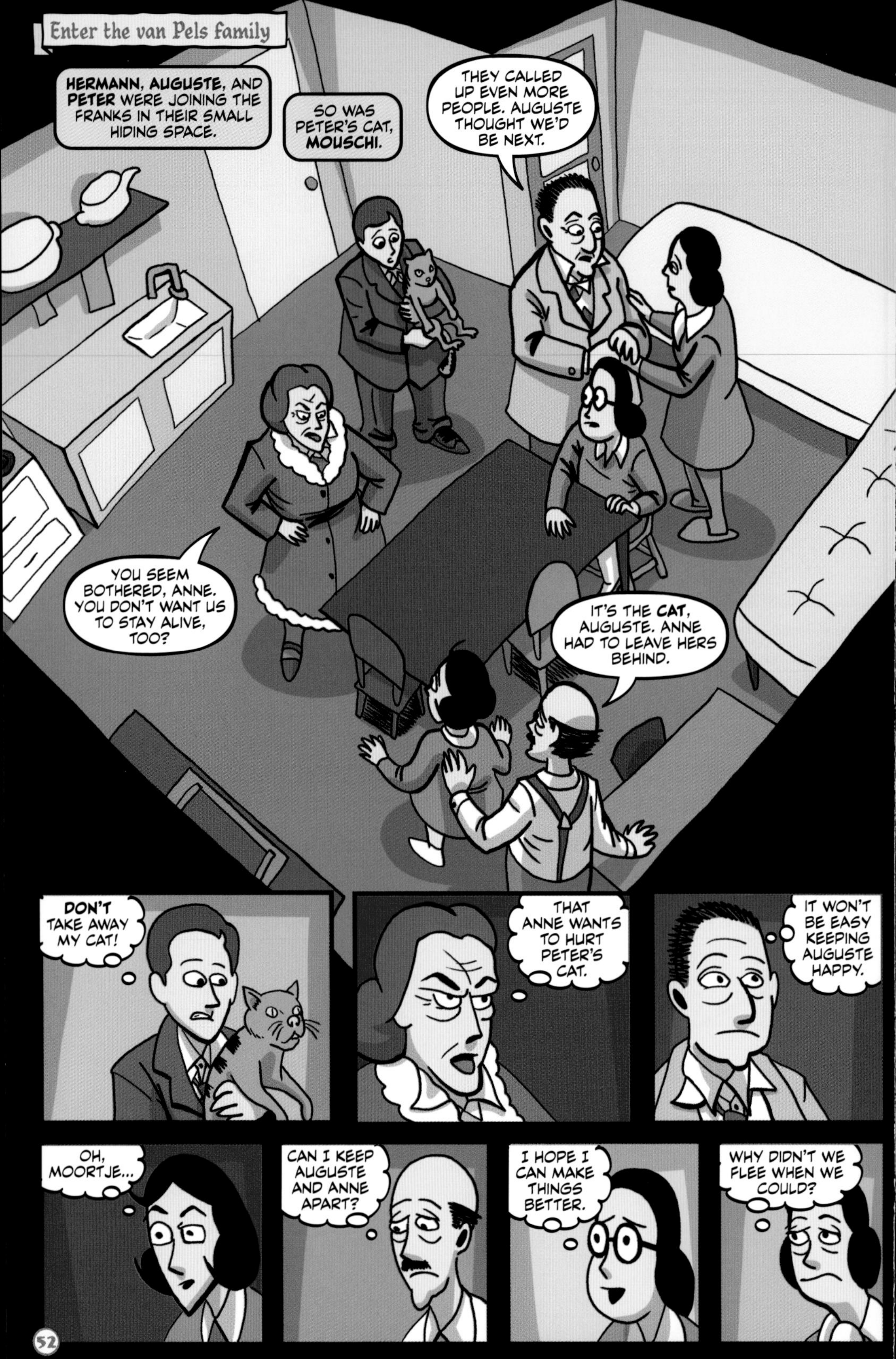
Enter the van Pels family
HERMANN, AUGUSTE, AND PETER WERE JOINING THE FRANKS IN THEIR SMALL HIDING SPACE.
SO WAS PETER'S CAT, MOUSCHI.
THEY CALLED UP EVEN MORE PEOPLE. AUGUSTE THOUGHT WE'D BE NEXT.
YOU SEEM BOTHERED, ANNE. YOU DON'T WANT US TO STAY ALIVE, TOO?
IT'S THE CAT, AUGUSTE. ANNE HAD TO LEAVE HERS BEHIND.
DON'T TAKE AWAY MY CAT!
THAT ANNE WANTS TO HURT PETER'S CAT.
IT WON'T BE EASY KEEPING AUGUSTE HAPPY.
OH, MOORTJE...
CAN I KEEP AUGUSTE AND ANNE APART?
I HOPE I CAN MAKE THINGS BETTER.
WHY DIDN'T WE FLEE WHEN WE COULD?

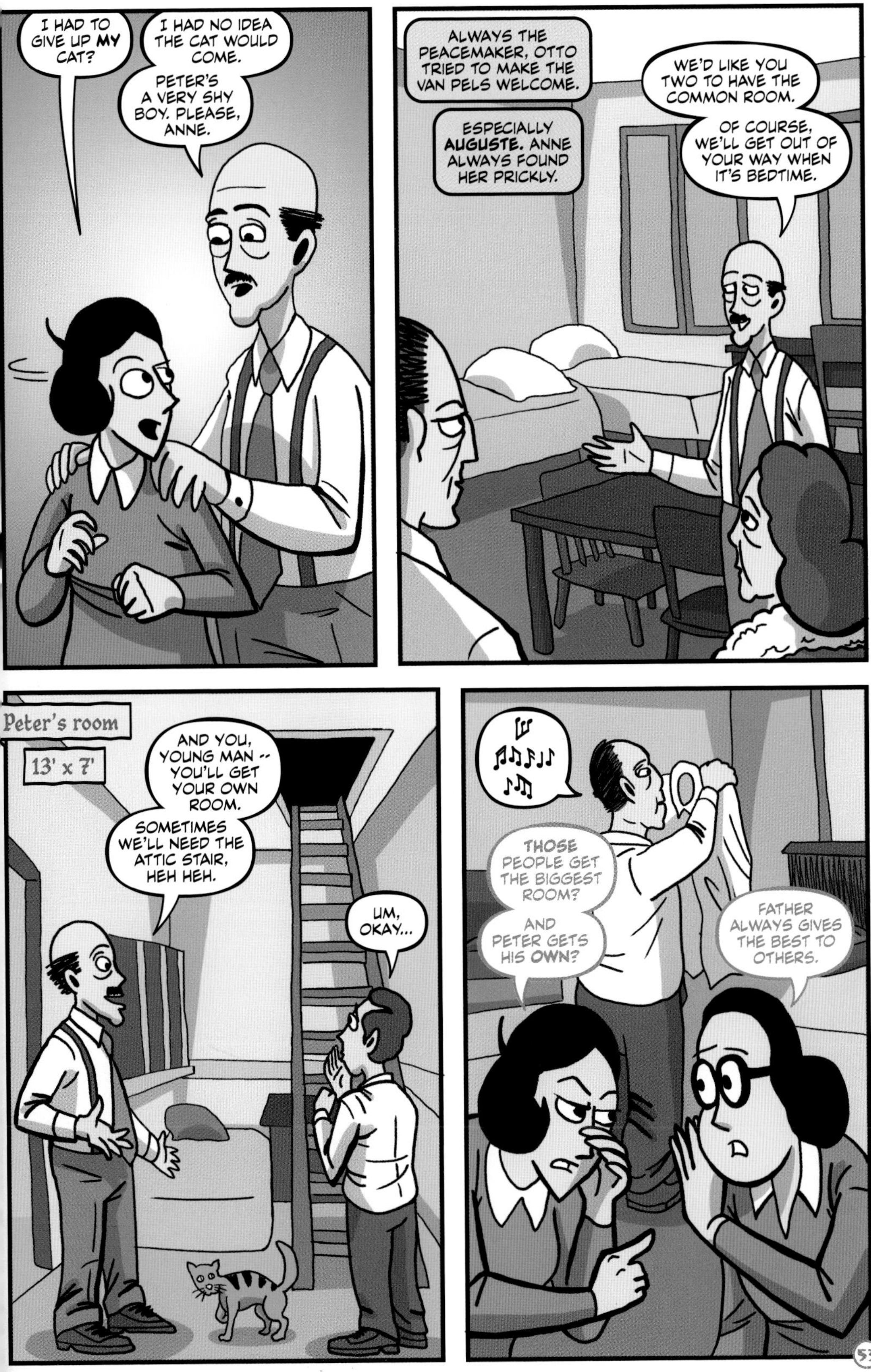
I HAD TO GIVE UP MY CAT?
I HAD NO IDEA THE CAT WOULD COME.
PETER'S A VERY SHY BOY. PLEASE, ANNE.
ALWAYS THE PEACEMAKER, OTTO TRIED TO MAKE THE VAN PELS WELCOME.
ESPECIALLY AUGUSTE. ANNE ALWAYS FOUND HER PRICKLY.
WE'D LIKE YOU TWO TO HAVE THE COMMON ROOM.
OF COURSE, WE'LL GET OUT OF YOUR WAY WHEN IT'S BEDTIME.
Peter's room
13' x 7'
AND YOU, YOUNG MAN -- YOU'LL GET YOUR OWN ROOM.
SOMETIMES WE'LL NEED THE ATTIC STAIR, HEH HEH.
UM, OKAY...
THOSE PEOPLE GET THE BIGGEST ROOM?
AND PETER GETS HIS OWN?
FATHER ALWAYS GIVES THE BEST TO OTHERS.

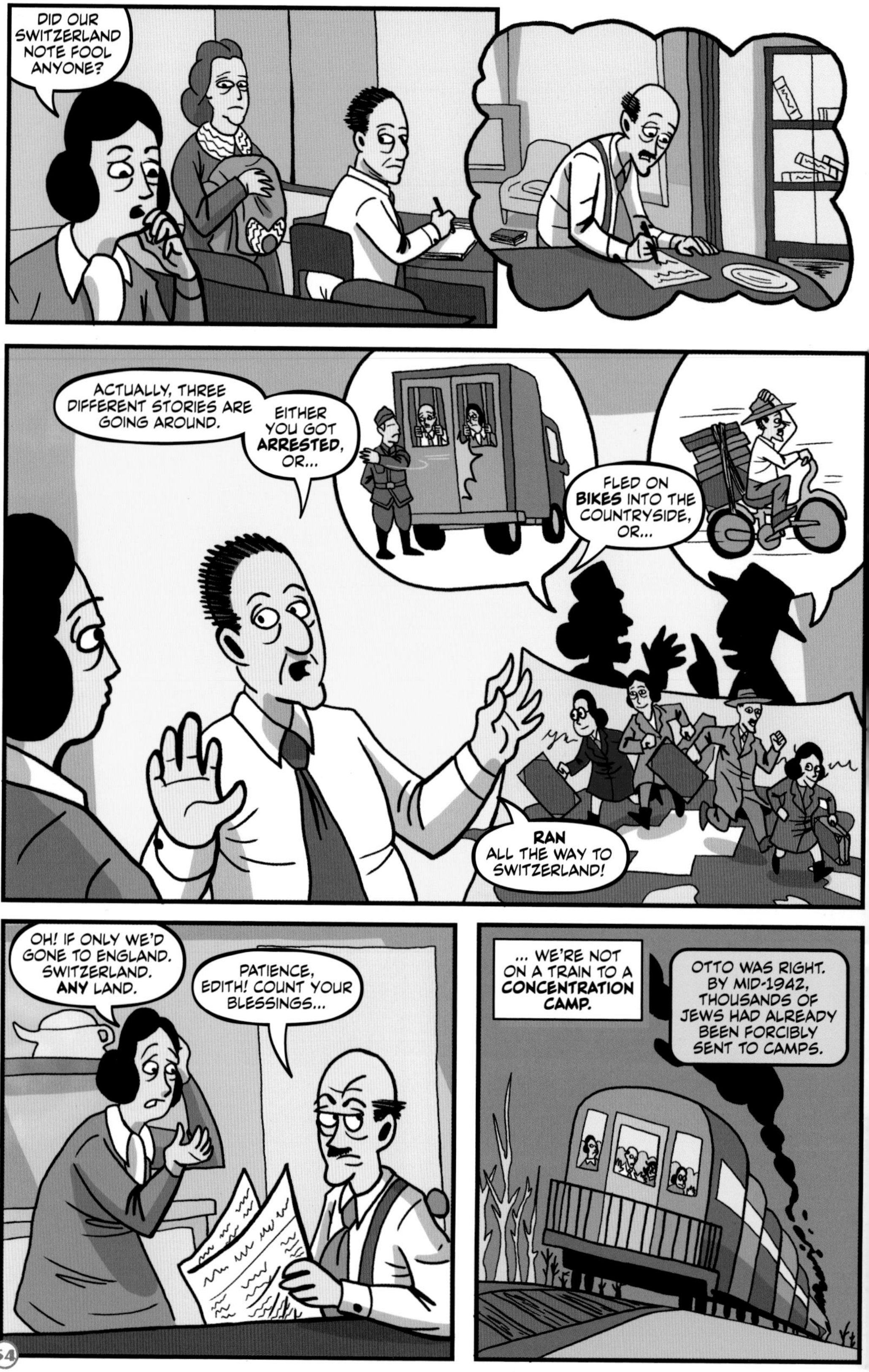
DID OUR SWITZERLAND NOTE FOOL ANYONE?
ACTUALLY, THREE DIFFERENT STORIES ARE GOING AROUND.
EITHER YOU GOT ARRESTED, OR...
FLED ON BIKES INTO THE COUNTRYSIDE, OR...
RAN ALL THE WAY TO SWITZERLAND!
OH! IF ONLY WE'D GONE TO ENGLAND. SWITZERLAND. ANY LAND.
PATIENCE, EDITH! COUNT YOUR BLESSINGS...
... WE'RE NOT ON A TRAIN TO A CONCENTRATION CAMP.
OTTO WAS RIGHT. BY MID-1942, THOUSANDS OF JEWS HAD ALREADY BEEN FORCIBLY SENT TO CAMPS.

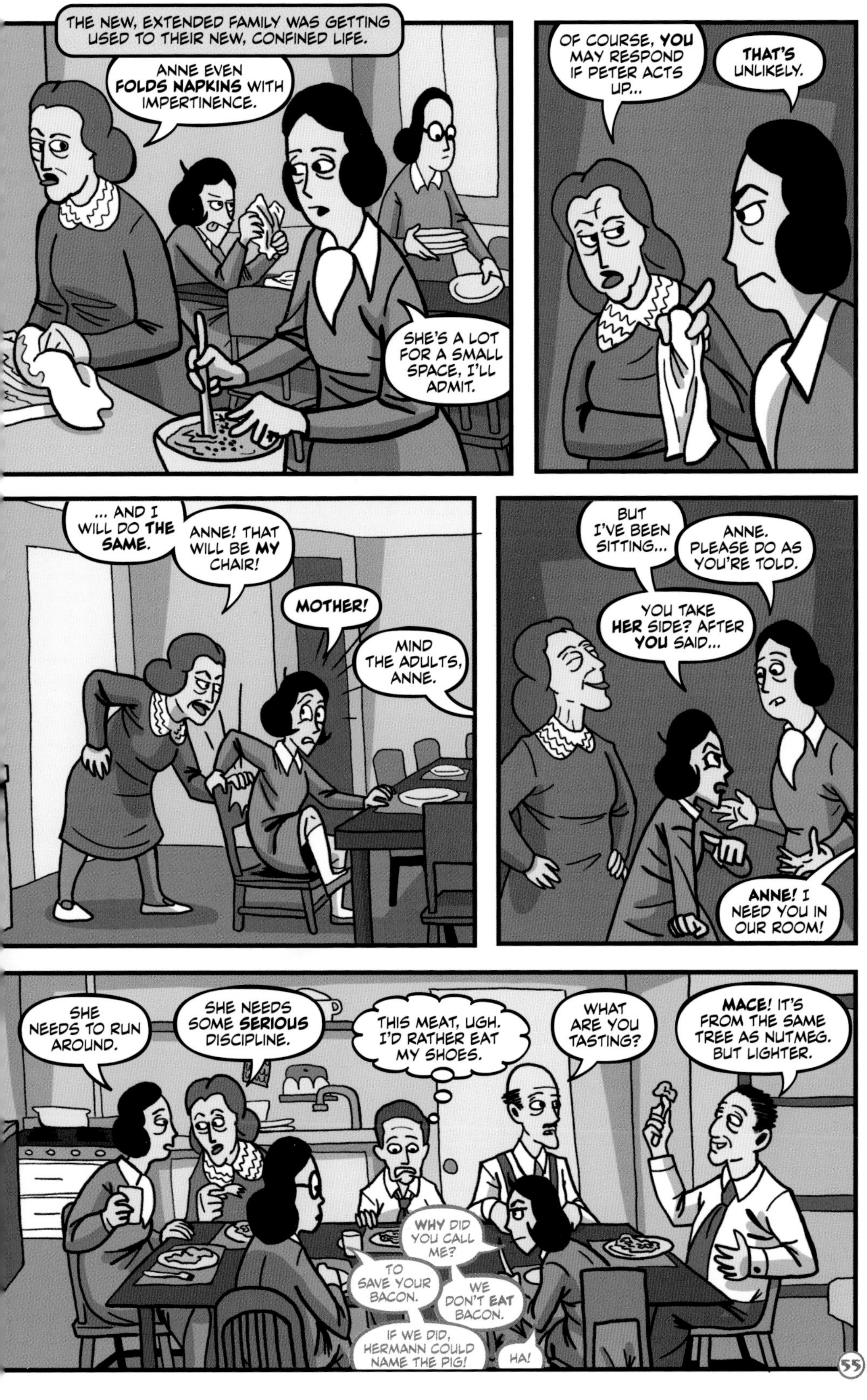
THE NEW, EXTENDED FAMILY WAS GETTING USED TO THEIR NEW, CONFINED LIFE.
ANNE EVEN **FOLDS NAPKINS** WITH IMPERTINENCE.
SHE'S A LOT FOR A SMALL SPACE, I'LL ADMIT.
OF COURSE, **YOU** MAY RESPOND IF PETER ACTS UP...
THAT'S UNLIKELY.
... AND I WILL DO **THE SAME.**
ANNE! THAT WILL BE **MY** CHAIR!
MOTHER!
MIND THE ADULTS, ANNE.
BUT I'VE BEEN SITTING...
ANNE. PLEASE DO AS YOU'RE TOLD.
YOU TAKE **HER** SIDE? AFTER **YOU** SAID...
ANNE! I NEED YOU IN OUR ROOM!
SHE NEEDS TO RUN AROUND.
SHE NEEDS SOME **SERIOUS** DISCIPLINE.
THIS MEAT, UGH. I'D RATHER EAT MY SHOES.
WHAT ARE YOU TASTING?
MACE! IT'S FROM THE SAME TREE AS NUTMEG. BUT LIGHTER.
WHY DID YOU CALL ME?
TO SAVE YOUR BACON.
WE DON'T **EAT** BACON.
IF WE DID, HERMANN COULD NAME THE PIG!
HA!

TWO FAMILIES. ONE SMALL SPACE.

NO WAY TO GET SUPPLIES.

WHAT WAS THE SECRET TO SURVIVAL IN THE SECRET ANNEX?

MEET THE HELPERS!

They worked for Opekta. And they risked it all to save people's lives.

Miep Gies

- Otto's invaluable assistant
- Opekta Customer Service manager
- Bringer of fresh food and books
- Chief organizer of the Annex and the helpers

Jan Gies

- Miep's husband, a social worker
- Became official non-Jewish "owner" of Opekta
- Agent in the Dutch Resistance
- Source for extra black market supplies

Bep Voskuijl

- At 23, the youngest helper and a friend to Anne
- Administrative assistant at Opekta
- Spent the most time in the Annex
- Managed bread, milk, and all "practical matters"

Victor Kugler

- Otto's longtime, trusted sales manager
- Kept Opekta running by adapting to the Nazis
- Always stressed out, couldn't tell his wife why
- Managed finances of the Annex

Johannes Kleiman

- Otto Frank's right-hand man since the Frank Bank
- After Opekta was "sold," became managing director
- Cheered up Annex folks while its stress made him ill
- Main communicator to and from outside world

Johan Voskuijl

- Opekta warehouse manager, and Bep's father
- Monitored warehouse employees and what they knew
- Made the waste from the Annex disappear
- Built the great bookcase door and much more

HELPING SEVEN PEOPLE HIDE FROM NAZIS WAS DANGEROUS.

Free Soup

VERY DANGEROUS. THEY HAD TO HIDE BUYING EXTRA THINGS WHEN MANY DUTCH HAD VERY LITTLE.

WITH SUPPLIES LOW, THEY BOUGHT ON THE **BLACK MARKET**, WHICH WAS HIGHLY ILLEGAL.

PRESCRIPTIONS HAD TO BE FORGED.

THE NAZIS PAID INFORMANTS TO WATCH FOR SUCH THINGS.

THEY NEEDED A NETWORK OF SHADY DEALERS JUST FOR THE **FOOD**.

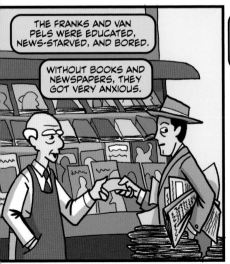

THE FRANKS AND VAN PELS WERE EDUCATED, NEWS-STARVED, AND BORED.

WITHOUT BOOKS AND NEWSPAPERS, THEY GOT VERY ANXIOUS.

ANNE'S DIARY DESCRIBES, IN LOVING DETAIL, THE INCREDIBLE GENEROSITY AND BRAVERY OF THEIR LOYAL HELPERS.

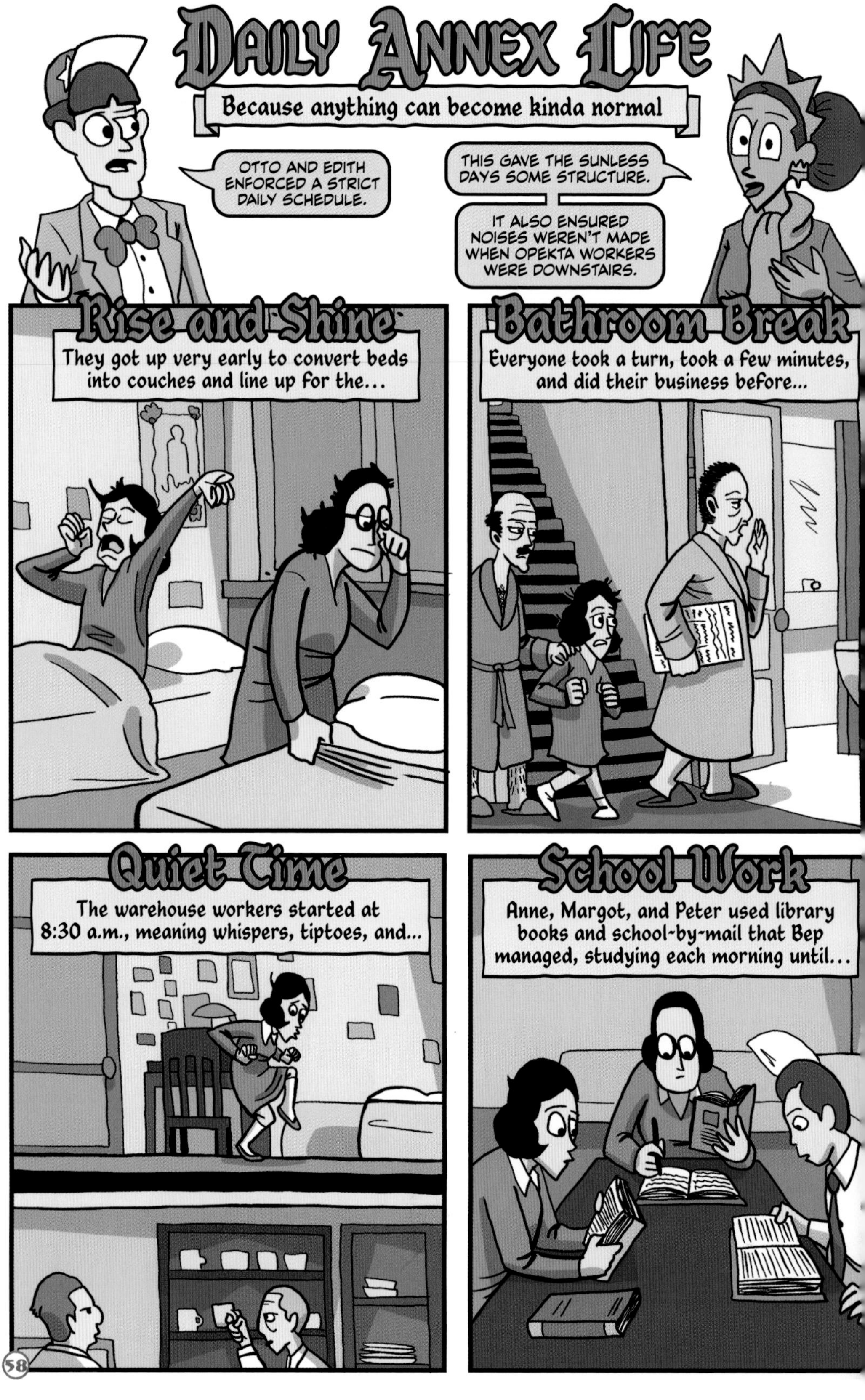

DAILY ANNEX LIFE
Because anything can become kinda normal
OTTO AND EDITH ENFORCED A STRICT DAILY SCHEDULE.
THIS GAVE THE SUNLESS DAYS SOME STRUCTURE.
IT ALSO ENSURED NOISES WEREN'T MADE WHEN OPEKTA WORKERS WERE DOWNSTAIRS.
Rise and Shine
They got up very early to convert beds into couches and line up for the...
Bathroom Break
Everyone took a turn, took a few minutes, and did their business before...
Quiet Time
The warehouse workers started at 8:30 a.m., meaning whispers, tiptoes, and...
School Work
Anne, Margot, and Peter used library books and school-by-mail that Bep managed, studying each morning until...

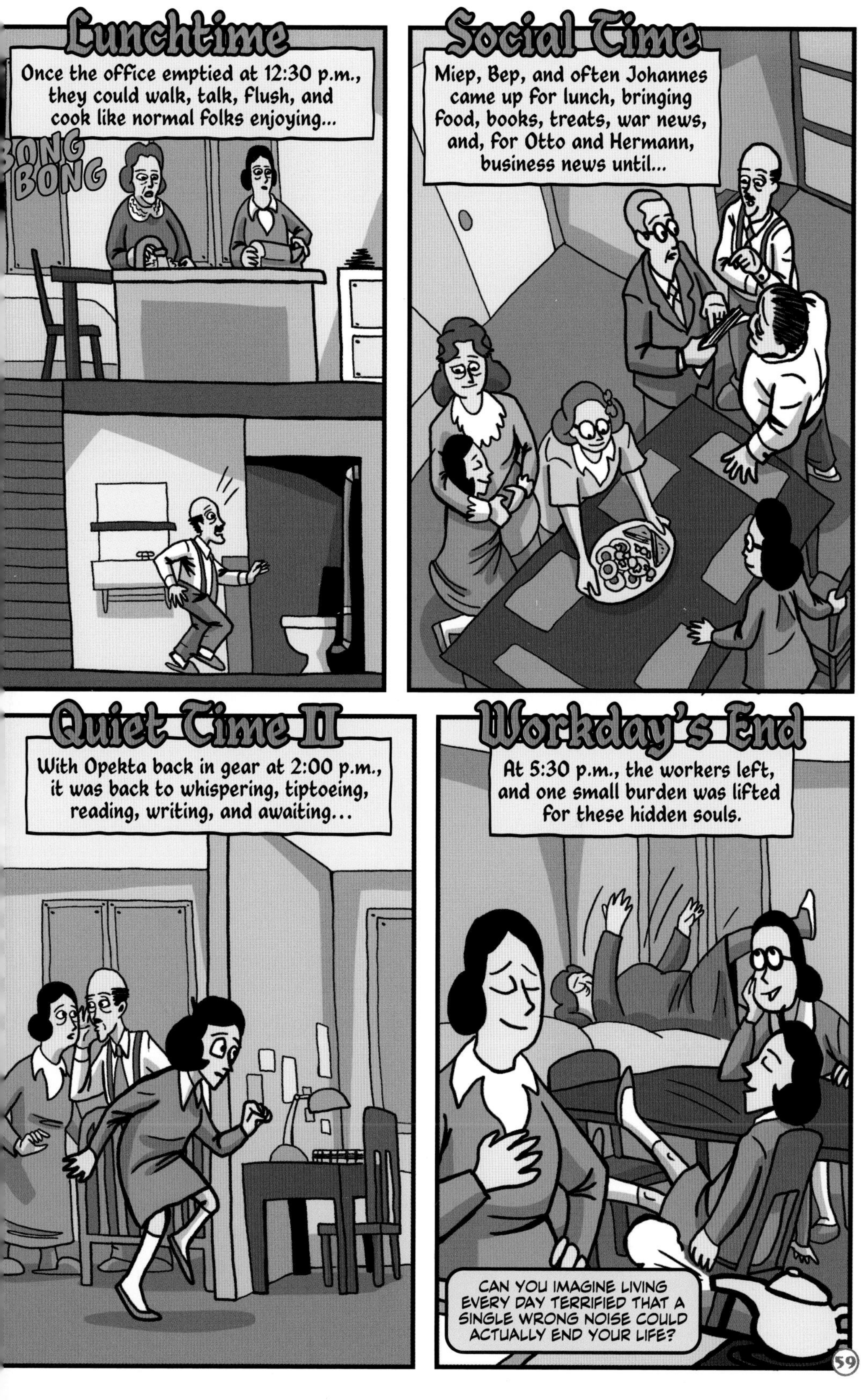
Lunchtime
Once the office emptied at 12:30 p.m., they could walk, talk, flush, and cook like normal folks enjoying...
BONG BONG
Social Time
Miep, Bep, and often Johannes came up for lunch, bringing food, books, treats, war news, and, for Otto and Hermann, business news until...
Quiet Time II
With Opekta back in gear at 2:00 p.m., it was back to whispering, tiptoeing, reading, writing, and awaiting...
Workday's End
At 5:30 p.m., the workers left, and one small burden was lifted for these hidden souls.
CAN YOU IMAGINE LIVING EVERY DAY TERRIFIED THAT A SINGLE WRONG NOISE COULD ACTUALLY END YOUR LIFE?

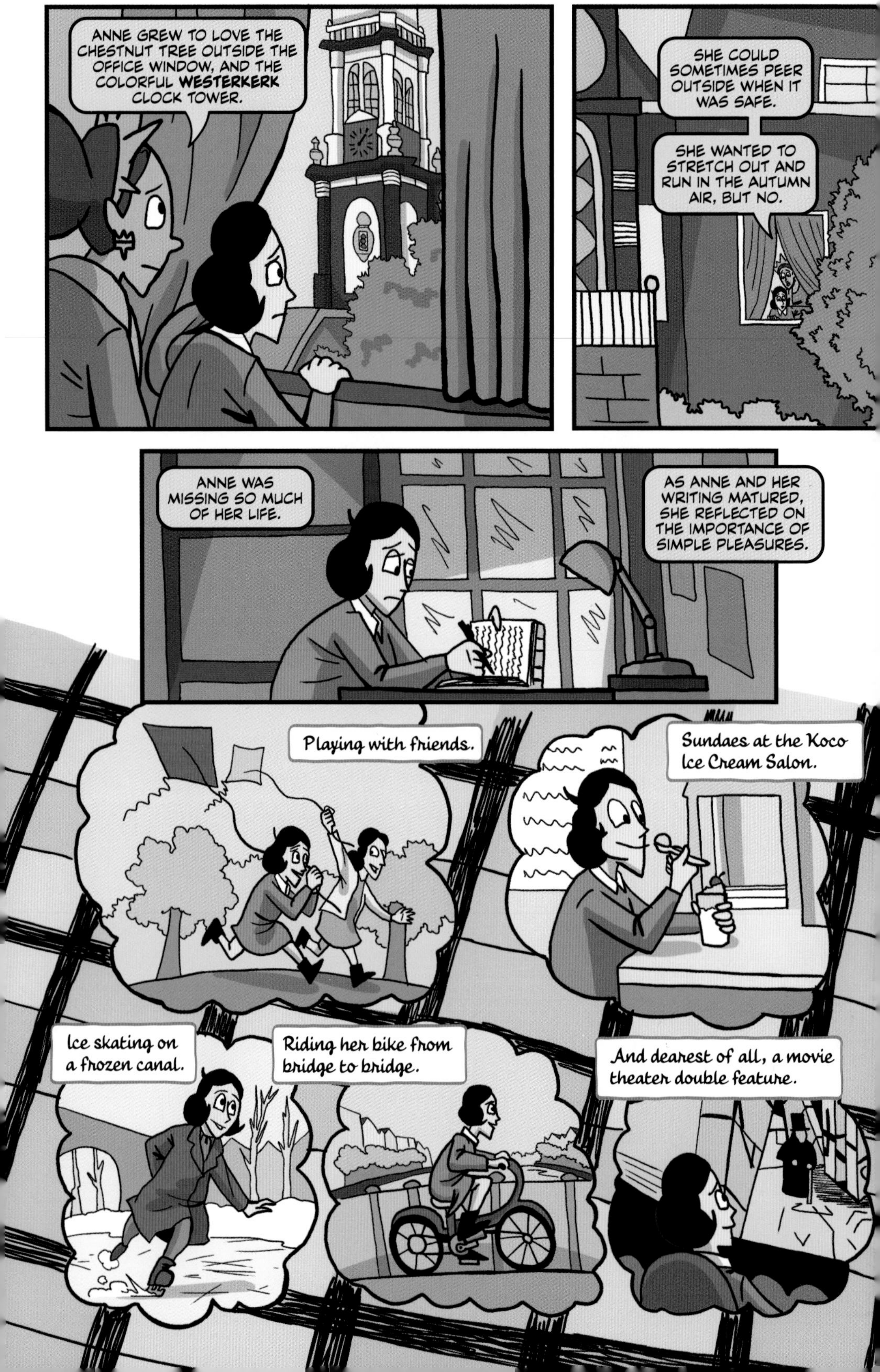

ANNE GREW TO LOVE THE CHESTNUT TREE OUTSIDE THE OFFICE WINDOW, AND THE COLORFUL **WESTERKERK** CLOCK TOWER.
SHE COULD SOMETIMES PEER OUTSIDE WHEN IT WAS SAFE.
SHE WANTED TO STRETCH OUT AND RUN IN THE AUTUMN AIR, BUT NO.
ANNE WAS MISSING SO MUCH OF HER LIFE.
AS ANNE AND HER WRITING MATURED, SHE REFLECTED ON THE IMPORTANCE OF SIMPLE PLEASURES.
Playing with friends.
Sundaes at the Koco Ice Cream Salon.
Ice skating on a frozen canal.
Riding her bike from bridge to bridge.
And dearest of all, a movie theater double feature.

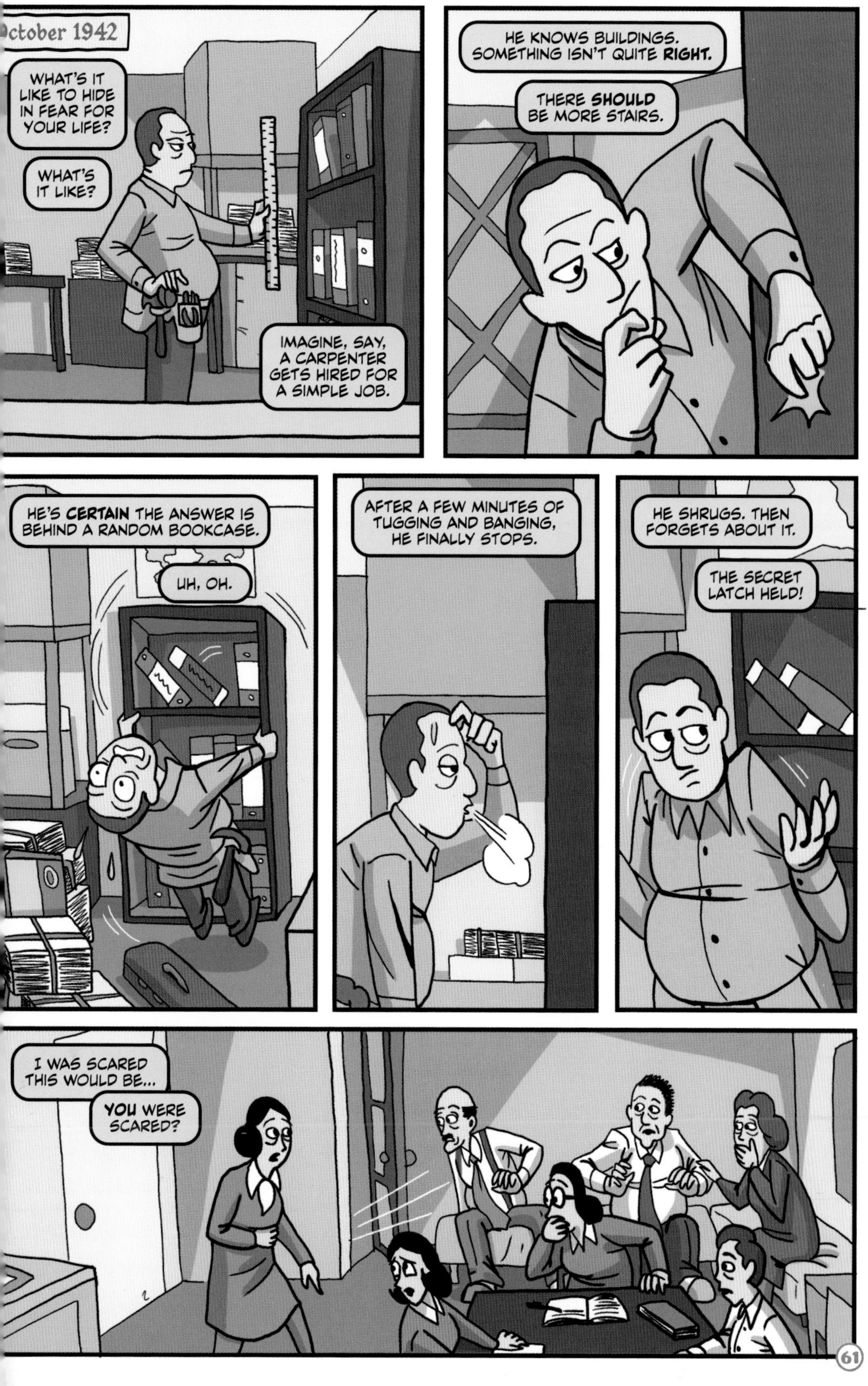

October 1942
WHAT'S IT LIKE TO HIDE IN FEAR FOR YOUR LIFE?
WHAT'S IT LIKE?
IMAGINE, SAY, A CARPENTER GETS HIRED FOR A SIMPLE JOB.
HE KNOWS BUILDINGS. SOMETHING ISN'T QUITE **RIGHT.**
THERE **SHOULD** BE MORE STAIRS.
HE'S **CERTAIN** THE ANSWER IS BEHIND A RANDOM BOOKCASE.
UH, OH.
AFTER A FEW MINUTES OF TUGGING AND BANGING, HE FINALLY STOPS.
HE SHRUGS. THEN FORGETS ABOUT IT.
THE SECRET LATCH HELD!
I WAS SCARED THIS WOULD BE...
YOU WERE SCARED?

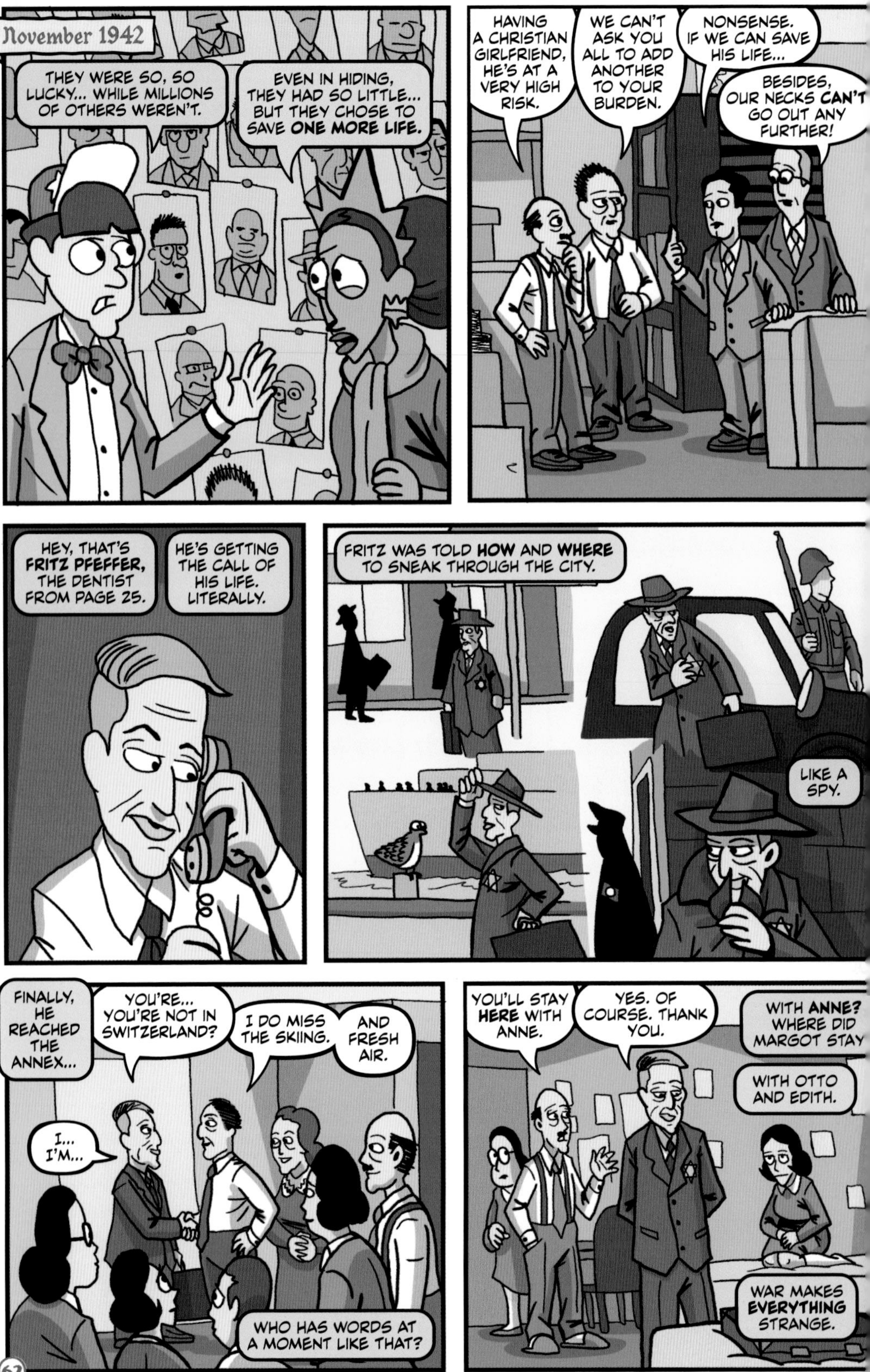
November 1942
THEY WERE SO, SO LUCKY... WHILE MILLIONS OF OTHERS WEREN'T.
EVEN IN HIDING, THEY HAD SO LITTLE... BUT THEY CHOSE TO SAVE ONE MORE LIFE.
HAVING A CHRISTIAN GIRLFRIEND, HE'S AT A VERY HIGH RISK.
WE CAN'T ASK YOU ALL TO ADD ANOTHER TO YOUR BURDEN.
NONSENSE. IF WE CAN SAVE HIS LIFE...
BESIDES, OUR NECKS CAN'T GO OUT ANY FURTHER!
HEY, THAT'S FRITZ PFEFFER, THE DENTIST FROM PAGE 25.
HE'S GETTING THE CALL OF HIS LIFE. LITERALLY.
FRITZ WAS TOLD HOW AND WHERE TO SNEAK THROUGH THE CITY.
LIKE A SPY.
FINALLY, HE REACHED THE ANNEX...
YOU'RE... YOU'RE NOT IN SWITZERLAND?
I DO MISS THE SKIING.
AND FRESH AIR.
I... I'M...
WHO HAS WORDS AT A MOMENT LIKE THAT?
YOU'LL STAY HERE WITH ANNE.
YES. OF COURSE. THANK YOU.
WITH ANNE? WHERE DID MARGOT STAY
WITH OTTO AND EDITH.
WAR MAKES EVERYTHING STRANGE.

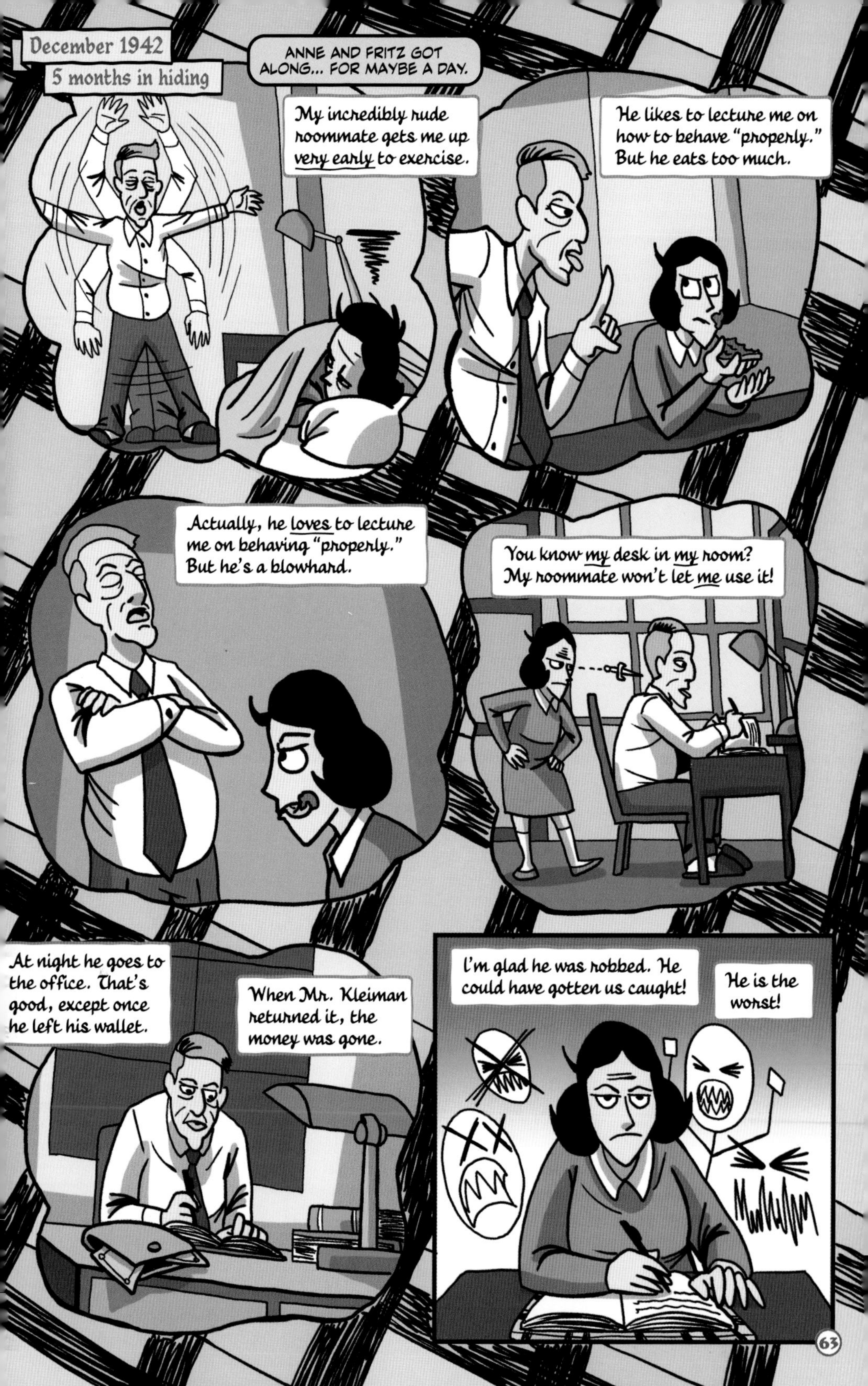
December 1942
5 months in hiding
ANNE AND FRITZ GOT ALONG… FOR MAYBE A DAY.
My incredibly rude roommate gets me up very early to exercise.
He likes to lecture me on how to behave "properly." But he eats too much.
Actually, he loves to lecture me on behaving "properly." But he's a blowhard.
You know my desk in my room? My roommate won't let me use it!
At night he goes to the office. That's good, except once he left his wallet.
When Mr. Kleiman returned it, the money was gone.
I'm glad he was robbed. He could have gotten us caught!
He is the worst!

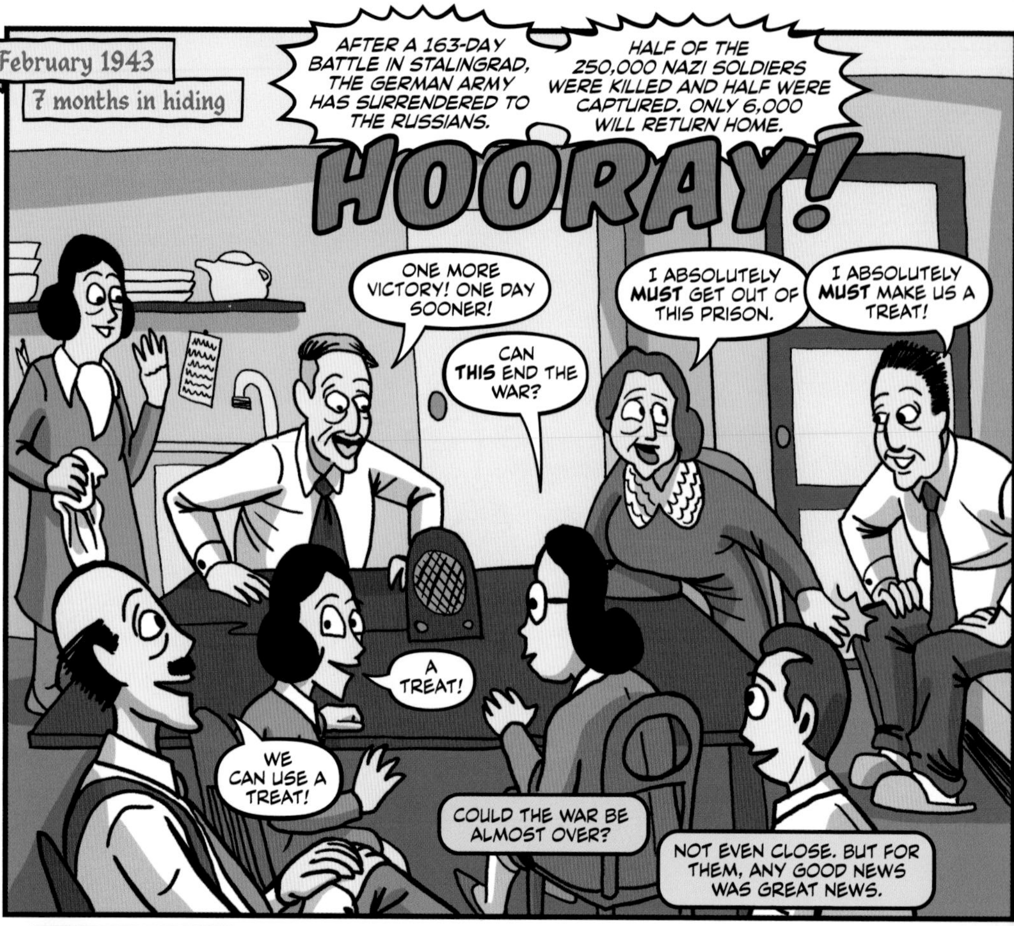
February 1943
7 months in hiding
AFTER A 163-DAY BATTLE IN STALINGRAD, THE GERMAN ARMY HAS SURRENDERED TO THE RUSSIANS.
HALF OF THE 250,000 NAZI SOLDIERS WERE KILLED AND HALF WERE CAPTURED. ONLY 6,000 WILL RETURN HOME.
HOORAY!
ONE MORE VICTORY! ONE DAY SOONER!
CAN THIS END THE WAR?
I ABSOLUTELY MUST GET OUT OF THIS PRISON.
I ABSOLUTELY MUST MAKE US A TREAT!
A TREAT!
WE CAN USE A TREAT!
COULD THE WAR BE ALMOST OVER?
NOT EVEN CLOSE. BUT FOR THEM, ANY GOOD NEWS WAS GREAT NEWS.

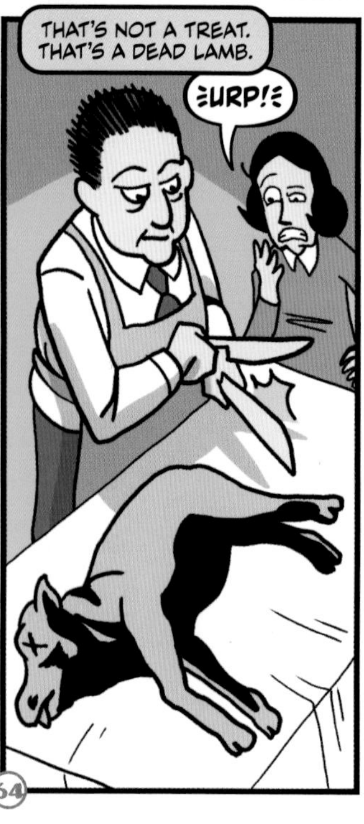
THAT'S NOT A TREAT. THAT'S A DEAD LAMB.
URP!

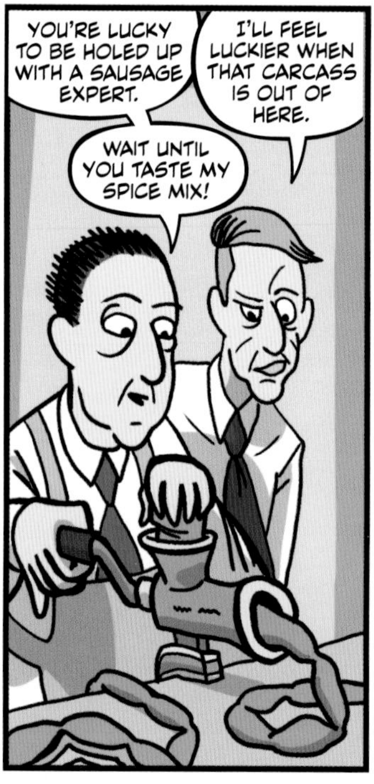
YOU'RE LUCKY TO BE HOLED UP WITH A SAUSAGE EXPERT.
I'LL FEEL LUCKIER WHEN THAT CARCASS IS OUT OF HERE.
WAIT UNTIL YOU TASTE MY SPICE MIX!

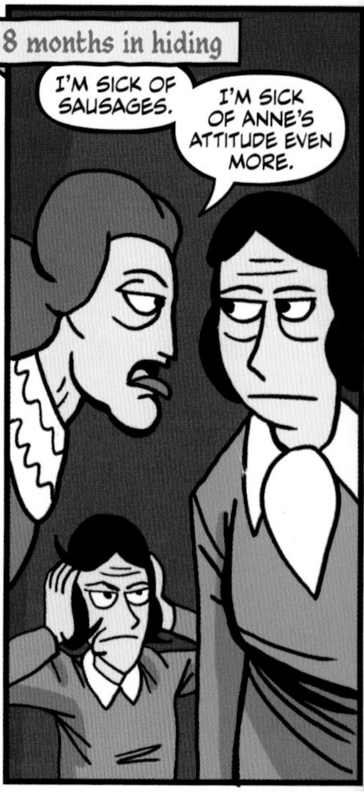
8 months in hiding
I'M SICK OF SAUSAGES.
I'M SICK OF ANNE'S ATTITUDE EVEN MORE.

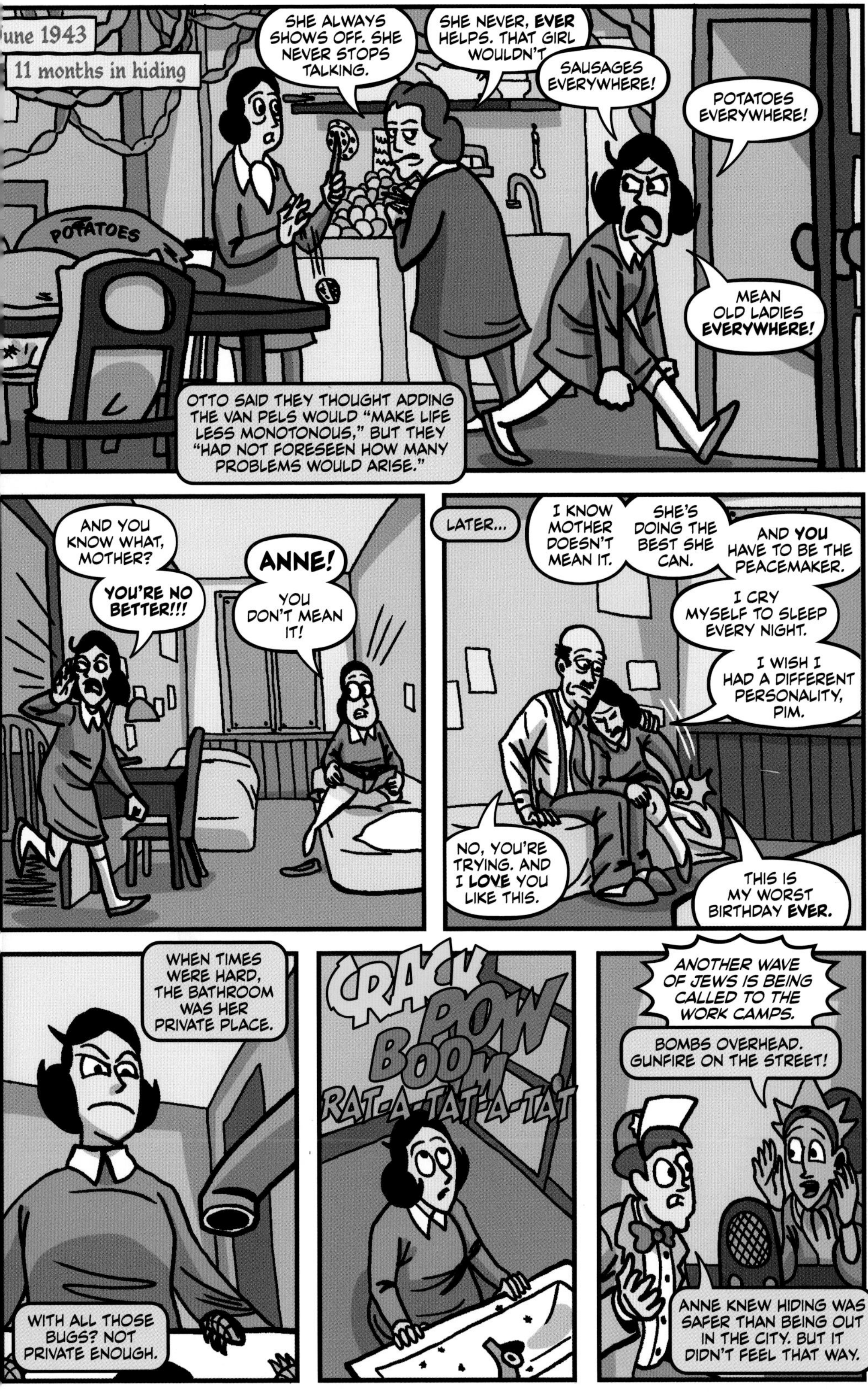

une 1943
11 months in hiding
SHE ALWAYS SHOWS OFF. SHE NEVER STOPS TALKING.
SHE NEVER, EVER HELPS. THAT GIRL WOULDN'T
SAUSAGES EVERYWHERE!
POTATOES EVERYWHERE!
POTATOES
MEAN OLD LADIES EVERYWHERE!
OTTO SAID THEY THOUGHT ADDING THE VAN PELS WOULD "MAKE LIFE LESS MONOTONOUS," BUT THEY "HAD NOT FORESEEN HOW MANY PROBLEMS WOULD ARISE."
AND YOU KNOW WHAT, MOTHER?
YOU'RE NO BETTER!!!
ANNE!
YOU DON'T MEAN IT!
LATER...
I KNOW MOTHER DOESN'T MEAN IT.
SHE'S DOING THE BEST SHE CAN.
AND YOU HAVE TO BE THE PEACEMAKER.
I CRY MYSELF TO SLEEP EVERY NIGHT.
I WISH I HAD A DIFFERENT PERSONALITY, PIM.
NO, YOU'RE TRYING. AND I LOVE YOU LIKE THIS.
THIS IS MY WORST BIRTHDAY EVER.
WHEN TIMES WERE HARD, THE BATHROOM WAS HER PRIVATE PLACE.
WITH ALL THOSE BUGS? NOT PRIVATE ENOUGH.
CRACK
POW
BOOM
RAT-A-TAT-A-TAT
ANOTHER WAVE OF JEWS IS BEING CALLED TO THE WORK CAMPS.
BOMBS OVERHEAD. GUNFIRE ON THE STREET!
ANNE KNEW HIDING WAS SAFER THAN BEING OUT IN THE CITY. BUT IT DIDN'T FEEL THAT WAY.

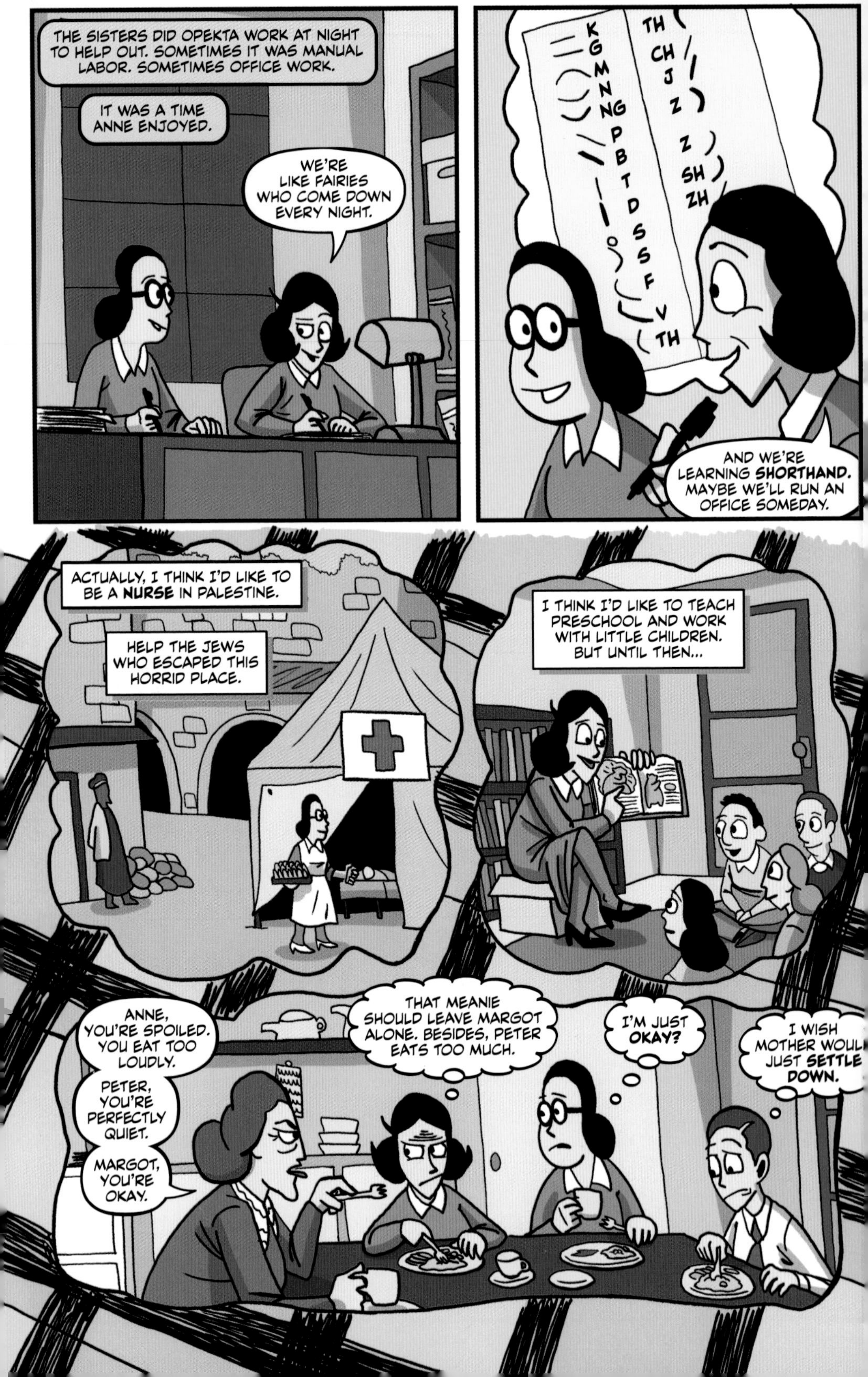

THE SISTERS DID OPEKTA WORK AT NIGHT TO HELP OUT. SOMETIMES IT WAS MANUAL LABOR. SOMETIMES OFFICE WORK.
IT WAS A TIME ANNE ENJOYED.
WE'RE LIKE FAIRIES WHO COME DOWN EVERY NIGHT.
K G M N NG P B T D S S F V TH
TH CH J Z Z SH ZH
AND WE'RE LEARNING **SHORTHAND.** MAYBE WE'LL RUN AN OFFICE SOMEDAY.
ACTUALLY, I THINK I'D LIKE TO BE A **NURSE** IN PALESTINE.
HELP THE JEWS WHO ESCAPED THIS HORRID PLACE.
I THINK I'D LIKE TO TEACH PRESCHOOL AND WORK WITH LITTLE CHILDREN. BUT UNTIL THEN...
ANNE, YOU'RE SPOILED. YOU EAT TOO LOUDLY.
PETER, YOU'RE PERFECTLY QUIET.
MARGOT, YOU'RE OKAY.
THAT MEANIE SHOULD LEAVE MARGOT ALONE. BESIDES, PETER EATS TOO MUCH.
I'M JUST **OKAY?**
I WISH MOTHER WOUL JUST **SETTLE DOWN.**

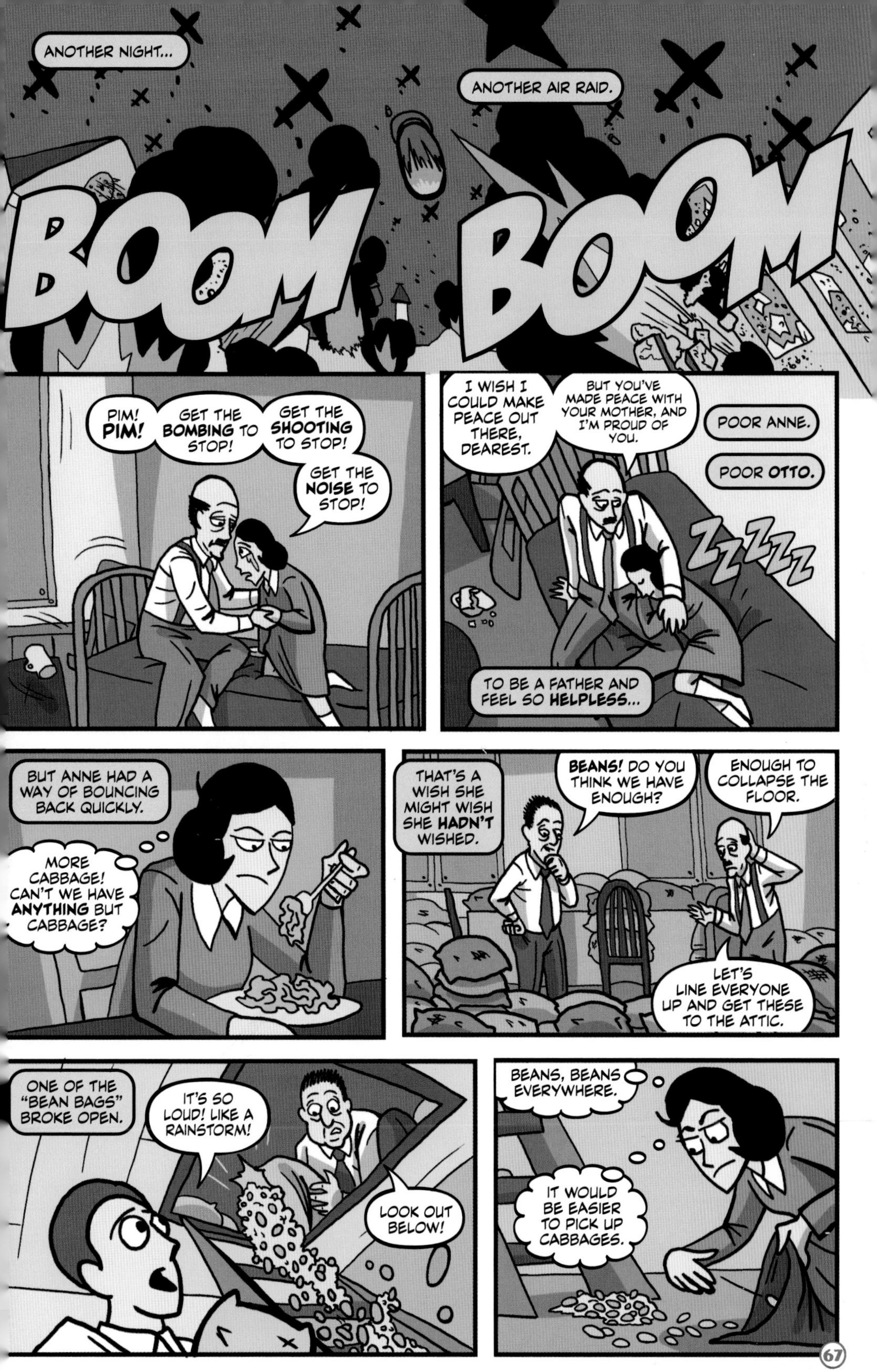

ANOTHER NIGHT...
ANOTHER AIR RAID.
BOOM
BOOM
PIM! PIM!
GET THE BOMBING TO STOP!
GET THE SHOOTING TO STOP!
GET THE NOISE TO STOP!
I WISH I COULD MAKE PEACE OUT THERE, DEAREST.
BUT YOU'VE MADE PEACE WITH YOUR MOTHER, AND I'M PROUD OF YOU.
POOR ANNE.
POOR OTTO.
ZZZZZ
TO BE A FATHER AND FEEL SO HELPLESS...
BUT ANNE HAD A WAY OF BOUNCING BACK QUICKLY.
MORE CABBAGE! CAN'T WE HAVE ANYTHING BUT CABBAGE?
THAT'S A WISH SHE MIGHT WISH SHE HADN'T WISHED.
BEANS! DO YOU THINK WE HAVE ENOUGH?
ENOUGH TO COLLAPSE THE FLOOR.
LET'S LINE EVERYONE UP AND GET THESE TO THE ATTIC.
ONE OF THE "BEAN BAGS" BROKE OPEN.
IT'S SO LOUD! LIKE A RAINSTORM!
LOOK OUT BELOW!
BEANS, BEANS EVERYWHERE.
IT WOULD BE EASIER TO PICK UP CABBAGES.

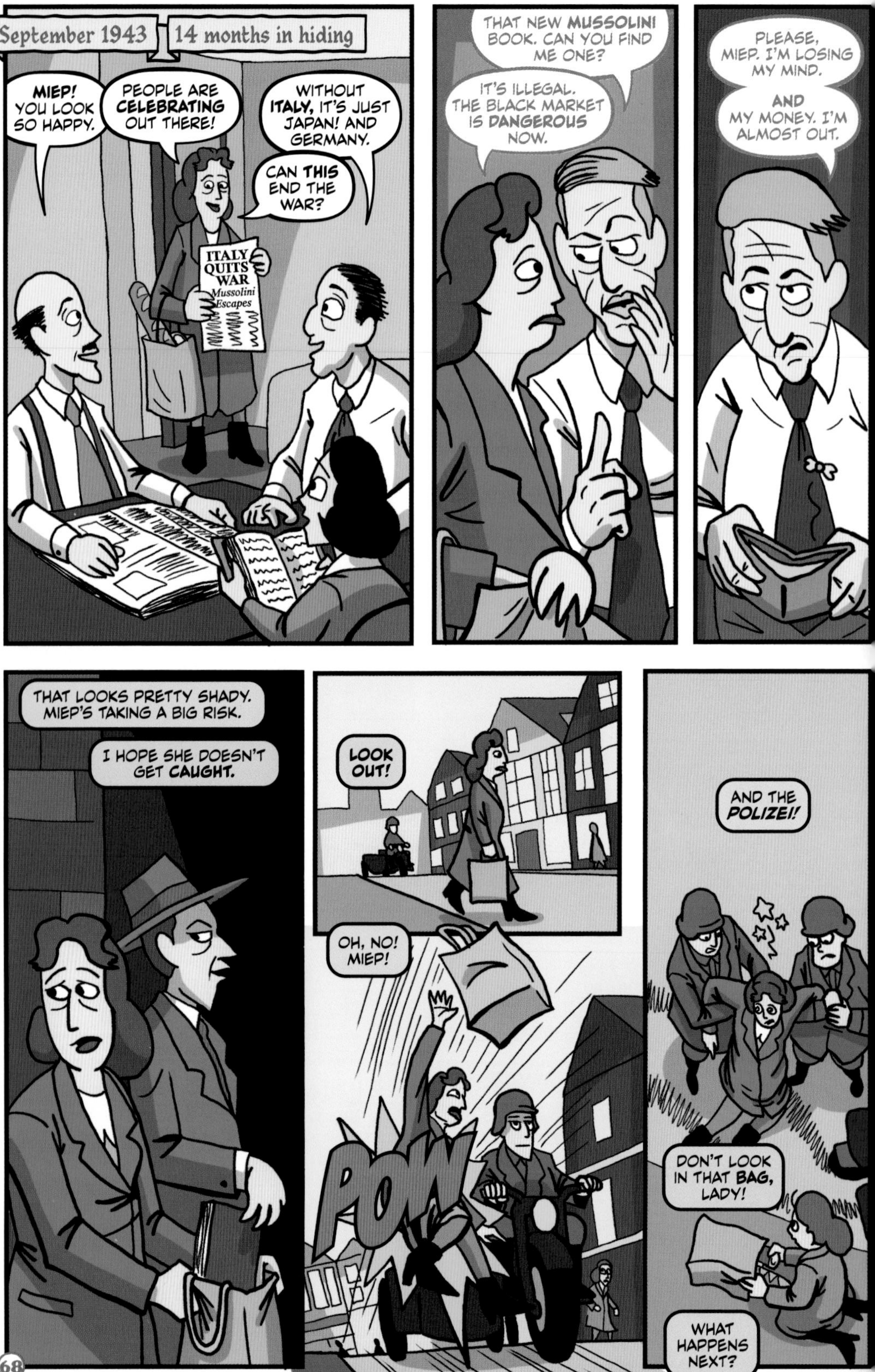
September 1943
14 months in hiding
MIEP! YOU LOOK SO HAPPY.
PEOPLE ARE CELEBRATING OUT THERE!
WITHOUT ITALY, IT'S JUST JAPAN! AND GERMANY.
CAN THIS END THE WAR?
ITALY QUITS WAR
Mussolini Escapes
THAT NEW MUSSOLINI BOOK. CAN YOU FIND ME ONE?
IT'S ILLEGAL. THE BLACK MARKET IS DANGEROUS NOW.
PLEASE, MIEP. I'M LOSING MY MIND.
AND MY MONEY. I'M ALMOST OUT.
THAT LOOKS PRETTY SHADY. MIEP'S TAKING A BIG RISK.
I HOPE SHE DOESN'T GET CAUGHT.
LOOK OUT!
OH, NO! MIEP!
POW
AND THE POLIZEI!
DON'T LOOK IN THAT BAG, LADY!
WHAT HAPPENS NEXT?

HOW MUCH WE DEPEND ON OUR HELPERS

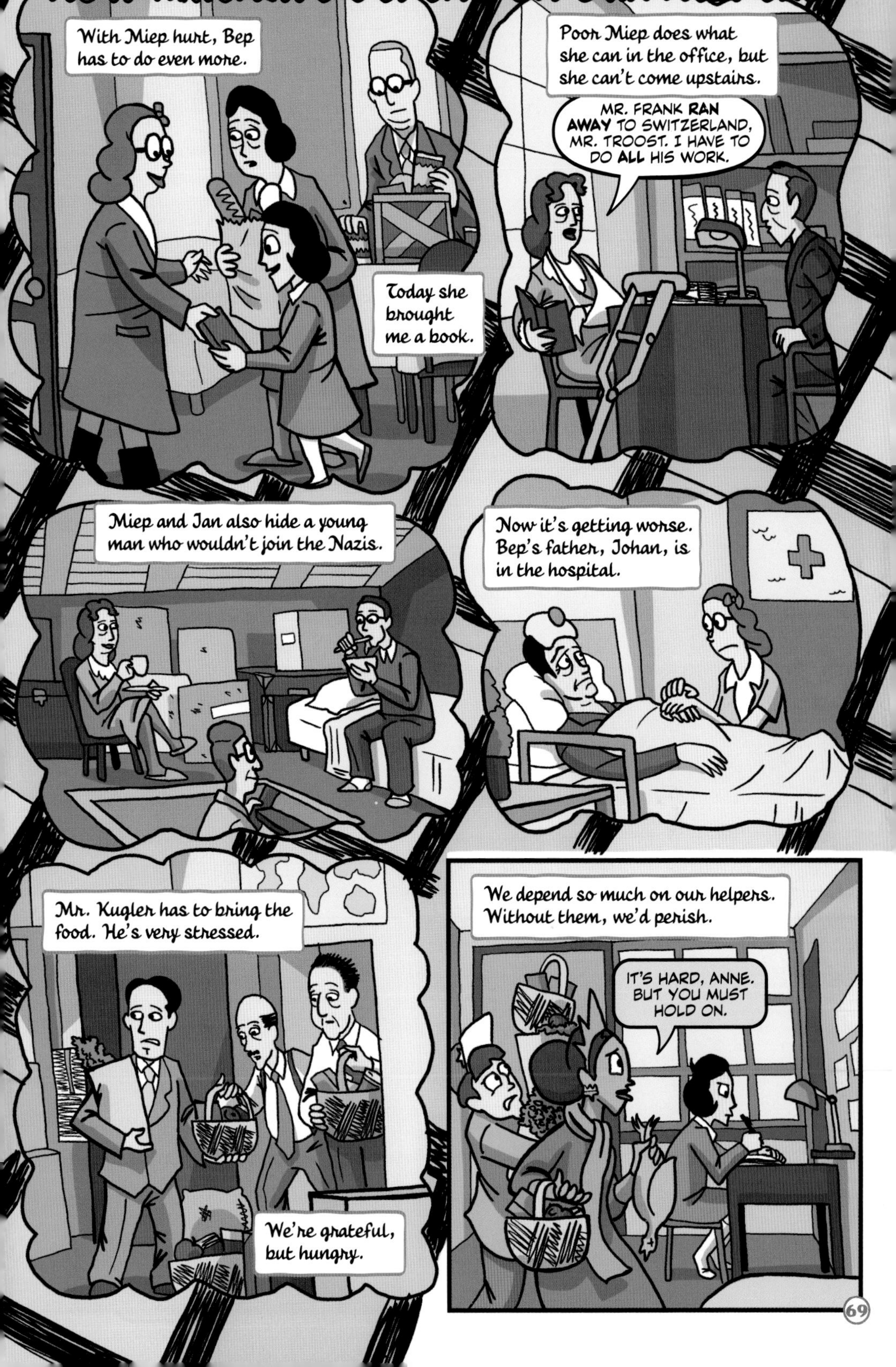
With Miep hurt, Bep has to do even more.
Today she brought me a book.
Poor Miep does what she can in the office, but she can't come upstairs.
MR. FRANK RAN AWAY TO SWITZERLAND, MR. TROOST. I HAVE TO DO ALL HIS WORK.
Miep and Jan also hide a young man who wouldn't join the Nazis.
Now it's getting worse. Bep's father, Johan, is in the hospital.
Mr. Kugler has to bring the food. He's very stressed.
We're grateful, but hungry.
We depend so much on our helpers. Without them, we'd perish.
IT'S HARD, ANNE. BUT YOU MUST HOLD ON.

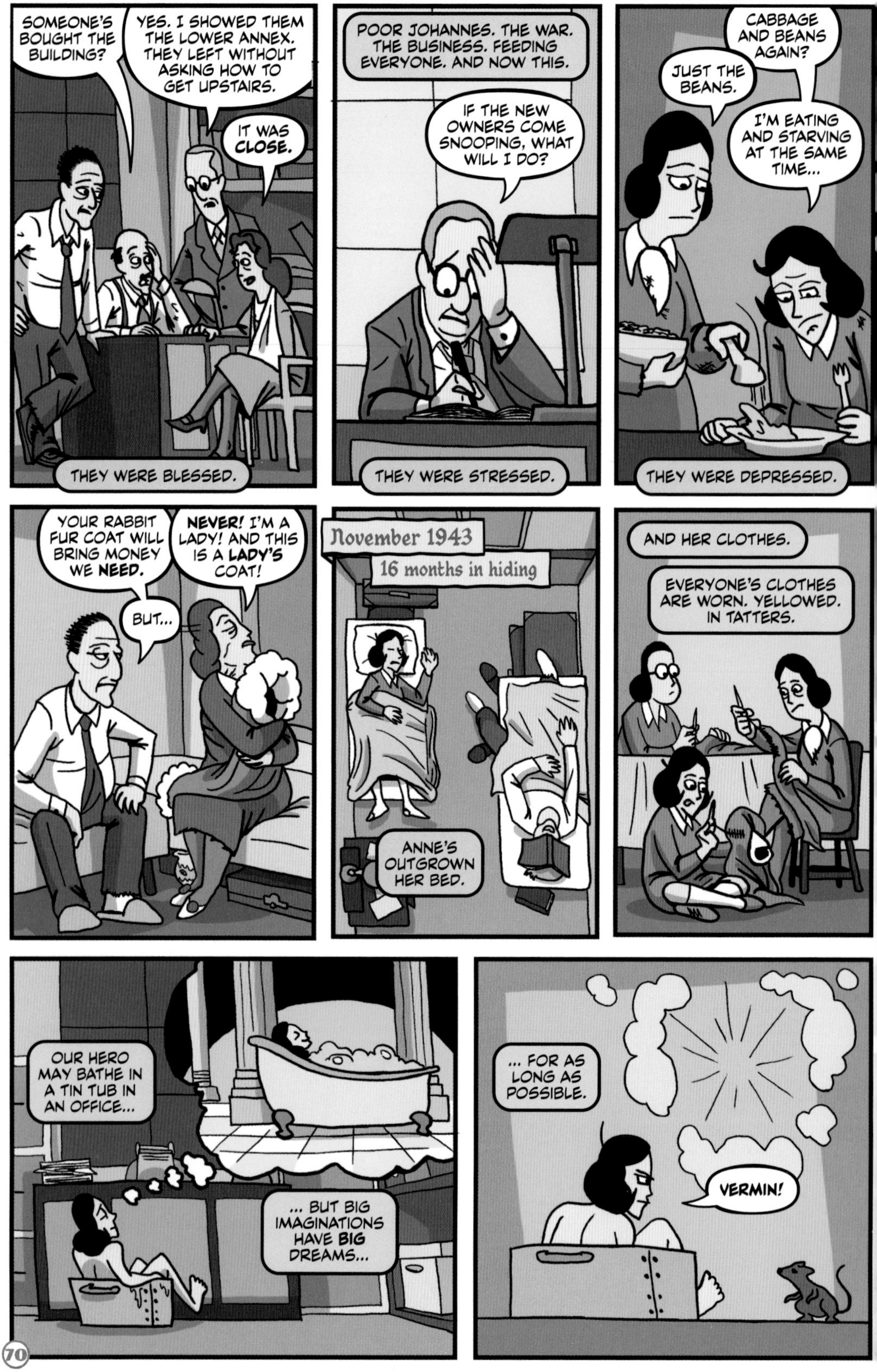
SOMEONE'S BOUGHT THE BUILDING?
YES. I SHOWED THEM THE LOWER ANNEX. THEY LEFT WITHOUT ASKING HOW TO GET UPSTAIRS.
IT WAS **CLOSE.**
THEY WERE BLESSED.
POOR JOHANNES. THE WAR. THE BUSINESS. FEEDING EVERYONE. AND NOW THIS.
IF THE NEW OWNERS COME SNOOPING, WHAT WILL I DO?
THEY WERE STRESSED.
CABBAGE AND BEANS AGAIN?
JUST THE BEANS.
I'M EATING AND STARVING AT THE SAME TIME...
THEY WERE DEPRESSED.
YOUR RABBIT FUR COAT WILL BRING MONEY WE **NEED.**
NEVER! I'M A LADY! AND THIS IS A **LADY'S** COAT!
BUT...
November 1943
16 months in hiding
ANNE'S OUTGROWN HER BED.
AND HER CLOTHES.
EVERYONE'S CLOTHES ARE WORN. YELLOWED. IN TATTERS.
OUR HERO MAY BATHE IN A TIN TUB IN AN OFFICE...
... BUT BIG IMAGINATIONS HAVE **BIG** DREAMS...
... FOR AS LONG AS POSSIBLE.
VERMIN!

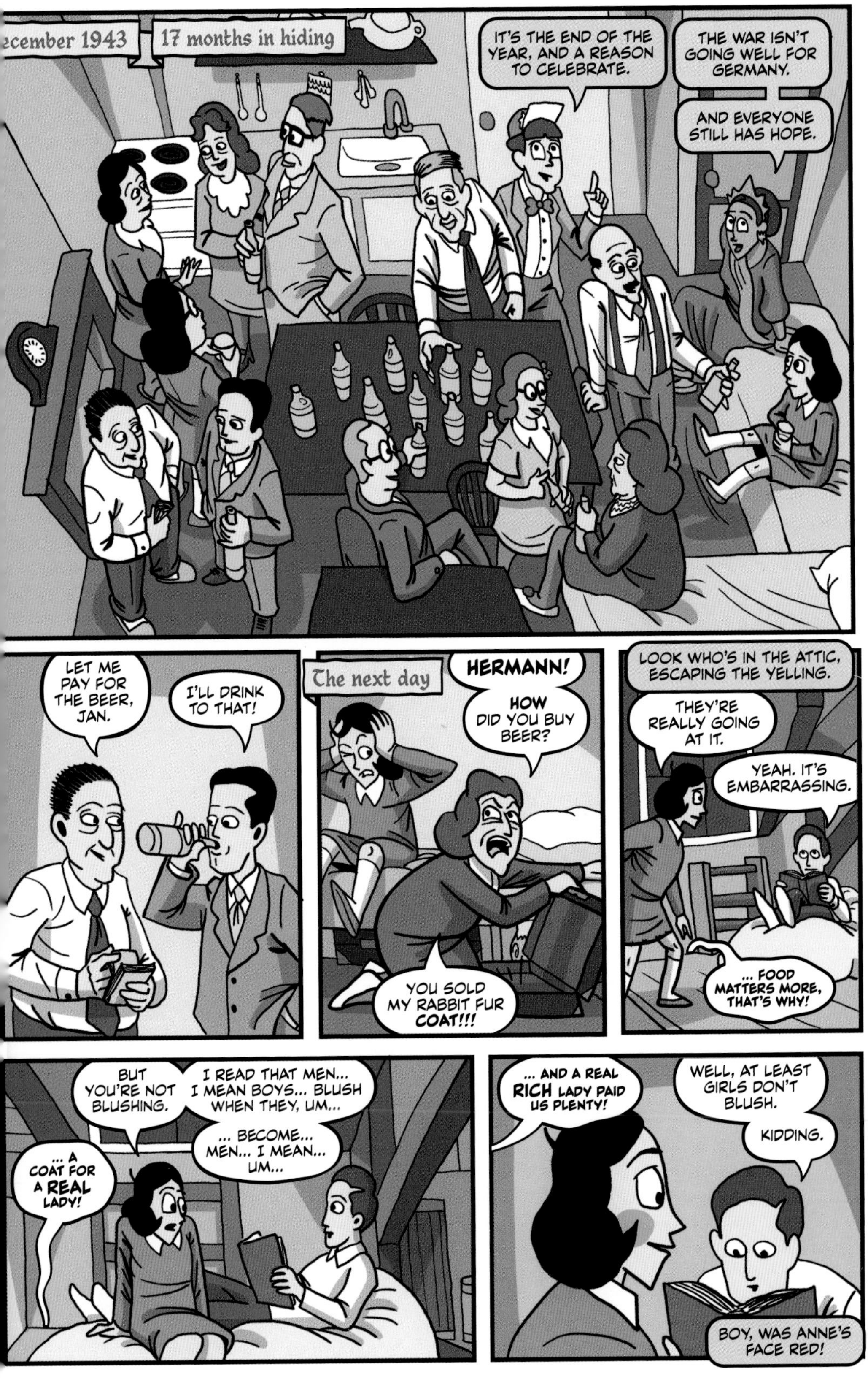
ecember 1943
17 months in hiding
IT'S THE END OF THE YEAR, AND A REASON TO CELEBRATE.
THE WAR ISN'T GOING WELL FOR GERMANY.
AND EVERYONE STILL HAS HOPE.
LET ME PAY FOR THE BEER, JAN.
I'LL DRINK TO THAT!
The next day
HERMANN!
HOW DID YOU BUY BEER?
YOU SOLD MY RABBIT FUR COAT!!!
LOOK WHO'S IN THE ATTIC, ESCAPING THE YELLING.
THEY'RE REALLY GOING AT IT.
YEAH. IT'S EMBARRASSING.
... FOOD MATTERS MORE, THAT'S WHY!
BUT YOU'RE NOT BLUSHING.
I READ THAT MEN... I MEAN BOYS... BLUSH WHEN THEY, UM...
... BECOME... MEN... I MEAN... UM...
... A COAT FOR A REAL LADY!
... AND A REAL RICH LADY PAID US PLENTY!
WELL, AT LEAST GIRLS DON'T BLUSH.
KIDDING.
BOY, WAS ANNE'S FACE RED!

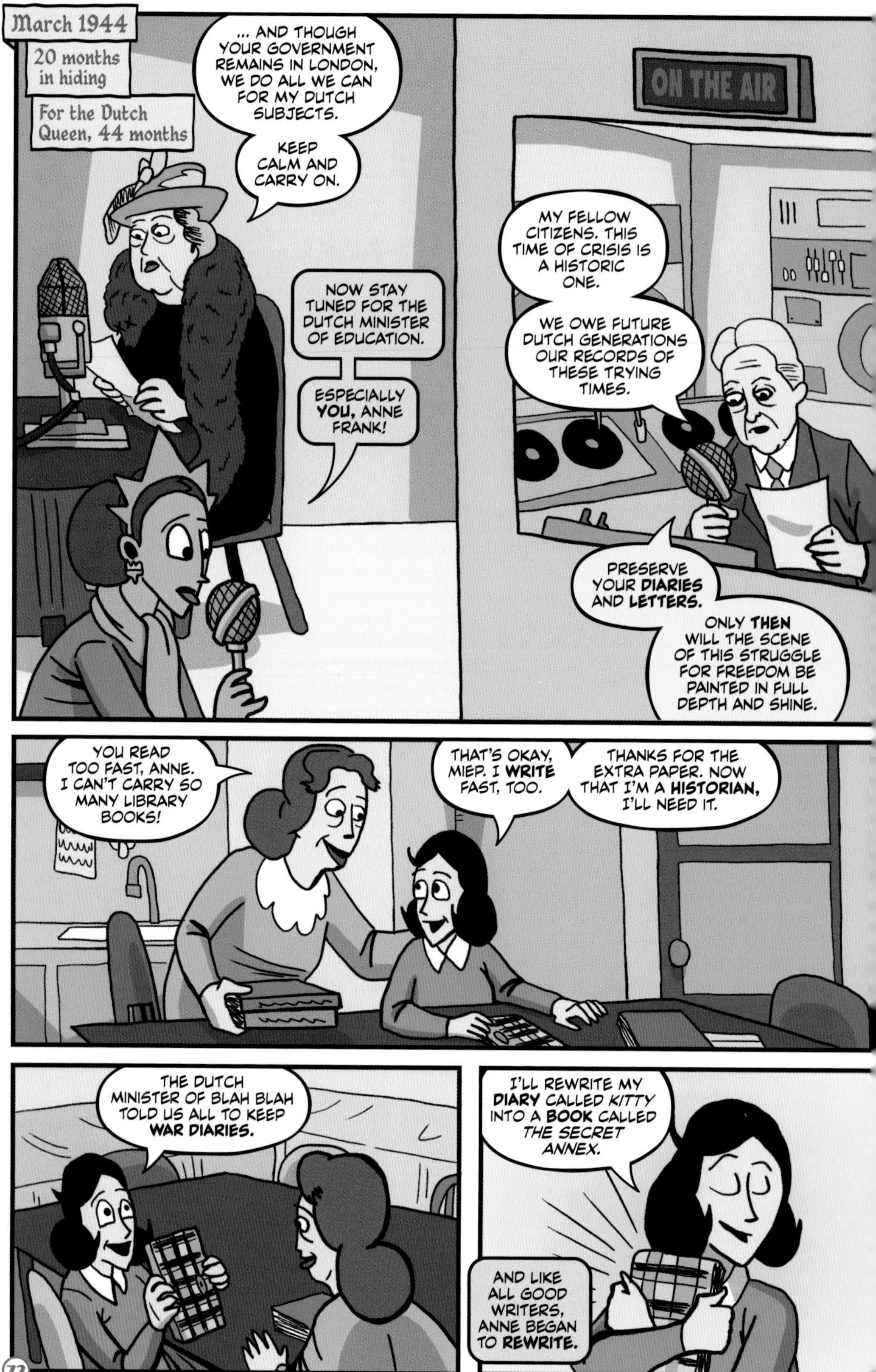
March 1944
20 months in hiding
For the Dutch Queen, 44 months
... AND THOUGH YOUR GOVERNMENT REMAINS IN LONDON, WE DO ALL WE CAN FOR MY DUTCH SUBJECTS.
KEEP CALM AND CARRY ON.
NOW STAY TUNED FOR THE DUTCH MINISTER OF EDUCATION.
ESPECIALLY **YOU,** ANNE FRANK!
ON THE AIR
MY FELLOW CITIZENS. THIS TIME OF CRISIS IS A HISTORIC ONE.
WE OWE FUTURE DUTCH GENERATIONS OUR RECORDS OF THESE TRYING TIMES.
PRESERVE YOUR **DIARIES** AND **LETTERS.**
ONLY **THEN** WILL THE SCENE OF THIS STRUGGLE FOR FREEDOM BE PAINTED IN FULL DEPTH AND SHINE.
YOU READ TOO FAST, ANNE. I CAN'T CARRY SO MANY LIBRARY BOOKS!
THAT'S OKAY, MIEP. I **WRITE** FAST, TOO.
THANKS FOR THE EXTRA PAPER. NOW THAT I'M A **HISTORIAN,** I'LL NEED IT.
THE DUTCH MINISTER OF BLAH BLAH TOLD US ALL TO KEEP **WAR DIARIES.**
I'LL REWRITE MY **DIARY** CALLED *KITTY* INTO A **BOOK** CALLED *THE SECRET ANNEX.*
AND LIKE ALL GOOD WRITERS, ANNE BEGAN TO **REWRITE.**

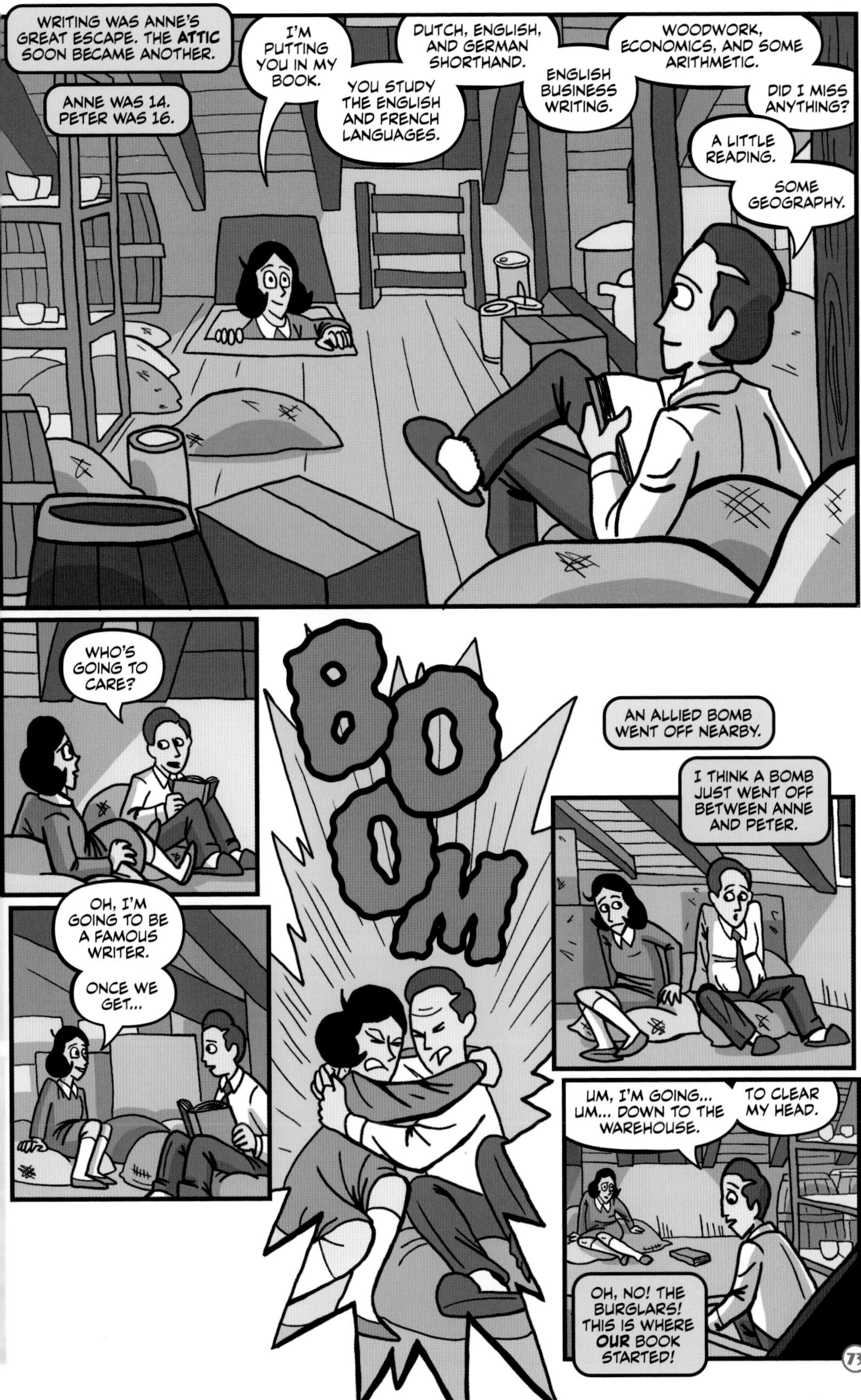

WRITING WAS ANNE'S GREAT ESCAPE. THE **ATTIC** SOON BECAME ANOTHER.
ANNE WAS 14. PETER WAS 16.
I'M PUTTING YOU IN MY BOOK.
YOU STUDY THE ENGLISH AND FRENCH LANGUAGES.
DUTCH, ENGLISH, AND GERMAN SHORTHAND.
ENGLISH BUSINESS WRITING.
WOODWORK, ECONOMICS, AND SOME ARITHMETIC.
DID I MISS ANYTHING?
A LITTLE READING.
SOME GEOGRAPHY.
WHO'S GOING TO CARE?
OH, I'M GOING TO BE A FAMOUS WRITER.
ONCE WE GET...
BOOM
AN ALLIED BOMB WENT OFF NEARBY.
I THINK A BOMB JUST WENT OFF BETWEEN ANNE AND PETER.
UM, I'M GOING... UM... DOWN TO THE WAREHOUSE.
TO CLEAR MY HEAD.
OH, NO! THE BURGLARS! THIS IS WHERE **OUR** BOOK STARTED!

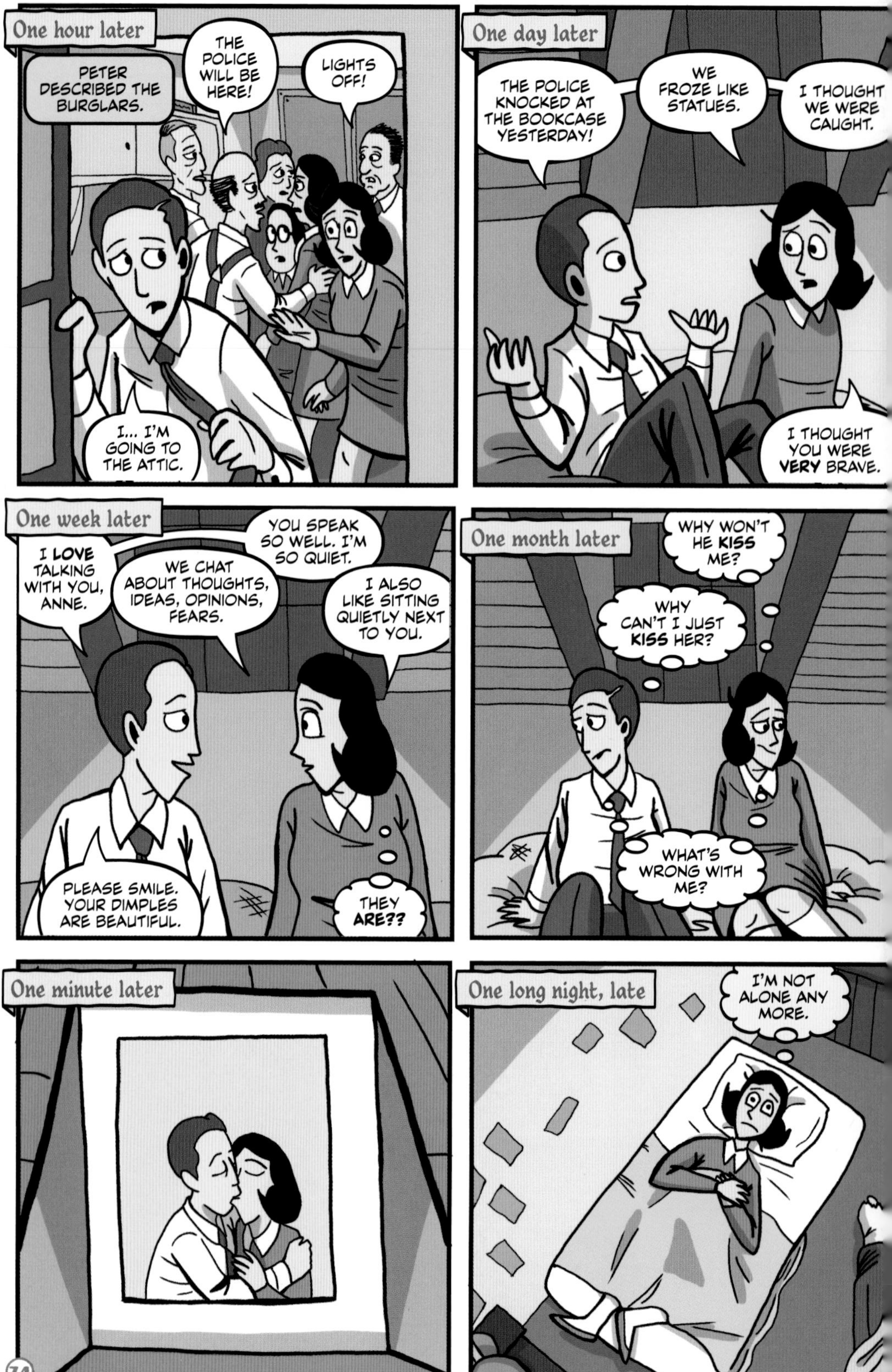
One hour later
PETER DESCRIBED THE BURGLARS.
THE POLICE WILL BE HERE!
LIGHTS OFF!
I... I'M GOING TO THE ATTIC.
One day later
THE POLICE KNOCKED AT THE BOOKCASE YESTERDAY!
WE FROZE LIKE STATUES.
I THOUGHT WE WERE CAUGHT.
I THOUGHT YOU WERE **VERY** BRAVE.
One week later
I **LOVE** TALKING WITH YOU, ANNE.
WE CHAT ABOUT THOUGHTS, IDEAS, OPINIONS, FEARS.
YOU SPEAK SO WELL. I'M SO QUIET.
I ALSO LIKE SITTING QUIETLY NEXT TO YOU.
PLEASE SMILE. YOUR DIMPLES ARE BEAUTIFUL.
THEY **ARE??**
One month later
WHY WON'T HE **KISS** ME?
WHY CAN'T I JUST **KISS** HER?
WHAT'S WRONG WITH ME?
One minute later
One long night, late
I'M NOT ALONE ANY MORE.

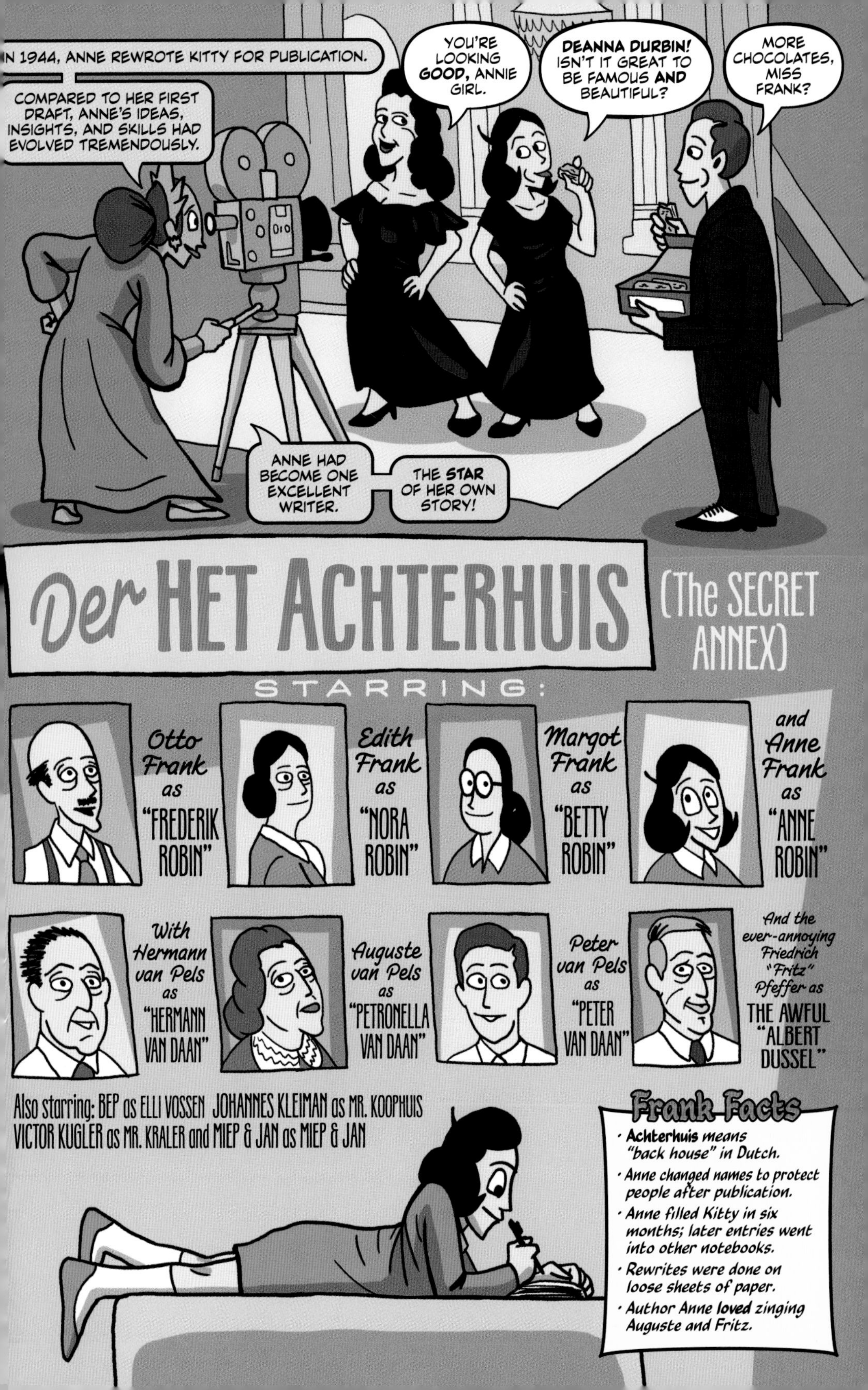
N 1944, ANNE REWROTE KITTY FOR PUBLICATION.
COMPARED TO HER FIRST DRAFT, ANNE'S IDEAS, INSIGHTS, AND SKILLS HAD EVOLVED TREMENDOUSLY.
YOU'RE LOOKING GOOD, ANNIE GIRL.
DEANNA DURBIN! ISN'T IT GREAT TO BE FAMOUS AND BEAUTIFUL?
MORE CHOCOLATES, MISS FRANK?
ANNE HAD BECOME ONE EXCELLENT WRITER.
THE STAR OF HER OWN STORY!
Der HET ACHTERHUIS (The SECRET ANNEX)
STARRING:
Otto Frank as "FREDERIK ROBIN"
Edith Frank as "NORA ROBIN"
Margot Frank as "BETTY ROBIN"
and Anne Frank as "ANNE ROBIN"
With Hermann van Pels as "HERMANN VAN DAAN"
Auguste van Pels as "PETRONELLA VAN DAAN"
Peter van Pels as "PETER VAN DAAN"
And the ever-annoying Friedrich "Fritz" Pfeffer as THE AWFUL "ALBERT DUSSEL"
Also starring: BEP as ELLI VOSSEN JOHANNES KLEIMAN as MR. KOOPHUIS VICTOR KUGLER as MR. KRALER and MIEP & JAN as MIEP & JAN
Frank Facts
· Achterhuis means "back house" in Dutch.
· Anne changed names to protect people after publication.
· Anne filled Kitty in six months; later entries went into other notebooks.
· Rewrites were done on loose sheets of paper.
· Author Anne loved zinging Auguste and Fritz.

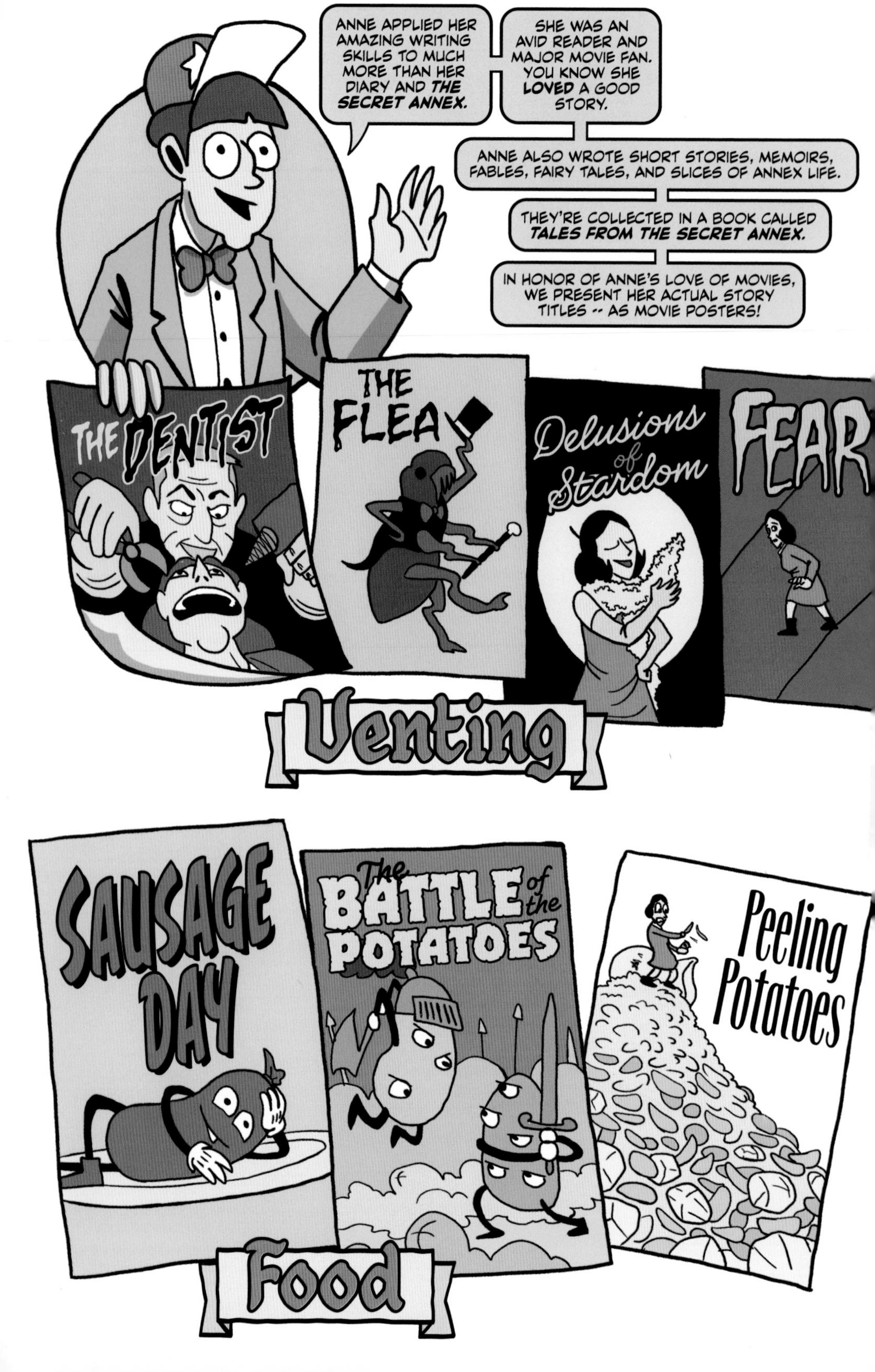
ANNE APPLIED HER AMAZING WRITING SKILLS TO MUCH MORE THAN HER DIARY AND ***THE SECRET ANNEX.***
SHE WAS AN AVID READER AND MAJOR MOVIE FAN. YOU KNOW SHE **LOVED** A GOOD STORY.
ANNE ALSO WROTE SHORT STORIES, MEMOIRS, FABLES, FAIRY TALES, AND SLICES OF ANNEX LIFE.
THEY'RE COLLECTED IN A BOOK CALLED ***TALES FROM THE SECRET ANNEX.***
IN HONOR OF ANNE'S LOVE OF MOVIES, WE PRESENT HER ACTUAL STORY TITLES -- AS MOVIE POSTERS!
THE DENTIST
THE FLEA
Delusions of Stardom
FEAR
Venting
SAUSAGE DAY
The BATTLE of the POTATOES
Peeling Potatoes
Food

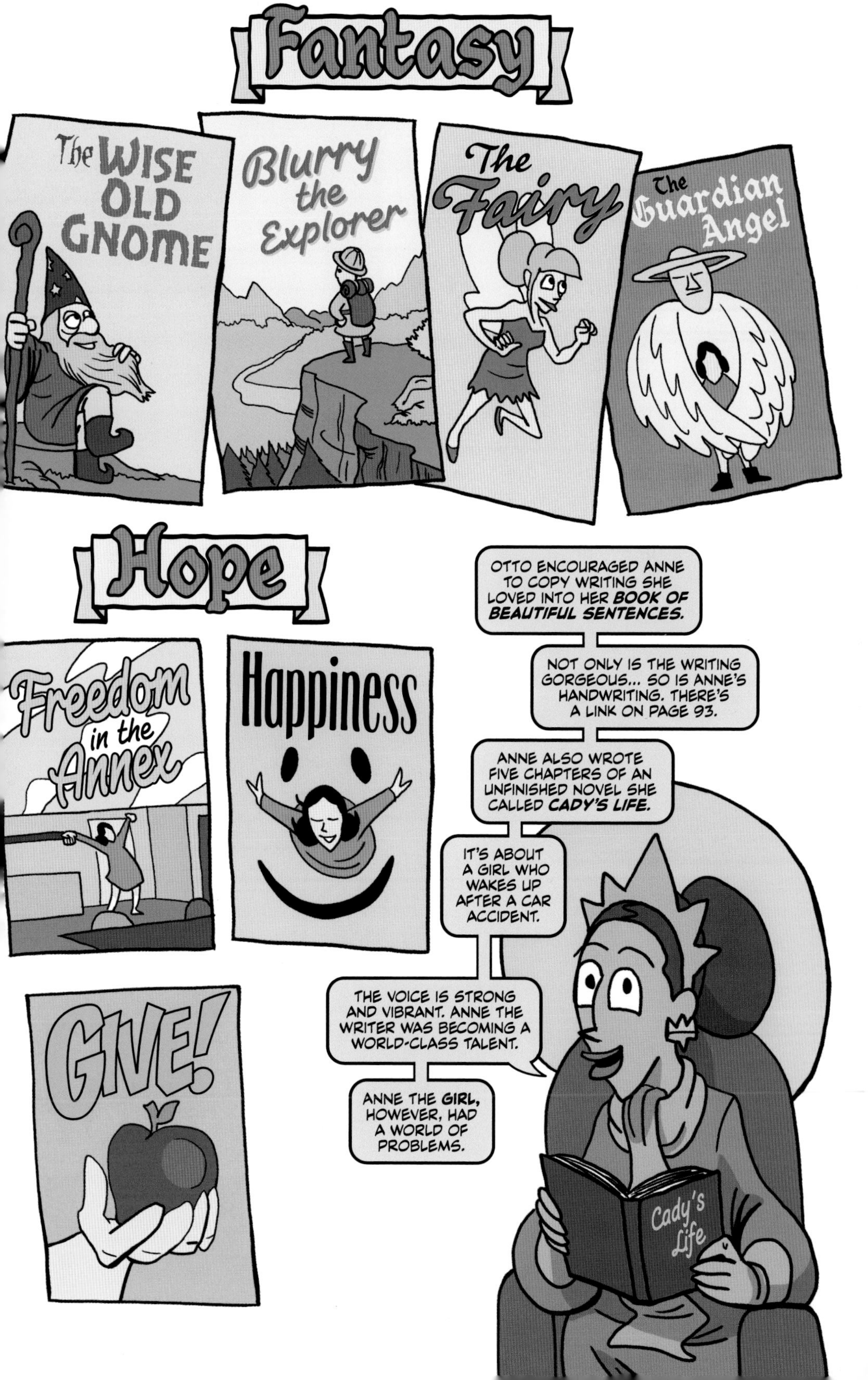

Fantasy
The Wise Old Gnome
Blurry the Explorer
The Fairy
The Guardian Angel
Hope
Freedom in the Annex
Happiness
GIVE!
OTTO ENCOURAGED ANNE TO COPY WRITING SHE LOVED INTO HER ***BOOK OF BEAUTIFUL SENTENCES.***
NOT ONLY IS THE WRITING GORGEOUS... SO IS ANNE'S HANDWRITING. THERE'S A LINK ON PAGE 93.
ANNE ALSO WROTE FIVE CHAPTERS OF AN UNFINISHED NOVEL SHE CALLED ***CADY'S LIFE.***
IT'S ABOUT A GIRL WHO WAKES UP AFTER A CAR ACCIDENT.
THE VOICE IS STRONG AND VIBRANT. ANNE THE WRITER WAS BECOMING A WORLD-CLASS TALENT.
ANNE THE **GIRL,** HOWEVER, HAD A WORLD OF PROBLEMS.
Cady's Life

MY MOTHER SAYS I'M BREAKING YOUR HEART.

MY MOTHER SAYS YOU'RE STEALING ME FROM HER.

MY **FATHER** IS AGAINST US KISSING.

SO? **STAND UP** FOR YOURSELF!

ANNE WAS CONFLICTED...

DEAR FATHER. YOU'RE DISAPPOINTED. YOU WANT US TO ACT OUR AGE.

BUT THIS **IS** OUR AGE.

WITH PETER, I'M FINALLY HAPPY!

THE REST OF US ARE ANYTHING **BUT** HAPPY.

THE NEW RULES:

GIVE IT A **REST**. DON'T GO UP THERE SO OFTEN.

YOU'RE A **GIRL**. DON'T FLIRT. DON'T ENCOURAGE HIM.

HE'S A **BOY**. MEN LEAD. WOMEN SET LIMITS.

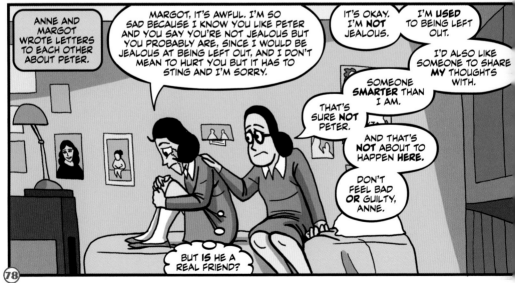

ANNE AND MARGOT WROTE LETTERS TO EACH OTHER ABOUT PETER.

MARGOT, IT'S AWFUL. I'M SO SAD BECAUSE I KNOW YOU LIKE PETER AND YOU SAY YOU'RE NOT JEALOUS BUT YOU PROBABLY ARE, SINCE I WOULD BE JEALOUS AT BEING LEFT OUT, AND I DON'T MEAN TO HURT YOU BUT IT HAS TO STING AND I'M SORRY.

IT'S OKAY. I'M **NOT** JEALOUS.

I'M **USED** TO BEING LEFT OUT.

I'D ALSO LIKE SOMEONE TO SHARE **MY** THOUGHTS WITH.

SOMEONE **SMARTER** THAN I AM.

THAT'S SURE **NOT** PETER.

AND THAT'S **NOT** ABOUT TO HAPPEN **HERE**.

DON'T FEEL BAD **OR** GUILTY, ANNE.

BUT **IS** HE A REAL FRIEND?

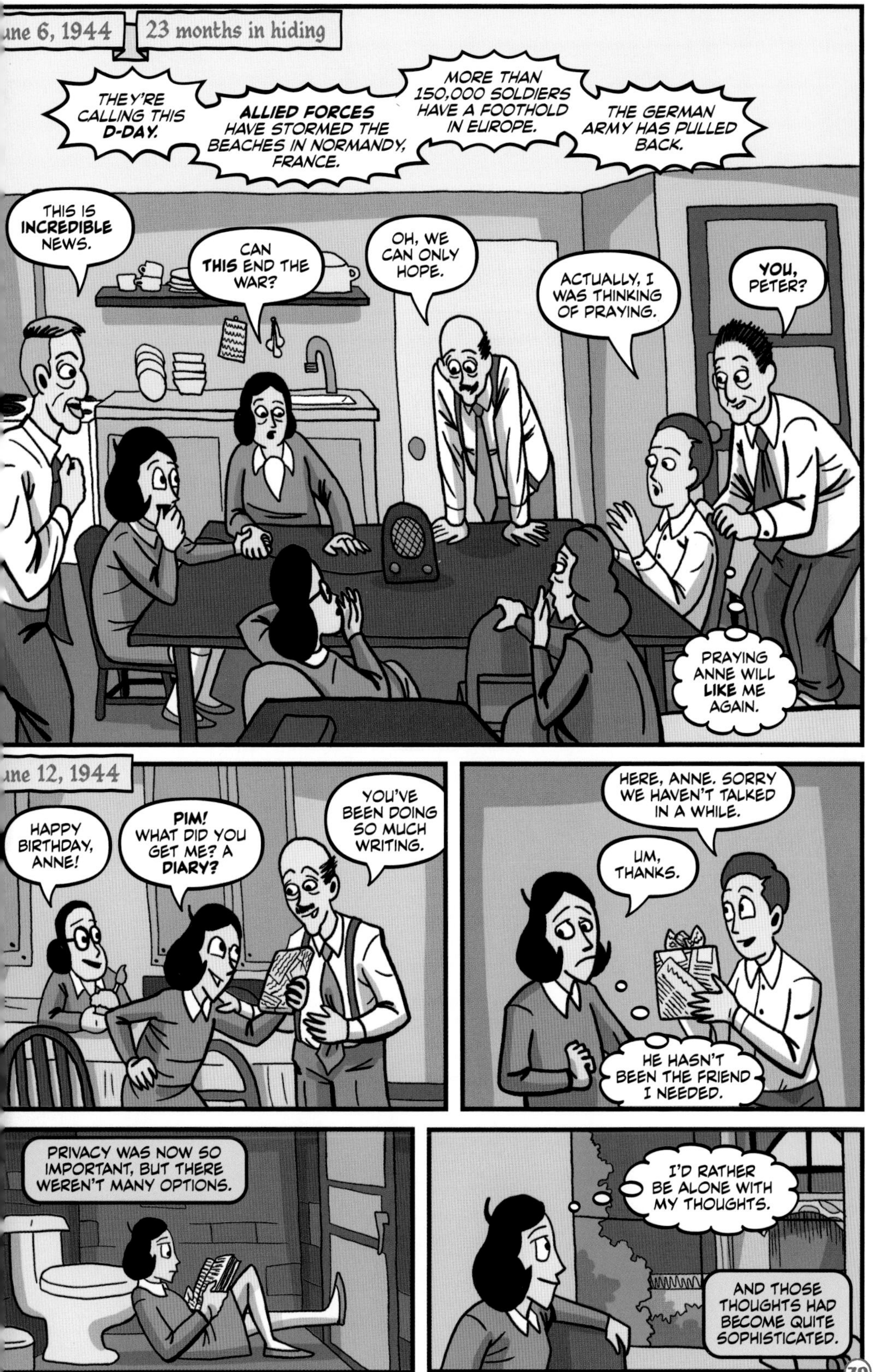
une 6, 1944
23 months in hiding
THEY'RE CALLING THIS D-DAY.
ALLIED FORCES HAVE STORMED THE BEACHES IN NORMANDY, FRANCE.
MORE THAN 150,000 SOLDIERS HAVE A FOOTHOLD IN EUROPE.
THE GERMAN ARMY HAS PULLED BACK.
THIS IS INCREDIBLE NEWS.
CAN THIS END THE WAR?
OH, WE CAN ONLY HOPE.
ACTUALLY, I WAS THINKING OF PRAYING.
YOU, PETER?
PRAYING ANNE WILL LIKE ME AGAIN.
une 12, 1944
HAPPY BIRTHDAY, ANNE!
PIM! WHAT DID YOU GET ME? A DIARY?
YOU'VE BEEN DOING SO MUCH WRITING.
HERE, ANNE. SORRY WE HAVEN'T TALKED IN A WHILE.
UM, THANKS.
HE HASN'T BEEN THE FRIEND I NEEDED.
PRIVACY WAS NOW SO IMPORTANT, BUT THERE WEREN'T MANY OPTIONS.
I'D RATHER BE ALONE WITH MY THOUGHTS.
AND THOSE THOUGHTS HAD BECOME QUITE SOPHISTICATED.

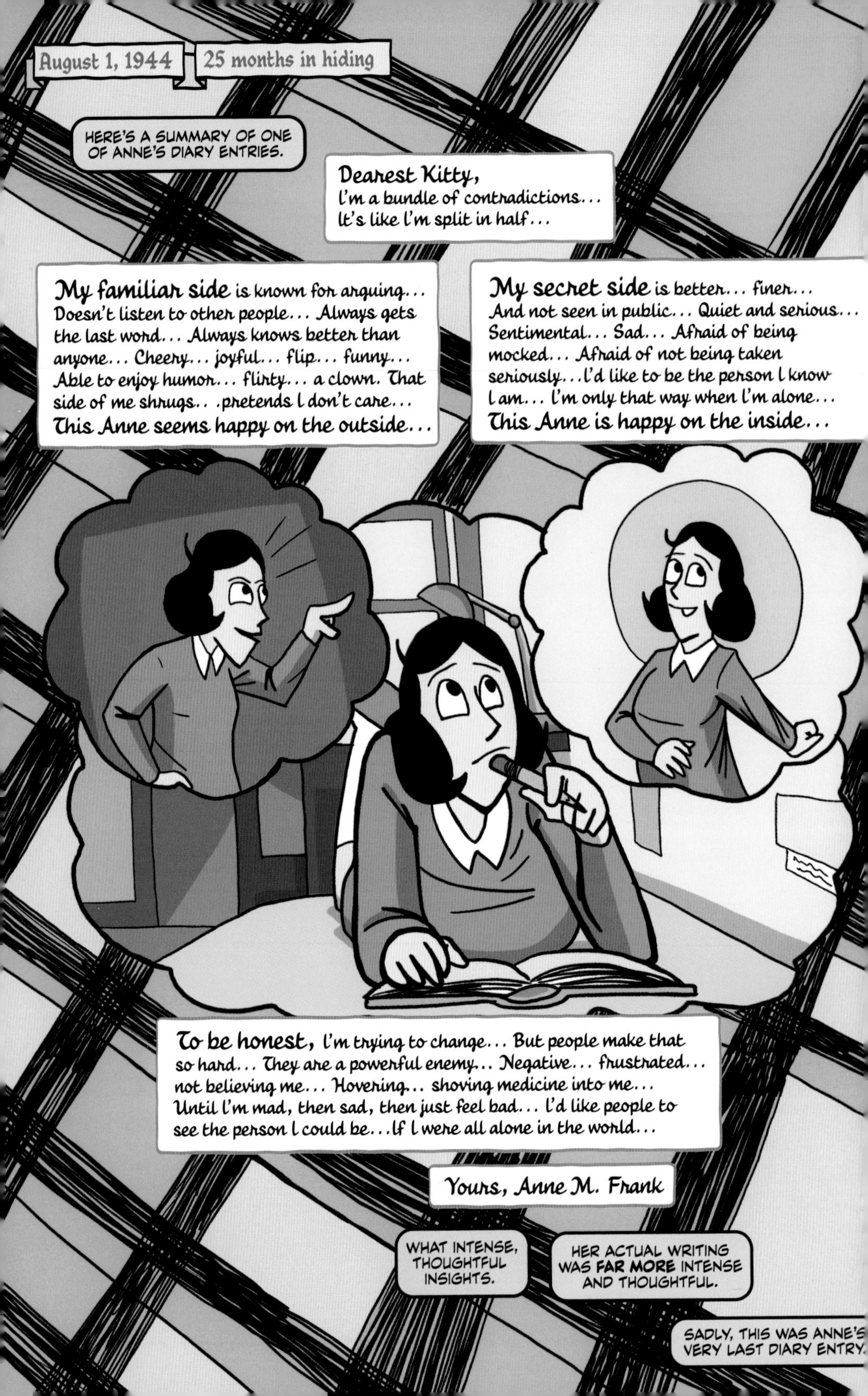

August 1, 1944
25 months in hiding
HERE'S A SUMMARY OF ONE OF ANNE'S DIARY ENTRIES.
Dearest Kitty, I'm a bundle of contradictions... It's like I'm split in half...
My familiar side is known for arguing... Doesn't listen to other people... Always gets the last word... Always knows better than anyone... Cheery... joyful... flip... funny... Able to enjoy humor... flirty... a clown. That side of me shrugs.. .pretends I don't care... This Anne seems happy on the outside...
My secret side is better... finer... And not seen in public... Quiet and serious... Sentimental... Sad... Afraid of being mocked... Afraid of not being taken seriously...I'd like to be the person I know I am... I'm only that way when I'm alone... This Anne is happy on the inside...
To be honest, I'm trying to change... But people make that so hard... They are a powerful enemy... Negative... frustrated... not believing me... Hovering... shoving medicine into me... Until I'm mad, then sad, then just feel bad... I'd like people to see the person I could be...If I were all alone in the world...
Yours, Anne M. Frank
WHAT INTENSE, THOUGHTFUL INSIGHTS.
HER ACTUAL WRITING WAS FAR MORE INTENSE AND THOUGHTFUL.
SADLY, THIS WAS ANNE'S VERY LAST DIARY ENTRY.

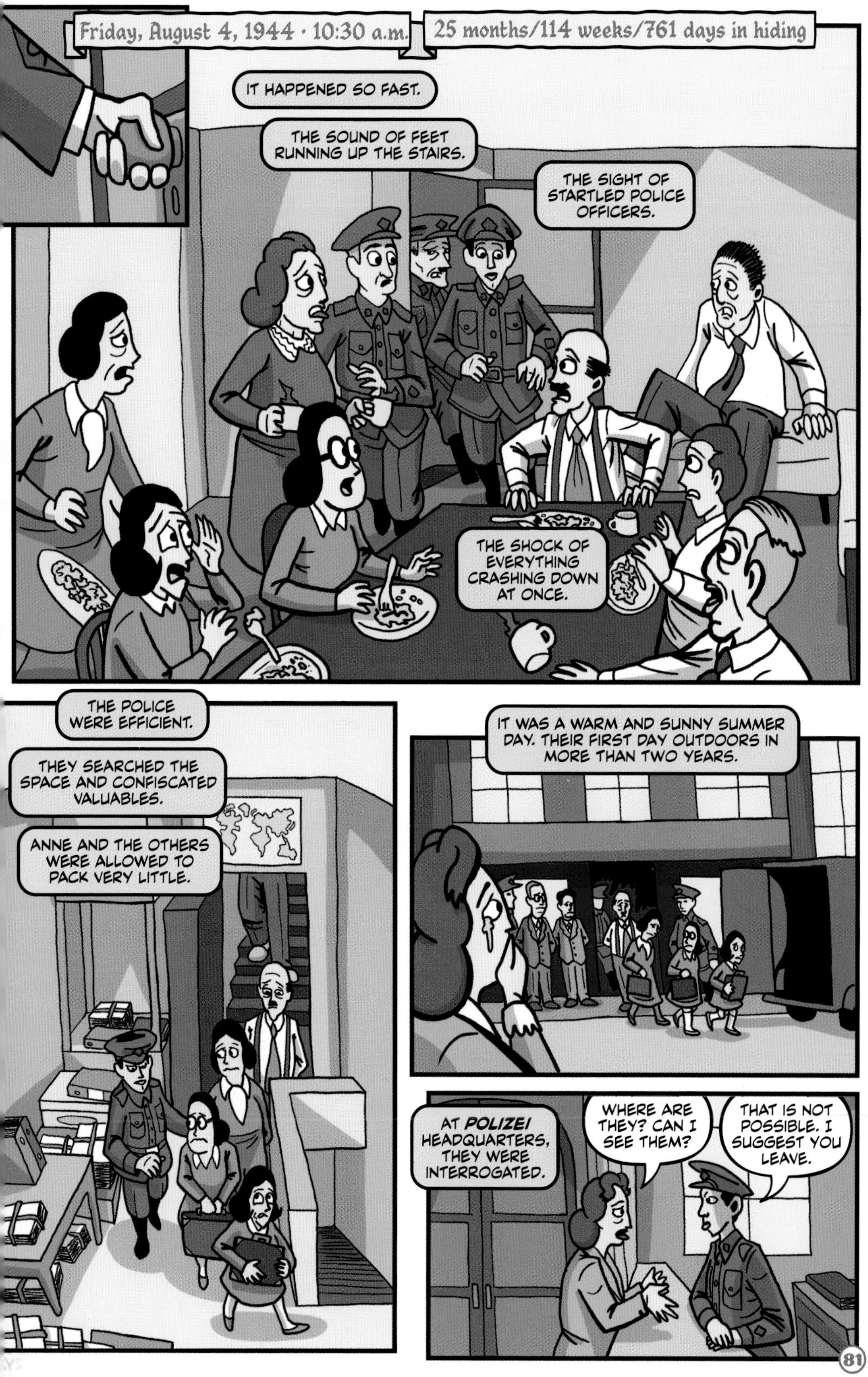
Friday, August 4, 1944 · 10:30 a.m.
25 months/114 weeks/761 days in hiding
IT HAPPENED SO FAST.
THE SOUND OF FEET RUNNING UP THE STAIRS.
THE SIGHT OF STARTLED POLICE OFFICERS.
THE SHOCK OF EVERYTHING CRASHING DOWN AT ONCE.
THE POLICE WERE EFFICIENT.
THEY SEARCHED THE SPACE AND CONFISCATED VALUABLES.
ANNE AND THE OTHERS WERE ALLOWED TO PACK VERY LITTLE.
IT WAS A WARM AND SUNNY SUMMER DAY. THEIR FIRST DAY OUTDOORS IN MORE THAN TWO YEARS.
AT *POLIZEI* HEADQUARTERS, THEY WERE INTERROGATED.
WHERE ARE THEY? CAN I SEE THEM?
THAT IS NOT POSSIBLE. I SUGGEST YOU LEAVE.

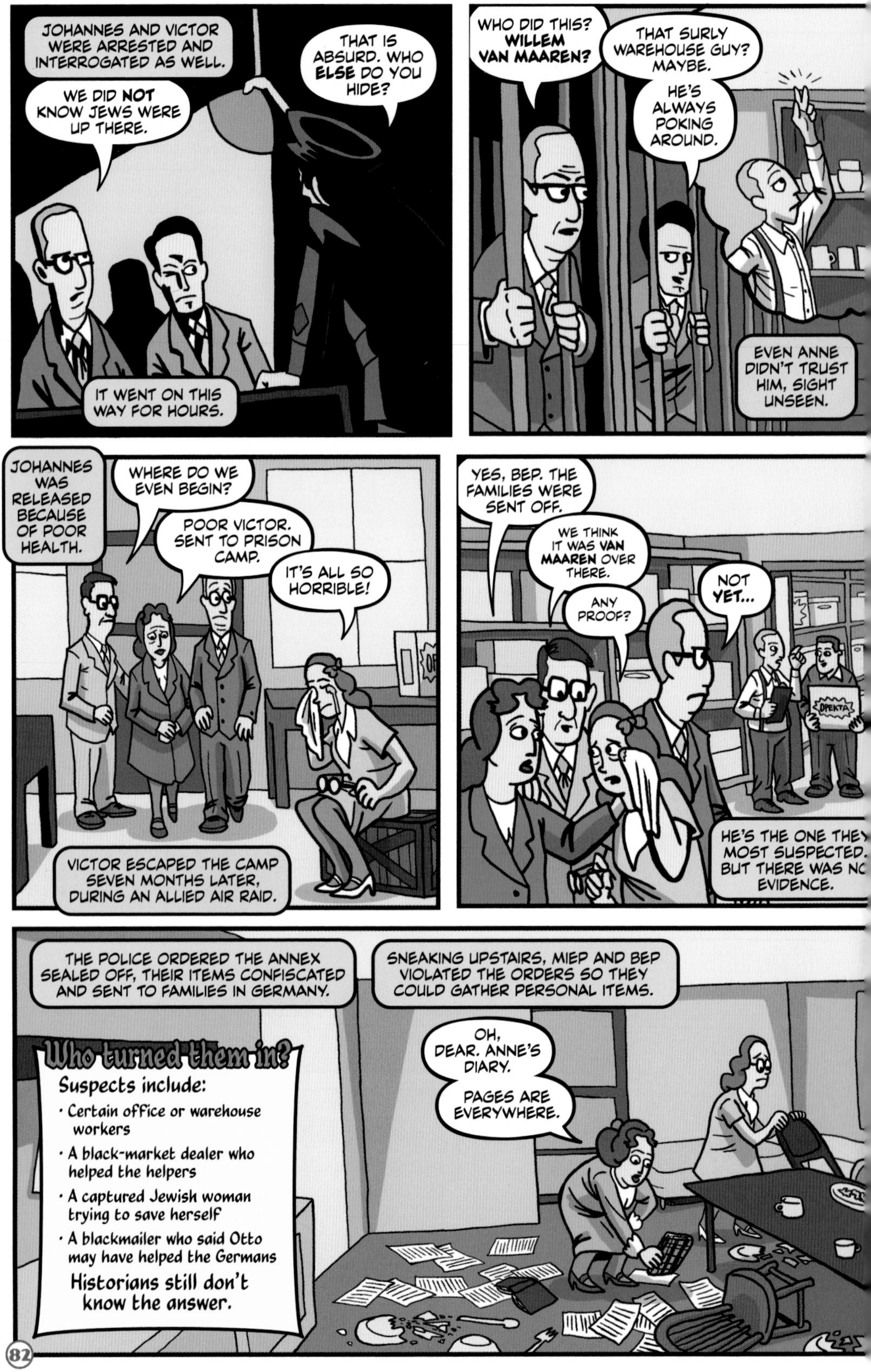
JOHANNES AND VICTOR WERE ARRESTED AND INTERROGATED AS WELL.
WE DID NOT KNOW JEWS WERE UP THERE.
THAT IS ABSURD. WHO ELSE DO YOU HIDE?
IT WENT ON THIS WAY FOR HOURS.
WHO DID THIS? WILLEM VAN MAAREN?
THAT SURLY WAREHOUSE GUY? MAYBE.
HE'S ALWAYS POKING AROUND.
EVEN ANNE DIDN'T TRUST HIM, SIGHT UNSEEN.
JOHANNES WAS RELEASED BECAUSE OF POOR HEALTH.
WHERE DO WE EVEN BEGIN?
POOR VICTOR. SENT TO PRISON CAMP.
IT'S ALL SO HORRIBLE!
VICTOR ESCAPED THE CAMP SEVEN MONTHS LATER, DURING AN ALLIED AIR RAID.
YES, BEP. THE FAMILIES WERE SENT OFF.
WE THINK IT WAS VAN MAAREN OVER THERE.
ANY PROOF?
NOT YET...
OPEKTA
HE'S THE ONE THEY MOST SUSPECTED. BUT THERE WAS NO EVIDENCE.
THE POLICE ORDERED THE ANNEX SEALED OFF, THEIR ITEMS CONFISCATED AND SENT TO FAMILIES IN GERMANY.
SNEAKING UPSTAIRS, MIEP AND BEP VIOLATED THE ORDERS SO THEY COULD GATHER PERSONAL ITEMS.
Who turned them in?
Suspects include:
· Certain office or warehouse workers
· A black-market dealer who helped the helpers
· A captured Jewish woman trying to save herself
· A blackmailer who said Otto may have helped the Germans
Historians still don't know the answer.
OH, DEAR. ANNE'S DIARY.
PAGES ARE EVERYWHERE.

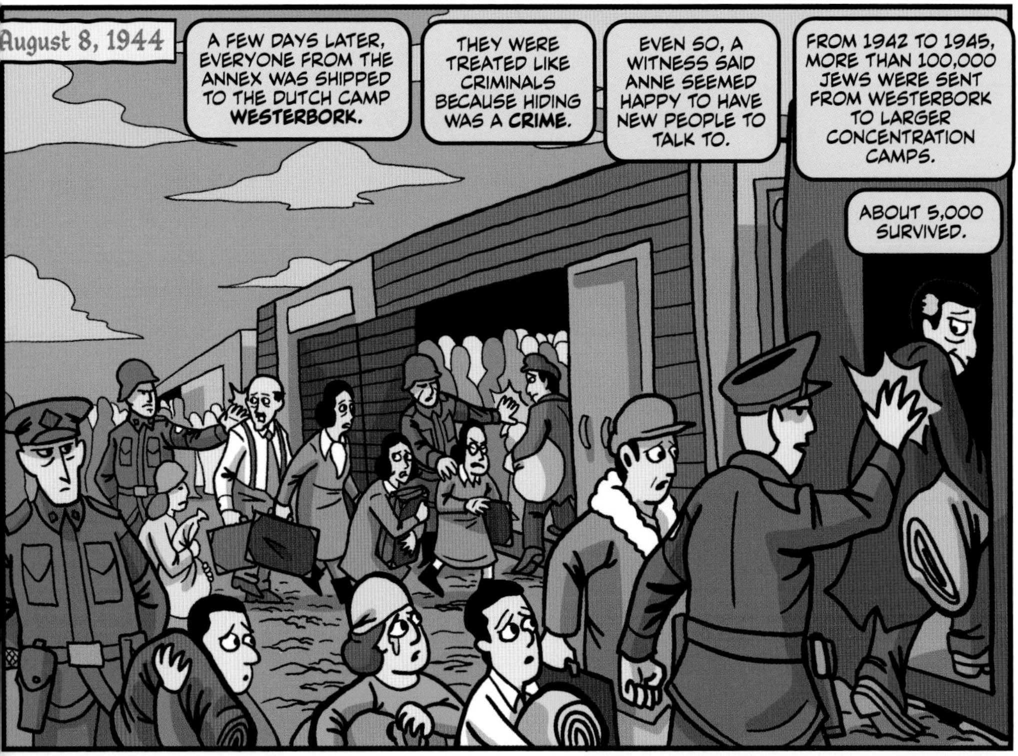
August 8, 1944
A FEW DAYS LATER, EVERYONE FROM THE ANNEX WAS SHIPPED TO THE DUTCH CAMP WESTERBORK.
THEY WERE TREATED LIKE CRIMINALS BECAUSE HIDING WAS A CRIME.
EVEN SO, A WITNESS SAID ANNE SEEMED HAPPY TO HAVE NEW PEOPLE TO TALK TO.
FROM 1942 TO 1945, MORE THAN 100,000 JEWS WERE SENT FROM WESTERBORK TO LARGER CONCENTRATION CAMPS.
ABOUT 5,000 SURVIVED.

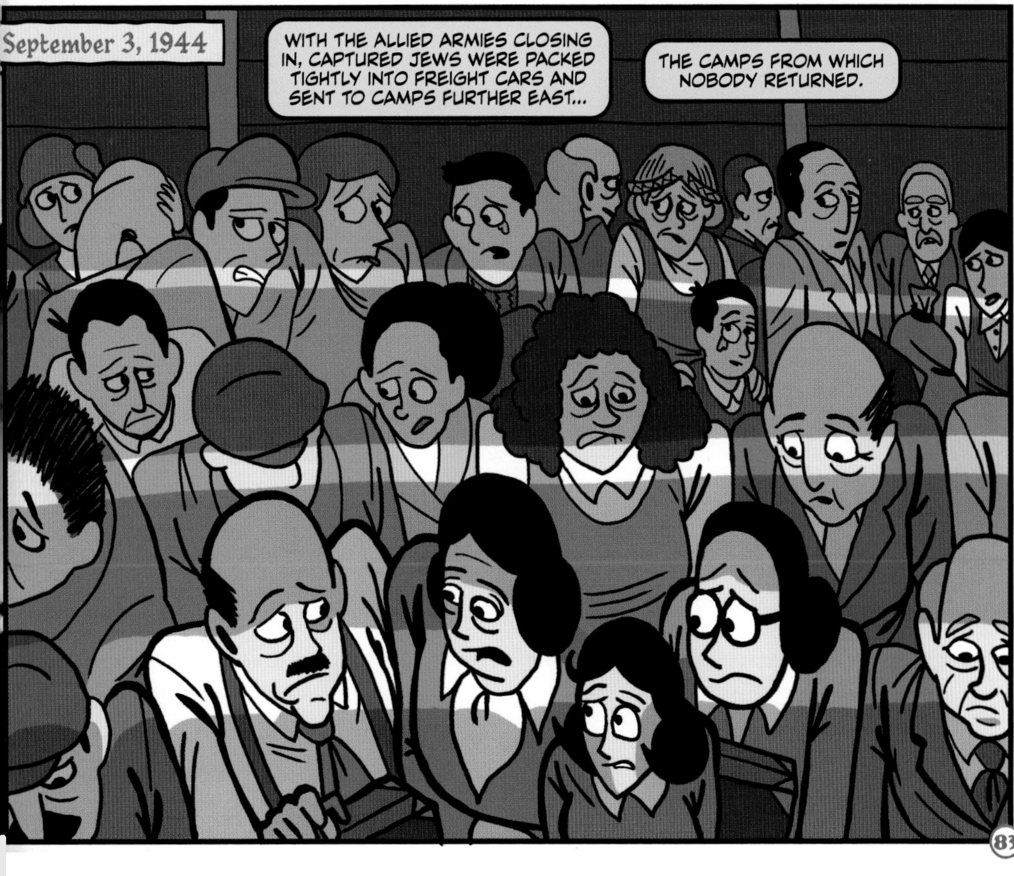
September 3, 1944
WITH THE ALLIED ARMIES CLOSING IN, CAPTURED JEWS WERE PACKED TIGHTLY INTO FREIGHT CARS AND SENT TO CAMPS FURTHER EAST...
THE CAMPS FROM WHICH NOBODY RETURNED.

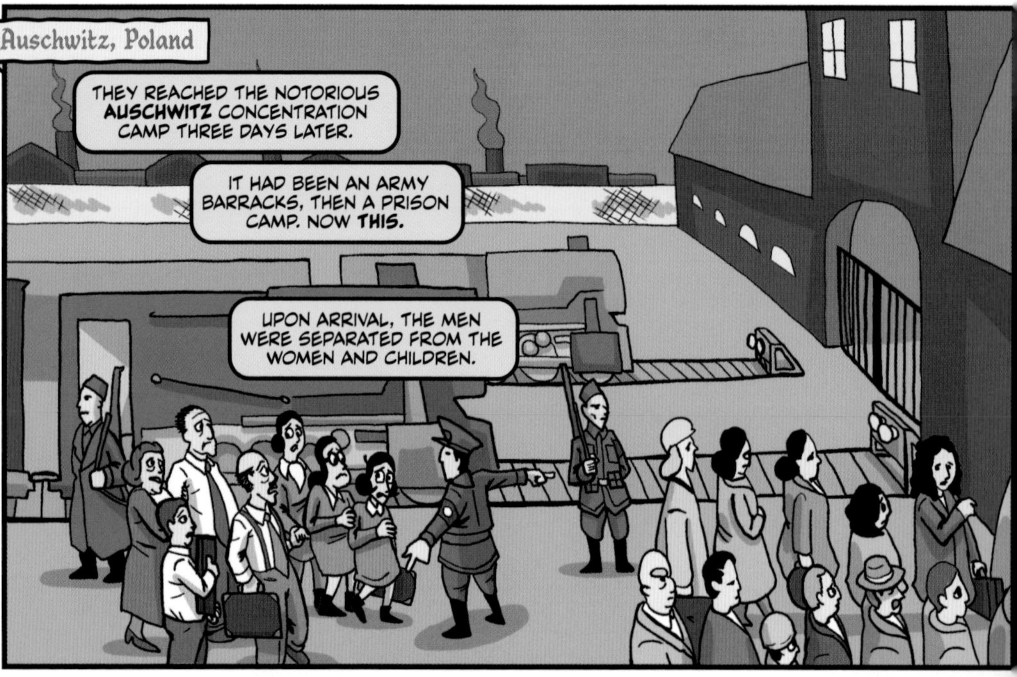
Auschwitz, Poland
THEY REACHED THE NOTORIOUS **AUSCHWITZ** CONCENTRATION CAMP THREE DAYS LATER.
IT HAD BEEN AN ARMY BARRACKS, THEN A PRISON CAMP. NOW **THIS.**
UPON ARRIVAL, THE MEN WERE SEPARATED FROM THE WOMEN AND CHILDREN.

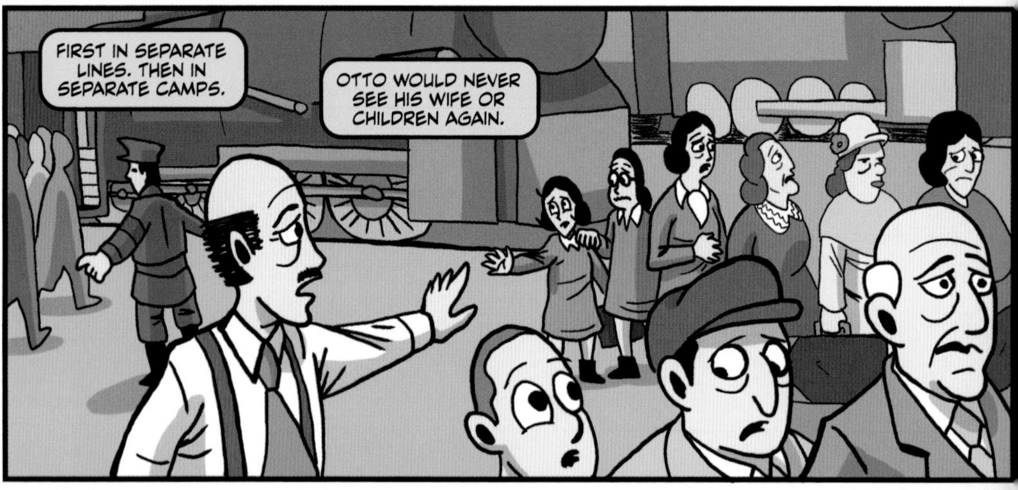
FIRST IN SEPARATE LINES. THEN IN SEPARATE CAMPS.
OTTO WOULD NEVER SEE HIS WIFE OR CHILDREN AGAIN.

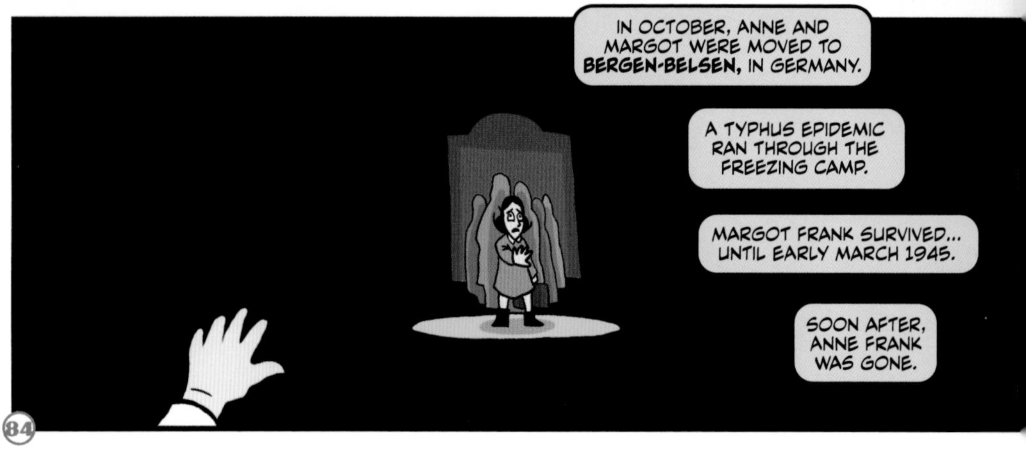
IN OCTOBER, ANNE AND MARGOT WERE MOVED TO **BERGEN-BELSEN,** IN GERMANY.
A TYPHUS EPIDEMIC RAN THROUGH THE FREEZING CAMP.
MARGOT FRANK SURVIVED... UNTIL EARLY MARCH 1945.
SOON AFTER, ANNE FRANK WAS GONE.

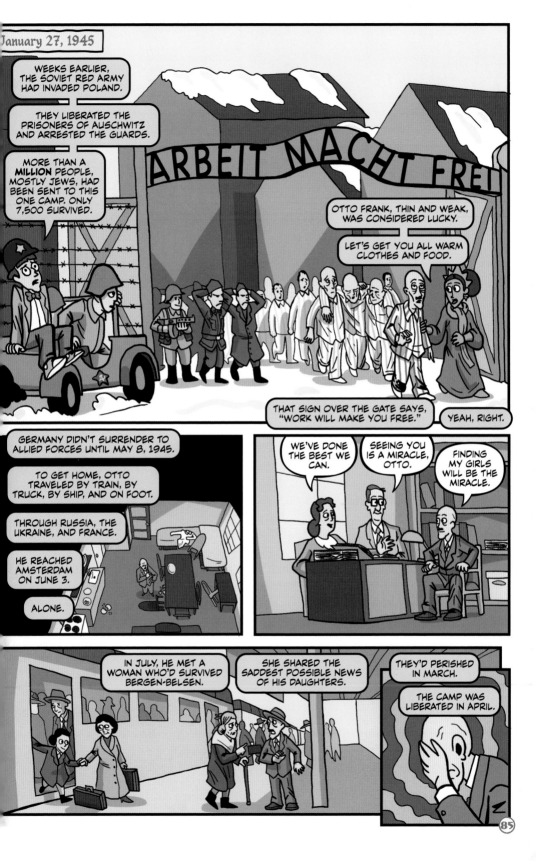

January 27, 1945

WEEKS EARLIER, THE SOVIET RED ARMY HAD INVADED POLAND.

THEY LIBERATED THE PRISONERS OF AUSCHWITZ AND ARRESTED THE GUARDS.

MORE THAN A MILLION PEOPLE, MOSTLY JEWS, HAD BEEN SENT TO THIS ONE CAMP. ONLY 7,500 SURVIVED.

ARBEIT MACHT FREI

OTTO FRANK, THIN AND WEAK, WAS CONSIDERED LUCKY.

LET'S GET YOU ALL WARM CLOTHES AND FOOD.

THAT SIGN OVER THE GATE SAYS, "WORK WILL MAKE YOU FREE."

YEAH, RIGHT.

GERMANY DIDN'T SURRENDER TO ALLIED FORCES UNTIL MAY 8, 1945.

TO GET HOME, OTTO TRAVELED BY TRAIN, BY TRUCK, BY SHIP, AND ON FOOT.

THROUGH RUSSIA, THE UKRAINE, AND FRANCE.

HE REACHED AMSTERDAM ON JUNE 3.

ALONE.

WE'VE DONE THE BEST WE CAN.

SEEING YOU IS A MIRACLE, OTTO.

FINDING MY GIRLS WILL BE THE MIRACLE.

IN JULY, HE MET A WOMAN WHO'D SURVIVED BERGEN-BELSEN.

SHE SHARED THE SADDEST POSSIBLE NEWS OF HIS DAUGHTERS.

THEY'D PERISHED IN MARCH.

THE CAMP WAS LIBERATED IN APRIL.

IN ONE WAY, ALL WAS NOT LOST.

I HID ANNE'S DIARIES AND STORIES AND PAPERS FROM THE POLICE.

KITTY? OH, MY...

IT WAS PAINFUL FOR OTTO TO READ ANNE'S WORDS.

WE CAN ONLY IMAGINE THE SORROW. BUT LOOK WHAT HE **FOUND.**

SO MANY MEMORIES.

SO MUCH LOSS.

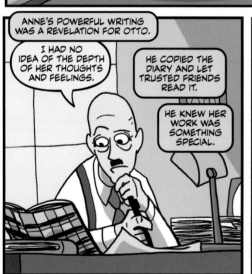

ANNE'S POWERFUL WRITING WAS A REVELATION FOR OTTO.

I HAD NO IDEA OF THE DEPTH OF HER THOUGHTS AND FEELINGS.

HE COPIED THE DIARY AND LET TRUSTED FRIENDS READ IT.

HE KNEW HER WORK WAS SOMETHING SPECIAL.

SO MANY PUBLISHERS SAID, "NO, SORRY, PEOPLE WANT TO FORGET THE WAR."

AT LEAST ANNE HAS THIS NEWSPAPER STORY.

I DON'T THINK ANNE WOULD HAVE STOPPED **THERE,** MR. FRANK.

April 3, 1946
HET PAROOL
A CHILD'S VOICE
by Anne Frank

BEP WAS RIGHT. THE NEWS STORY CONVINCED A PUBLISHER TO PRINT THE BOOK.

SO BIG? ALL THESE PAGES ON THE SAME LARGE PAPER?

DON'T WORRY, WE'LL CUT THE PAGES TO REGULAR SIZE.

IF SHE HAD BEEN HERE, ANNE WOULD HAVE BEEN SO PROUD.

"THE SECRET ANNEX."

ONE GIRL'S WISDOM, EMOTIONS, AND VIEW OF THE WAR... IT STRUCK A CHORD.

EXACTLY THE TITLE ANNE WANTED.

ANNE'S WRITING WAS AN INSTANT SENSATION.

FOR OTTO, THE SURVIVAL OF ANNE'S BOOK WAS A MIRACLE.

ANNE FRANK
Het Achter-huis
DAGBOEKBRIEVEN VAN 14 JUNI 1942 – 1 AUGUSTUS 1944

FOR THE WORLD'S JEWS, THERE WAS ANOTHER MIRACLE OF SURVIVAL.

TRANSLATION: *THE SECRET ANNEX. DIARY LETTERS FROM 14 JUNE 1942 - 1 AUGUST 1944*

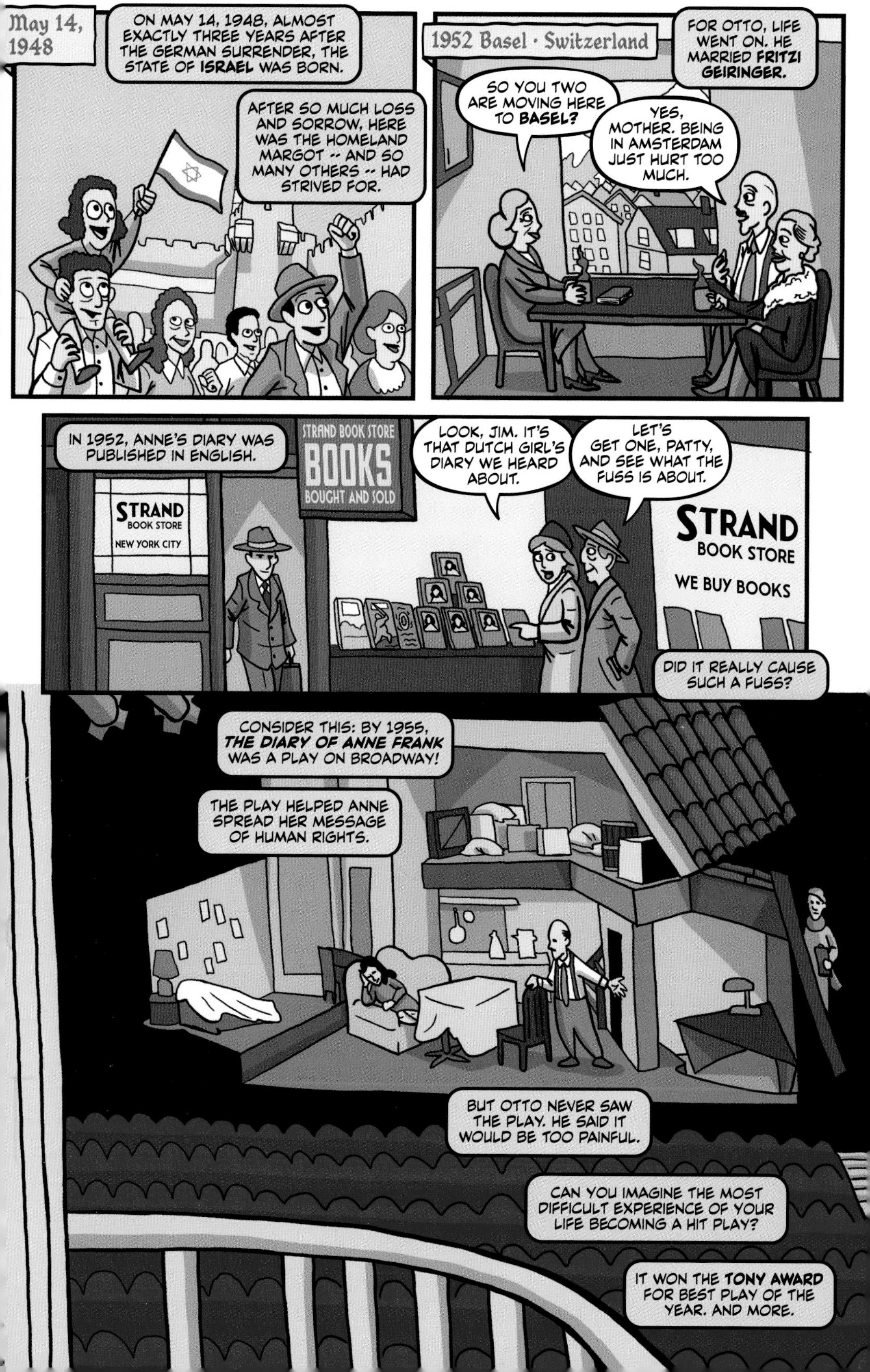
May 14, 1948
ON MAY 14, 1948, ALMOST EXACTLY THREE YEARS AFTER THE GERMAN SURRENDER, THE STATE OF ISRAEL WAS BORN.
AFTER SO MUCH LOSS AND SORROW, HERE WAS THE HOMELAND MARGOT -- AND SO MANY OTHERS -- HAD STRIVED FOR.
1952 Basel · Switzerland
FOR OTTO, LIFE WENT ON. HE MARRIED FRITZI GEIRINGER.
SO YOU TWO ARE MOVING HERE TO BASEL?
YES, MOTHER. BEING IN AMSTERDAM JUST HURT TOO MUCH.
IN 1952, ANNE'S DIARY WAS PUBLISHED IN ENGLISH.
STRAND BOOK STORE BOOKS BOUGHT AND SOLD
STRAND BOOK STORE NEW YORK CITY
LOOK, JIM. IT'S THAT DUTCH GIRL'S DIARY WE HEARD ABOUT.
LET'S GET ONE, PATTY, AND SEE WHAT THE FUSS IS ABOUT.
STRAND BOOK STORE WE BUY BOOKS
DID IT REALLY CAUSE SUCH A FUSS?
CONSIDER THIS: BY 1955, THE DIARY OF ANNE FRANK WAS A PLAY ON BROADWAY!
THE PLAY HELPED ANNE SPREAD HER MESSAGE OF HUMAN RIGHTS.
BUT OTTO NEVER SAW THE PLAY. HE SAID IT WOULD BE TOO PAINFUL.
CAN YOU IMAGINE THE MOST DIFFICULT EXPERIENCE OF YOUR LIFE BECOMING A HIT PLAY?
IT WON THE TONY AWARD FOR BEST PLAY OF THE YEAR. AND MORE.

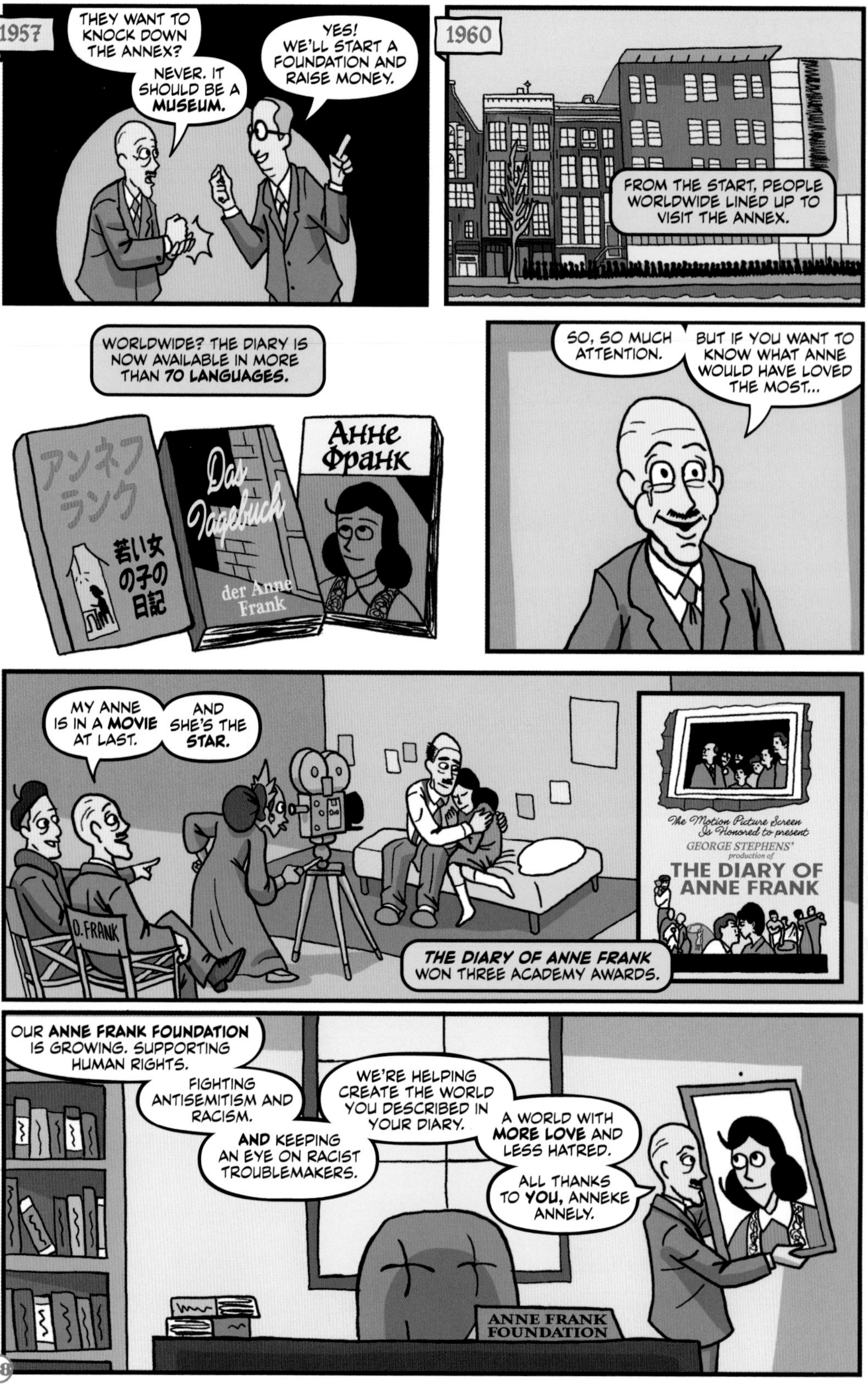
1957
THEY WANT TO KNOCK DOWN THE ANNEX?
NEVER. IT SHOULD BE A **MUSEUM.**
YES! WE'LL START A FOUNDATION AND RAISE MONEY.
1960
FROM THE START, PEOPLE WORLDWIDE LINED UP TO VISIT THE ANNEX.
WORLDWIDE? THE DIARY IS NOW AVAILABLE IN MORE THAN **70 LANGUAGES.**
アンネフランク
若い女の子の日記
Das Tagebuch der Anne Frank
Анне Франк
SO, SO MUCH ATTENTION.
BUT IF YOU WANT TO KNOW WHAT ANNE WOULD HAVE LOVED THE MOST...
MY ANNE IS IN A **MOVIE** AT LAST.
AND SHE'S THE **STAR.**
O. FRANK
The Motion Picture Screen Is Honored to present
GEORGE STEPHENS' production of
THE DIARY OF ANNE FRANK
THE DIARY OF ANNE FRANK WON THREE ACADEMY AWARDS.
OUR **ANNE FRANK FOUNDATION** IS GROWING. SUPPORTING HUMAN RIGHTS.
FIGHTING ANTISEMITISM AND RACISM.
AND KEEPING AN EYE ON RACIST TROUBLEMAKERS.
WE'RE HELPING CREATE THE WORLD YOU DESCRIBED IN YOUR DIARY.
A WORLD WITH **MORE LOVE** AND LESS HATRED.
ALL THANKS TO **YOU,** ANNEKE ANNELY.
ANNE FRANK FOUNDATION

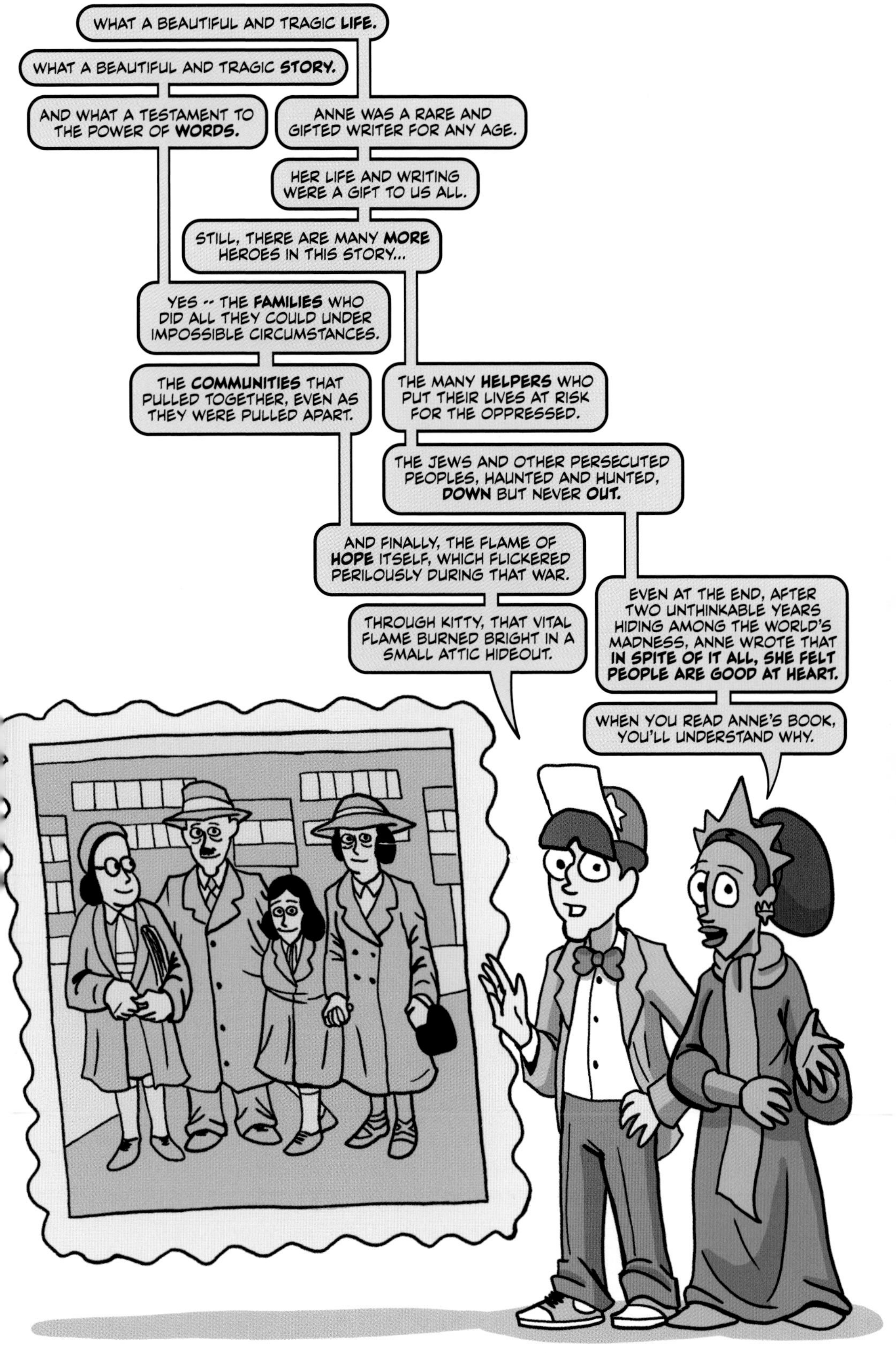

WHAT A BEAUTIFUL AND TRAGIC **LIFE.**
WHAT A BEAUTIFUL AND TRAGIC **STORY.**
AND WHAT A TESTAMENT TO THE POWER OF **WORDS.**
ANNE WAS A RARE AND GIFTED WRITER FOR ANY AGE.
HER LIFE AND WRITING WERE A GIFT TO US ALL.
STILL, THERE ARE MANY **MORE** HEROES IN THIS STORY...
YES -- THE **FAMILIES** WHO DID ALL THEY COULD UNDER IMPOSSIBLE CIRCUMSTANCES.
THE **COMMUNITIES** THAT PULLED TOGETHER, EVEN AS THEY WERE PULLED APART.
THE MANY **HELPERS** WHO PUT THEIR LIVES AT RISK FOR THE OPPRESSED.
THE JEWS AND OTHER PERSECUTED PEOPLES, HAUNTED AND HUNTED, **DOWN** BUT NEVER **OUT.**
AND FINALLY, THE FLAME OF **HOPE** ITSELF, WHICH FLICKERED PERILOUSLY DURING THAT WAR.
THROUGH KITTY, THAT VITAL FLAME BURNED BRIGHT IN A SMALL ATTIC HIDEOUT.
EVEN AT THE END, AFTER TWO UNTHINKABLE YEARS HIDING AMONG THE WORLD'S MADNESS, ANNE WROTE THAT **IN SPITE OF IT ALL, SHE FELT PEOPLE ARE GOOD AT HEART.**
WHEN YOU READ ANNE'S BOOK, YOU'LL UNDERSTAND WHY.

HIDDEN HEROES OF WORLD WAR II

MIEP AND THE OTHER ANNEX HELPERS WERE NOT ALONE IN THEIR BRAVERY. DURING THE WAR, MANY "REGULAR" PEOPLE RISKED THEIR OWN LIVES TO HELP SAVE THE LIVES OF THE OPPRESSED. HERE ARE A FEW WHO ARE REMEMBERED.

VARIAN FRY was an American sent to help Jewish refugees in Nazi-occupied Marseille, France. Despite threats and arrests, Fry illegally helped at least 4,000 Jews, smuggling about 1,000 out of the country to freedom.

JOHAN VAN HULST was a Dutch teacher who hid Jewish children in his school, then helped smuggle about 600 of them out of the Netherlands... hidden in bags, boxes, and baskets.

CARL LUTZ worked for the Swiss government. Though Switzerland was officially neutral, not choosing sides in the war, Lutz saved more than 60,000 Hungarian Jews. He issued official Swiss papers that kept them from being sent to the camps.

OSKAR SCHINDLER was a businessman who rescued more than 1,000 Polish Jews. A member of the Nazi party, he knew that if he put the Jews to work in his factories, they wouldn't be killed. He is remembered in the film *Schindler's List*.

ELLEN MARGRETHE THOMPSON ran an inn on the northern coast of the Netherlands with her husband Henry. Working with Dutch fishermen, they helped about 1,000 Jews flee to safety in Sweden. Henry was arrested for smuggling and died in a camp.

RAOUL WALLENBERG, who worked for the Swedish embassy in Hungary, arranged for 650 Jews to become Swedish citizens and live in houses protected by Sweden, saving them from forced labor.

DR. JAN ZABINSKI was director of Poland's Warsaw Zoo, hiding a dozen Jews on the zoo grounds, as well as burying and preserving a war diary similar to Anne's.

ANNE FRANK TIMELINE

1929 Anne is born in Frankfurt, Germany, to Otto and Edith Frank.

1933 Adolf Hitler becomes Chancellor of Germany in January. His Nazi government begins to identify and repress opponents. By July, Otto moves to Amsterdam, in the Netherlands, to start a company (Opekta) and a new life for his family, away from Nazi persecution of Jews. Edith soon follows, then Margot.

1934 In March, after living several months with Otto's mother, Anne, 4, becomes the last Frank to join Otto in Germany.

1935 Germany's Nuremberg Laws remove citizenship protection from Jews. Anti-Jewish sentiments also rise in Amsterdam. Anne begins school.

1938 Jews across Germany are arrested, and their property attacked, on a night known as *Kristallnacht*, "the night of broken glass." Life in the Netherlands for Jews is also getting harder.

1939 Germany invades Poland on September 1, starting World War II in Europe. Edith and Otto consider leaving the country. Anne becomes a big fan of the movies.

1940 On May 10, Germany invades the Netherlands, Belgium, and Luxembourg, followed shortly by France. Anne's world is now under Nazi rule. In October, new laws are passed forbidding Jews from owning homes and businesses, working for the government, and much more. Like many, the Franks adapt.

1941 By October, all Jews under Nazi control must wear a yellow Jewish star as identification. Anne and Margot now attend the Jewish day school.

1942 For Anne's 13th birthday, she's given a diary that she names "Kitty." She becomes an avid writer of her life and times. The book is full within 6 months. On July 16, Margot is called up to be deported. The next day, Otto leads his family to a hideout he built in a back annex of his office building. Soon they are joined by Otto's partner, Hermann van Pels, and his family, Auguste and Peter. Otto and Hermann soon ask their dentist, Fritz Pfeffer, to hide with their families in the Annex.

1943 Survival in the Annex is dependent on Otto's loyal office workers, who risk their lives for extra bread, milk, vegetables, and many other rationed items.

1944 On August 4, after 26 months of hiding, everyone in the Annex is arrested. The Franks are sent to a series of concentration camps: Westerbork (in the Netherlands), then Auschwitz (in Poland). Anne and Margot are soon transferred to Bergen-Belsen in Germany.

1945 In March, Margot and Anne do not survive a typhus epidemic, passing away just a month before their camp is liberated. Of the eight who hid in the Annex, only Otto Frank survives.

GLOSSARY

ANNEX: An addition to a building.

ANTISEMITISM: A racist position against Jewish people.

BLACK MARKET: An illegal network for making purchases.

CONCENTRATION CAMP: A prison camp.

CURFEW: A specific time when people are not allowed outside.

DEPORT: To forcibly send someone away.

JUDAISM: The religion of the Jewish people.

KOSHER: An ancient set of dietary laws followed by many Jews.

LYCEUM, MONTESSORI: Types of schools.

OCCUPIED COUNTRY: A nation under the control of an invading force.

POGROM: An organized attack on a Jewish community.

POLIZEI: The Nazi police force in occupied countries.

PUPPET GOVERNMENT: A weak government supported by a nation's invaders.

THE RESISTANCE: Civilians using any means to thwart their invaders.

SHORTHAND: A written alphabet for capturing spoken words very quickly.

VANDALIZE: To destroy intentionally.

VOOR JODEN VERBODEN: Dutch for "Jews are Forbidden."

FIND OUT MORE

BOOKS

Frank, Anne. *Diary of a Young Girl.* New York: Doubleday, 1952.

Frank, Anne. *Tales from the Secret Annex.* New York: Bantam Books, 2003.

Folman, Ari (author) and David Polonsky (illustrator). *Anne Frank's Diary: The Graphic Adaptation.* New York: Pantheon Books, 2018.

Gies, Miep, and Alison Gold. *Anne Frank Remembered.* New York: Simon & Schuster, 1987.

Goslar, Hannah, and Alison Gold. *Memories of Anne Frank: Reflections of a Childhood Friend.* New York: Scholastic, 1999.

ONLINE

Anne Frank House
The official website of the Anne Frank house. Biographies, history, photos, Anne's handwriting, and a virtual 3D walk-through of the Annex.
www.AnneFrank.org

VIDEO

Stevens, George, dir. *The Diary of Anne Frank.* Los Angeles: 20th Century Fox, 1959.

Dornhelm, Robert, dir. *Anne Frank: The Whole Story.* Los Angeles: ABC/Walt Disney, 2001.

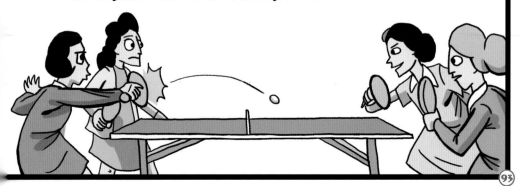

SHOW ME HISTORY!

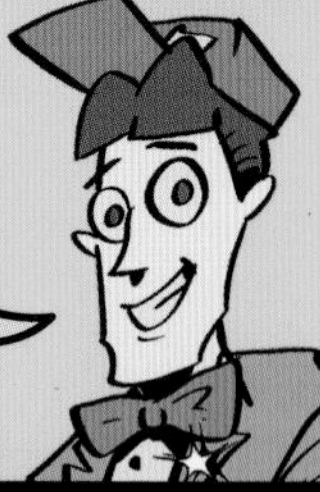
COLLECT EVERY BOOK IN THE SERIES AND FIND THE *STORY* IN HISTORY!

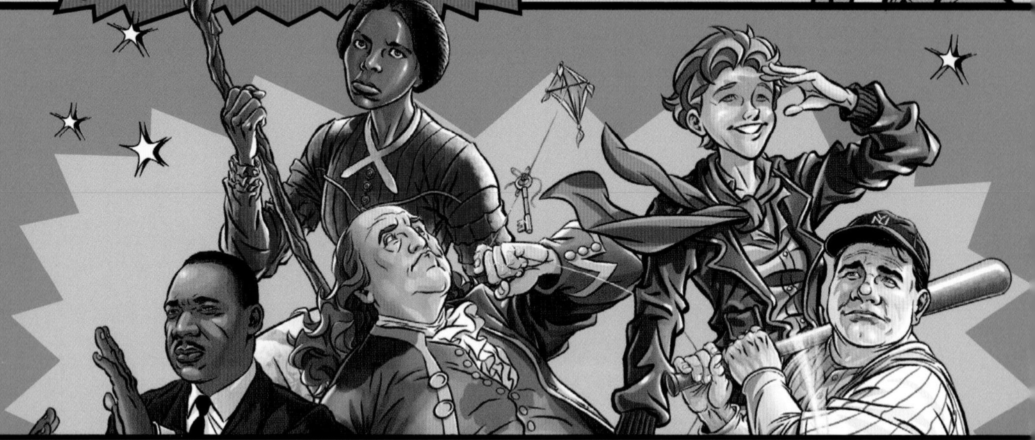

ABRAHAM LINCOLN
DEFENDER OF THE UNION!

ALBERT EINSTEIN
GENIUS OF SPACE AND TIME!

ALEXANDER HAMILTON
THE FIGHTING FOUNDING FATHER!

AMELIA EARHART
PIONEER OF THE SKY!

ANNE FRANK
WITNESS TO HISTORY!

BABE RUTH
BASEBALL'S ALL-TIME BEST!

BENJAMIN FRANKLIN
INVENTOR OF THE NATION!

GEORGE WASHINGTON
SOLDIER AND STATESMAN!

HARRIET TUBMAN
FIGHTER FOR FREEDOM!

HELEN KELLER
INSPIRATION TO EVERYONE!

JESUS
MESSENGER OF PEACE!

MARTIN LUTHER KING JR.
VOICE FOR EQUALITY!

MUHAMMAD ALI
THE GREATEST OF ALL TIME!

SACAGAWEA
COURAGEOUS TRAILBLAZER!

SUSAN B. ANTHONY
CHAMPION FOR VOTING RIGHTS!

WALT DISNEY
THE MAGICAL INNOVATOR!

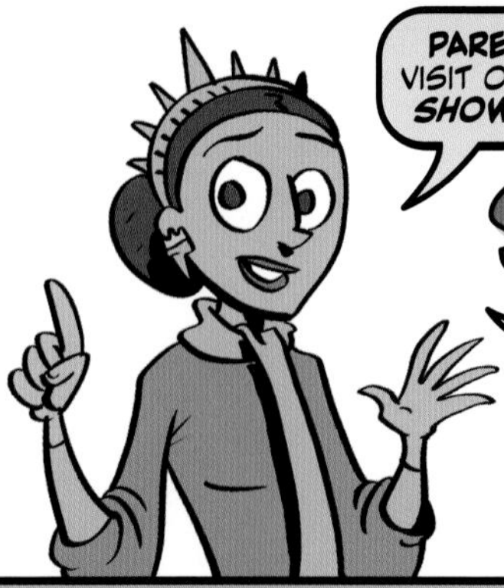
PARENTS AND TEACHERS: VISIT OUR WEBSITE FOR MORE *SHOW ME HISTORY!* FUN...
SHOWMEHISTORY.COM
... WHERE YOU CAN LEARN MORE ABOUT THE AUTHORS, SIGN UP FOR OUR EMAIL NEWSLETTER, AND DOWNLOAD OUR READING GUIDES!
ALSO FOLLOW US ON **SOCIAL MEDIA!**

@showmehistorybooks
www.facebook.com/portablepress
www.pinterest.com/portablepress
@portablepress

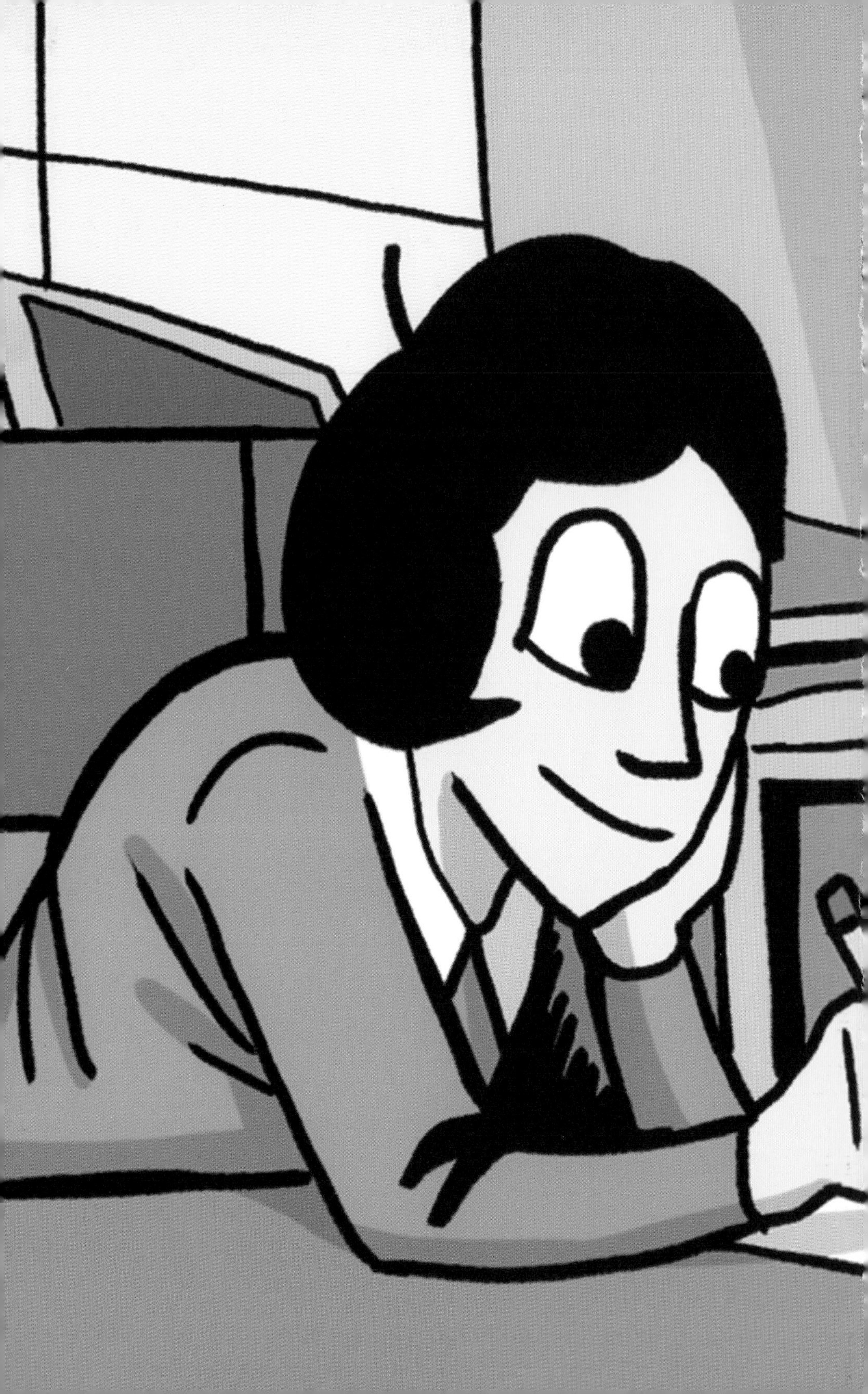